USAGE

A Workbook for Students of English

by

Thomas S. La Farge

(Horace Mann School, Riverdale NY)

WAYSIDE PUBLISHING
Suite #5
11 Jan Sebastian Way
Sandwich MA 02563
(888) 302-2519

ISBN 1-877653-88-8

Table of Contents

Introduction

"I didn't do nothin'."

In some situations, the grammar of the line that students, both guilty and innocent, have used for generations is perfectly acceptable. In fact, it is beautifully emphatic. So are these statements, which you might hear in the cafeteria: "Him and me are going out for pizza. Wanna come?" Or when you press your cell phone to your ear: "Hi, it's me." However, the same expressions are not acceptable in formal writing. So the first thing to get clear is your goal in using this book: not to reform your everyday speech but to master the usage appropriate to formal situations.

What is "usage" and why do you have to learn it? Usage sets rules for using English clearly and correctly. If you're a dancer, a tennis player, a violinist, a painter, then you know the importance of good form and good technique, which you can fall back upon to do whatever you want – leap, serve, play arpeggios, or make a painted figure come to life – with minimal effort. Usage is good form and good technique in language.

You may not dance or play tennis, but everyone has to write. You want your reader to follow what you're saying, not to become distracted by your errors. Look at the following sentence:

"Mr. Schlooter feeds his dog more than his wife."

Oh? How sad for Mrs. Schlooter. Or wait, is it sad for the dog? Did this writer mean, "Mr. Schlooter feeds his dog more than he feeds his wife"? Or did the writer mean, "Mr. Schlooter feeds his dog more than his wife does"? Sometimes you can figure out the answer from context. But as a writer, what do you want your reader to do, stop and figure out what you're saying or concentrate on your meaning? Your reader can't hear you, can't see your face. All he or she gets is your words, and if those aren't clear, the reader has to stop to work them out. If a reader has to do this too often, he or she will lose the thread of what you're saying. This workbook is designed to enable you to express yourself clearly, elegantly, unambiguously in writing.

Another important reason to study correct formal usage: you have to convince your readers to believe you. To do this, you need to give them reason to think you're someone they should pay attention to. Your teacher will have told you how important it is to come across as reasonable and informed in your writing or public speaking. You back up your views with evidence and reasons. You're articulate, consistent, organized, someone to take seriously. But in deciding whether to accept your views, your listeners and readers will also judge the way you speak and write. If they can't follow you or are distracted by your usage errors, your great points may simply not land with the impact you expected, and the mistakes may even spoil the beauty of your case.

You will need to use common sense and patience while you learn. Some rules are going to seem arbitrary; some will generate statements that sound completely weird. "It is I, your teacher, who am telling you this." (*Am* has to agree with *I*.) Grammar is not an exact science, and you will find situations in which it is hard to see the application of a rule that elsewhere is clear. Finally, the issues in this workbook are not always matters of correct or incorrect usage. Often, especially in the later chapters, it's a question of better or worse, and better almost always means more concise. Even where there is clearly a wrong answer, there may be some right answers that are better than others. Keep in mind that you are being asked to memorize rules and do drill exercises not only to prepare for quizzes, tests, and the SAT (although this book will help you to do that) but primarily to improve as a writer and as an editor of your own writing.

In this book twelve topics have been chosen in which writing errors are commonly made. Some of the more complex topics are divided into two or more lessons. In each lesson I explain the rules and give several examples. You will find shaded boxes highlighting "rules of thumb" helpful to usage students, and there are some extended "Writer's Reference" lessons to help you apply the principles to your own essay-writing.

All the exercises have the same instructions: read the sentence and fix it if it is wrong – the same thing to do when you edit your own writing. The first exercise in any lesson tells you which rule applies in each sentence; for this "guided" exercise we have provided an answer key at the back of the book so that you can check your work. Then there follows an additional exercise without the rule numbers. Finally, each chapter after the first ends with a cumulative exercise, in which you are tested on your mastery of all the rules learned up to that point. Following the last lesson you'll find a section called "Words to Watch Out For" with explanations and exercises to teach you how to correct some of the most common errors in word-usage. Then a last set of review exercises. Finally a battery of SAT-style exercises to help you get a feel for that test.

The sentences in this book come from current and past Horace Mann English teachers and students and have been field-tested by them over seven years. Heartfelt thanks to them for their help, criticism and inspiration, and thanks too to Larry Weiss, former Head of the Upper School at Horace Mann, and to the school's Curriculum Grant committee for their ongoing encouragement and support of this project. Looking through stacks of old papers, I found a long tradition of comic, even satirical sentences. No one ever said that grammar is exciting, but I hope you will smile from time to time as you use *Usage*.

To the teachers who use this book

Dear colleagues,

In 1996 another teacher and I were given the charge of finding an English usage workbook for use by students, to support them as writers by allowing them to avoid or correct the most common types of usage error. We looked at many texts and were dissatisfied with all of them. Some were just too costly. Some were too complex, offering far more topics than our students would want or need to pay attention to. Some included usage topics briefly in what was otherwise a descriptive grammar. And none offered what we thought key: an abundance of exercises by means of which students can build mastery and confidence.

My experience is that grammar is far more easily learned than taught. English usage in particular, with its inconsistencies and gray areas, is nearly impossible to explain to anyone who doesn't already have a good instinct for it. As in the physical training athletes, artists, and musicians undergo, mastering usage is much more a matter of imitation, repetition, and self-correction than of instruction.

So I decided to write our own book, one with short, clear explanations of the principles that apply in the cases most commonly met in writing, followed by enough problems to give even an unconfident student some feel for the sorts of error that can spoil a sentence and some method for avoiding them. I wanted the problem-sentences to be engaging enough to overcome the resistance that grammar naturally excites in all right-thinking people, so I have tried to appeal to the experience of adolescents and to their sense of the absurd. At the same time I have kept the sentences within the bounds of formal practice. That is the book I have tried, with much help from others, to create.

In the lessons you will notice places where our prescriptions go contrary to much of what is practiced in ordinary language. I am holding the line on some issues where you may feel the battle has been lost. Is there really any ambiguity about the sentence, "She only smiles at me if I smile at her first"? We correct that to: "She smiles at me only…" and explain the correction by asserting that *only* modifies the clause, not the verb. Vague *which*; *due to* used adverbially; anyone's everyday experience is riddled with examples of these errors, so why hold out? For me the issue is not so much the purity of the language as my sense that rules are what you fall back on when in doubt. You want a clear basis for judgment, especially in those writing situations where the language must be formally correct, as in an essay for a college application. And clear rules reduce the grammar litigation that can eat up a teacher's time, energy, and sanity.

What I hope I have given you is a workbook you will not have to teach, one that will reduce your work to that of answering the questions that naturally come up in the course of going over the exercises. I hope as well that the book will be an occasion for you and your students to share an occasional laugh.

I. Punctuation with Apostrophes

(apos, poss)

Apostrophes give us all headaches. In two of the three situations where you use them – possessives and plurals – they are sometimes right to use and sometimes wrong. In the third – contractions – the forms created with them sound exactly like possessives that don't use them: *who's/whose, they're/their, it's/its.* The only remedy is to know the rules.

1. **Apostrophes are used in contractions when two words have been made into one, or when one word has been shortened by leaving out letters.** Some examples:

can't = cannot	*won't = will not*	*don't = do not*
they're = they are	*who's = who is*	*it's = it is*

   Apart from contractions, no regular verb form ends in apostrophe + s.

   Wrong: She *look's* angry. (*looks* is the regular form, not a contraction.)
   Right: Let's go have lunch. (*Let's* is the contraction of *let us*.)

   Contractions of years also use an apostrophe:

   My sister was born in '83.

2. **Apostrophes are used to show the possessive form of all nouns but no pronouns.**
   First, nouns. To form the possessive of a singular noun that does not end in *s* or *x*, add *'s*.

the demon's laugh	*Pascal's triangle*	*Manhattan's streets*

   To form the possessive form of a singular noun that does end in *s* or *x*, it is permissible to add the apostrophe without the *s*:

   Marx' writing or *Marx's writing*
   the witness' story or *the witness's story*

   To form the possessive form of a plural noun that ends with *s*, add just the apostrophe:

workers' uprising	*horses' tails*	*neighbors' demands*

   Some nouns, however, do not form their plural with *s*. In these cases add *'s*.

women's lounge	*geese's cackle*	*data's errors*

   No pronoun ever forms its possessive form with an apostrophe.

   Wrong: That green bookbag is *her's*. (*Hers* is already a possessive.)
   Right: Noah is a neighbor of *ours*. (No apostrophe.)

3. **An apostrophe may also be used to mean "of" or "for"** when used in phrases like *Men's room*. The phrase *Men's room* does not really show possession; the men don't own that room, but it is a room for men only. *Children's books* are books **for** children. *A year's growth* is the growth **of** (during) a year. Handle these situations exactly as you would the possessive case.

4. **When two or more entities possess something jointly, use the apostrophe and s only after the last of them.**

   > *I slept the night on Bill and Hillary's couch.*   [They both own the couch.]
   > *Sacco and Vanzetti's trial caused an uproar.*   [S and V were tried together.]

   But:
   > *The Rosenbergs' and Alger Hiss's trials both produced questionable verdicts.*
   > [The Rosenbergs and Alger Hiss were tried at different times.]

5. **Use the apostrophe and s after the last word of hyphenated compound nouns to show possession.**

   > *Phil did not want the vice-chairman's job.*
   > *The commander-in-chief's decision is final.*

6. **Use an apostrophe and *s* to form the plural of numerals, letters, symbols, abbreviations, or words used out of context.**

   These items will often be italicized, a fact that should make your task easier. **This is the only situation in which the apostrophe is used to form a plural.**

   > *Richard uses too many **however's** in his writing.*
   > *E-mail addresses have people typing lots of **@'s**.*
   > *There are four **i's** in verisimilitude.*
   > *The car service we use has seven **7's** in its phone number.*
   > *Wally invested all his money in **CD's**; unfortunately, they're the musical not the financial kind.*

   Wake-up call: This rule seems to be evolving. Some publishers now omit the apostrophe for the rule of letters and symbols. You may see *1960s* as well as *1960's*, *IPOs* as well as *IPO's*.

I. Apostrophes: Guided Exercise

Some of the sentences below are correct, and some have an error in apostrophes. If the sentence is correct, write "C." If the sentence contains an error, cross out the incorrect word and write the correct word at the end of the sentence. The number in parentheses at the end of each sentence refers to a rule you have just learned.

1. I know there still in the locker room, but they have changed out of their uniforms and are ready to go home. (1)

2. Its hard to believe that we are already in ninth grade! (1)

3. Aren't you tired of hearing about their' party? (2)

4. Mira's new dress is made of red silk, but its collar is woven cotton. (2)

5. The abbess' story about the missing halibut sounds fishy to me. (2)

6. Are you going to the Womens' Issues Club meeting? (2)

7. The best snow sculpture is their's, but because they were nasty to the referee, they did not win the prize. (2)

8. How much is a month's wage for that position? (3)

9. Its a shame that the dog hurt its paw, but luckily the vet is there to help. (1)

10. Julius and Ethel's trial was considered a travesty by many observers, but the two of them were executed anyway. (4)

11. It's a shame the way Mrs. Nagy let's Irene's and Igor's clothes get mixed up. (1)

12. The collaboration went through some rough moments, but Wong and Chou's new play is now a hit on Broadway. (4)

13. Computer Associates' new chip is expected to earn huge profits for the manufacturer. (2)

14. My mother-in-laws' brother is the nicest relative I have, but I don't see him as often as I'd like. (5)

15. How many s's are there in Mississippi? (6)

16. Norman Thomas does not want the vice-president's job, but there going to nominate him anyway. (1)

17. The sheeps' little hooves patter merrily across the barn floor all night long. (2)

18. The Secretary-General's long speech was not so popular as hers'. (2)

19. Do you believe that George's and Martha's bed at Mount Vernon is a valuable antique? (4)

20. Now that all five million auto workers have voted "yes," the workers' new contract will take effect on June 22nd. (2)

21. Wine that was bottled in '83 is probably ready to be poured today. (1)

22. The girl's bathroom on the third floor is always crowded. (2)

23. Mr. Castleman's and Dr. Weiss's offices are very close to each other. (4)

24. They're polished table is shining in a single shaft of sunlight. (1)

25. The commander-in-chief's signature is already on that document, but the senators' name is not. (2)

(Answer key on page 229.)

I. Apostrophes: More Practice Sentences

Some of the sentences below are correct, and some have an error in apostrophes. If the sentence is correct, write "C." If the sentence contains an error, cross out the incorrect word and write the correct word at the end of the sentence.

1. The Native Americans' right to run casino gambling is now being challenged in California.

2. The boy's locker room smells like socks that have not been washed in a month's time.

3. The Class of '97 is already in college, and the Class of '98 is planning it's graduation now.

4. Ms. Jacobs' class is the most interesting in the school; all the ninth graders in her class say that no one else has a literary experience as interesting as theirs'.

5. Billy's and Bob's tennis match resulted in a tie because they are so equally matched in skill and stamina.

6. The vice-chairmans' speech to the club was applauded wildly.

7. Make your *r*'s larger than your *n*'s.

8. Gilbert's and Sullivan's great operetta *The Mikado* was a triumph, even though the duo were barely speaking to one another when they wrote it.

9. The teacher told Egbert that no one's writing should contain so many *herein*'s.

10. Is your dog as noisy as her's?

11. I hope that they're going to repave the highway soon; its very bumpy.

12. The convicted felons' invitations to try out as extras in the movie *Rocky* were actually a trick by the district attorney.

13. Karl Marx' papers are all in a library in London, but John Lennons' are not.

14. The childrens' books were brightly illustrated and contained interesting stories.

15. When I write *1 1*'s, I try to make the strokes parallel, but her's are very sloppy.

16. The handwriting expert thinks that his strokes are better than yours'.

17. I do'nt like their attitude, but since I have to deal with them, I will accept every insult with a smile.

18. Those three senator's proposals for rent control deregulation differ in almost every detail.

19. The Vice-President's plane is known as "Airforce Two."

20. Whose in the pantry looking for canned peas?

21. The *and's* in your first paragraph are used incorrectly.

22. Is'nt it wonderful to see all those orphans' new parents?

23. The cat's food has to be placed in three separate rooms because otherwise the cute little kitties fight.

24. The year's severance pay was very helpful to the worker who had been laid off.

25. Do you think that an hour's study will prepare you for that final?

26. Eve doesn't know who's apple she ate, but she does know that it gave her indigestion.

27. I wish that Otto and Osmundine's wedding were'nt on September 1st.

28. Otto's and Osmundine's rings were made by the best jeweler in the city.

29. Two *O's* are engraved on each ring.

30. I cant believe that they're actually getting married!

31. The guests' cars will have to be parked in the lower parking lot.

32. The choirs' music is already in place on the conductor's podium.

33. The preacher's robe has been ironed, but theres no way to keep it from getting wrinkled as he moves around the altar.

34. Do you know the O'Malley's or their son Hugh, who's married to a cousin of yours?

35. Osmundine's sister wont be a bridesmaid because Osmundine thinks the ceremony should be very simple.

36. However, its Osmundine's idea to have the Mormon Tabernacle Choir sing six *amen's* at the end of the ceremony.

37. Years from now everyone will be talking about the marriage of '05.

38. The patients' healthcare concerns were of great interest to they're insurer.

39. Ms. Harkness' pavilion is paved with gold.

40. The couple who are being honored will dance on top of the gold, but they're relatives will have to stay on the carpet.

41. The hour's wage for each musician is set by the union.

42. Its not hard to imagine a giant bill for this event.

43. Dr. Hill's wedding is not so lavish as theirs.

44. His two hour's planning resulted in a simple but meaningful day.

45. The elephants' large feet thundered across the hardened dust as the herd ran to it's traditional breeding ground.

46. The data's significance is not immediately apparent.

47. She doesn't make her *a*'s in the traditional way.

48. The Revolution of '48 was aimed at cutting taxation.

49. Fifteen minute's wait at the tunnel is not bad!

50. Arent you glad you finished your grammar exercise?

II. Subject-Verb Agreement

(agr / sv)

When we say that in an English sentence the subject and the verb have to "agree," we mean one simple thing: either they both must be singular or they both must be plural. Most agreement errors arise because a writer is not clear about what the subject is and matches a plural verb with a singular subject or vice versa.

Always know what the subject is and whether it is singular or plural.

LESSON A. LINKING THE SUBJECT TO THE VERB CORRECTLY

…WHEN THE SUBJECT AND A PREDICATE NOMINATIVE ARE DIFFERENT IN NUMBER

7. **A verb must agree with its subject, not with a noun that follows a linking verb.**

   Sometimes a linking verb connects a singular subject with a plural predicate nominative, or vice versa. Which is correct?

   Taxes is/are my biggest expense.
   Olive's worst problem is/are her teeth.

   In the first example *taxes* is plural and *expense* is singular. The verb agrees with the subject; the subject is *taxes*; therefore the verb has to be *are*. Work out the second.

…WHEN ORDINARY SENTENCE STRUCTURE IS INVERTED

Normally in an English sentence the verb follows the subject, but this is not always the case. The general rule:

> **In the situation where normal sentence structure is inverted, be sure that you can identify the subject that the verb is to agree with.**

8. **In questions and some exclamations the subject follows or interrupts the verb:**

   Why **doesn't** <u>your brother</u> like jai-alai?
   Have <u>Max and Nora</u> gotten out of school yet?
   Has <u>Max or Nora</u> gotten out of school yet?
   How wild **are** my <u>dreams</u>! [an old-fashioned phrasing]

9. **In sentences written in inverted order, look for the subject after the verb.**

   Near the river **stands** a stunted <u>tree</u>.
   Carved on that tree **are** some <u>obscenities</u>.

10. *Here* and *There* are never subjects. When you see a sentence beginning with these words, look for the subject after the verb.

This is called the "expletive construction."

> Here **lies** <u>Edgar Allan Poe.</u> [Poe is the subject: "Poe lies here."]
> There **were** three bloodstained <u>gloves</u> in the shoebox. [Gloves are the subject: "Gloves were in the shoebox."]

...WHEN WORDS COME IN BETWEEN SUBJECT AND VERB

The intervening expressions may contain nouns and pronouns that seem to be the subject because they are closer to the verb than the true subject. Some intervening expressions will be set off by commas, but others are not. The rule of thumb:

> **The verb agrees with the subject, not with any words that come between. A useful trick: identify those words and mentally put them in parentheses.**

Find the true subject and make the verb agree with it.

> Rashid, like many others, prefers/prefer to study in a quiet room.
> Rashid (like many others) **prefers** to study in a quiet room.

11. **An intervening prepositional or participial phrase doesn't affect the number of the verb**:

> Olive's bag <u>of old shoes</u> **smells** rank.
> The snakes <u>in Otto's bathtub</u> **are** mostly harmless.
> The hen <u>raised by the schoolchildren</u> **likes** nothing better than Twinkies.

These phrases are dangerous because they are rarely set off by commas.

12. **Expressions that begin in the following ways have no effect on the number of the subject:**

> *as well as, accompanied by, together with, including, excluding, in company with, along with, no less than, in addition to, followed by, assisted by.*

> Olive, <u>assisted by her children,</u> **is** able to name all fifty states.
> James, <u>no less than his elected representatives,</u> **supports** mass transit.

13. **Intervening negative expressions don't affect the number of the subject:**

> Olga, <u>not Nancy,</u> **was** the writer of that poem.
> Ana, <u>rather than her rivals,</u> **is** the candidate we should vote for.

14. **The nouns in intervening adjective clauses don't affect the number of the subject:**

> The drivers <u>who use the Henry Hudson Parkway</u> **seem** to like to drive fast.

II A. Subject-Verb Agreement: Guided Exercise

Some of the sentences below are correct, and some have an error in subject-verb agreement. If the sentence is correct, write "C." If the sentence contains an error, cross out the verb and write the correct verb at the end of the sentence. The number in parentheses at the end of each sentence refers to a rule you have just learned.

1. That magazine's outstanding feature are its illustrations. (7)

2. Tom, who is one of my friends, sticks up for me whenever I meet the bully. (14)

3. Near the tracks beside the hills that surround all the towns are my house. (9)

4. There is rarely, if ever, any peanuts left after Otto has been watching football. (10)

5. Does Mary really need her little lambs today? (8)

6. Tamara, as well as four other scientists, was invited to speak to the ant farm convention. (12)

7. The cafeteria's worst flaw are the uncomfortable chairs. (7)

8. A large box of long fireplace matches are on the floor, far too close to the flames. (11)

9. There is several ways to make an omelet, but all involve broken eggs. (10)

10. Nancy, along with her three friends and the entire freshman class, were invited to try out for the part of Ophelia in the musical version of *Hamlet*. (12)

11. A box of firecrackers have been stacked with the ammunition. (11)

12. Because James loves new recipes, a set of 4,599 cookbooks sit on his bookshelf. (11)

13. Stan's greatest fear is snakes. (7)

14. The effects of caffeine lasts from two to six hours, just enough to get you through gym class. (11)

15. Does the smell of onions make you cry? (8, 11)

16. Sal's attitude, not his grades, have improved lately. (13)

17. The special effects in *Jurassic Park* and *The Lost World* was created by computers. (11)

18. The kids who sniffle constantly during every test needs to lay out some money for tissues. (14)

19. Here's the various methods for remembering all these grammar rules. (10)

20. The best part of the school day, Daphne asserts, are the lunches. (11)

21. On the bulletin board at the back of the room was a completely blank sign-up sheet for cafeteria duty. (9)

22. The major subjects, not the minor, are graded. (13)

23. Does science really explain the sighting of a UFO? (8)

24. I believe that Jack, along with his accomplices Jill and Raji, are going to ace the biology test. (12)

25. Is there any old magazines in the cellar? (8)

(Answer key on page 229.)

II A. Subject-Verb Agreement: More Practice Sentences

If the sentence is correct, write "C." If the sentence contains an error in subject-verb agreement, cross out the verb and write the correct verb at the end of the sentence.

1. Despite extra-help programs, one out of every twenty students are dropped from the frisbee team each term.

2. Near the wealthiest section of many cities stand miserable slums.

3. Surprisingly, Alfred, instead of the class show-offs, has won the prize.

4. Martha, together with her traveling companion Nkeisha, were listening to the bus driver, who diligently pointed out local landmarks such as the supermarket, the fire engine, and the pond.

5. The boxes stacked on the far side of the room has been burned.

6. The effect of movie violence on young viewers are not so terrible as you have been led to believe.

7. The expert who cited endless statistics were shown to be wrong.

8. The frequency of taxi-pedestrian accidents is rising each year.

9. In the past, close cooperation among students in pre-exam study sessions have brought higher grades for all.

10. Here's the best newspaper articles I could find on that topic.

11. Only one of his many excuses were accepted by his stern, unforgiving mother.

12. Along the banks of the Nile were found some beads from Aida's necklace.

13. There's Mike's three favorite hats!

14. The bottom of these soda cans are made of reinforced aluminum.

15. One of the greatest challenges teachers face are students who won't admit their own weaknesses.

16. Here are a list of good reasons for postponing college.

17. There was no water in the house after T. Rex stepped on the roof.

18. Chinese cooking, along with the cuisine of many cultures, are more popular now that supermarkets sell the ingredients.

19. Students in a nearby school has earned money selling toy dinosaurs designed to teach pre-historic anatomy.

20. The evening news on Channel Five usually concern local events.

21. There's only a few days of school left before vacation!

22. Does that book, as well as the red one, contain information about soccer?

23. It came as a relief that an elected leader and not greedy bureaucrats were in charge of the government.

24. The essays, excluding the brilliantly original piece written by Juliet, were repetitive and dull.

25. The chairperson's remarks, transmitted over a malfunctioning public address system, was difficult to hear.

26. What the nature of the political contributions were I do not know.

27. One of the packages was mailed, and the other went by UPS.

28. The television industry, no less than other industries, make wide use of celebrity endorsements.

29. The welfare of these starving children depends on your generosity.

30. The problem with Jon's homework are the pizza stains on the margins.

31. Here is at least fifteen books written by this English class.

32. Mara, along with her sister Lydia, are going to visit the penguins in the zoo tomorrow.

33. The people who are in the club with Justin think he will be a good president.

34. Near the kindergarten down the street from the nuclear reactor is the waste containers for the plutonium and uranium.

35. David's mimeograph machine, not his computer or his instant-fax machines, was the most useful item in the office.

36. Occasionally Dr. Deboss herself, without her top aides, attend the Governing Council meetings.

37. Weekends are tough for Harold when there is no football games on television.

38. A major factor in the ability to tolerate another's faults are one's own secret vices.

39. The only thing that worries me about the Yankees are their relief pitching.

40. The Office of Official Officers have a number of problems with those elections.

41. Only Yuka's smallest toes fits into that tiny shoe.

42. Do the mail boxes have to be painted green?

43. Screaming with fear and searching for his loved ones was Fred Flintstone.

44. Here is the most important pieces of jewelry in the entire collection.

45. With such force does Lady Macbeth argue with her husband!

46. The point of all these grammar exercises are to make sure you speak well.

47. I don't know about you, but I think the problem with grammar are the exercises.

48. There is a box of melted crayons on the desk next to the candle.

49. Cynthia's favorite possession is her baseball cards.

50. At the end of the exercise and close to the bottom of the page are at least three more problems.

LESSON B. AGREEMENT WITH A COMPOUND SUBJECT

Compound subjects are subjects in which two or more nouns or pronouns are joined by a conjunction.

15. **If compound singular subjects are joined by *and*, then the subject is considered plural and demands a plural verb.**

> *Martha and I **were** invited to speak at the assembly.*
> *The living-room, den, and dining-room **are** being redecorated.*

16. **But if the compound subjects identify the same entity, they are considered singular and demand a singular verb.**

If you can imagine the whole subject phrase with hyphens in it, then this rule probably applies.

> *Ham and eggs **is** Otto's favorite breakfast.*

Here you can see that "ham-and-eggs" is a single dish, one item on a menu rather than two. "Peanut-butter-and-jelly" works the same way. Sometimes two separate nouns are used to name the same person or thing:

> *The captain and quarterback **has** been injured.*

This sentence works only if the captain and quarterback are the same person. If they were different, a second *the* would probably precede the second subject.

> *The king and the queen **were** crowned together.*

17. **Names of stores or firms take a singular verb even if the name appears plural or includes several names joined by *and* or & .**

> *Simon & Schuster **is** my mother's publisher.*
> *Dean & Deluca **is** the most expensive grocery store in New York.*
> *Sears **is** having a sale.*

18. **Subject-items meant to be considered separately take a singular verb, even though the conjunction that joins them is *and*.**

The signal is the use of the adjectives *each* or *every* at the beginning of the subject.

> *Every student, teacher, and staff member **looks** forward to vacations.*
> *Each actor and stagehand **has** been warned about the blackout after Act One.*

> *Each* **and** *every* **are always singular.**

19. Two singular subjects joined by *or, nor, either...or, whether...or, neither...nor* are considered singular and demand a singular verb. But if such a conjunction joins a singular and a plural subject, the verb agrees with the nearer subject.

You're thinking about only one of these subjects at a time, instead of both together. (These conjunctions are really *disjunctive*: they disjoin alternatives.)

*Either Mrs. Schwartz or her eldest daughter **is** coming at three.*

*I can't remember whether Otto or Sam **was** the one who scored.*

*Neither Ruth nor Raquel **knows** where the stamps are kept.*

*Neither the teachers nor the security guards **see** what goes on in those bushes.*

*Neither Raoul nor his buddies **have** a clue about the Superbowl.*

*Either the students or their teacher **is** writing bad words on the blackboard.*

*Whether a gas leak or frayed electrical cables **were** the cause of it, that fire brought the building down.*

***Does** either Leonardo or the sailors wear scuba gear in that scene?*

***Do** either the sailors or Leonardo know how to swim?*

II B. Subject-Verb Agreement: Guided Exercise

Some of the sentences below are correct, and some have an error in subject-verb agreement. If the sentence is correct, write "C." If the sentence contains an error, cross out the verb and write the correct verb at the end of the sentence. The number in parentheses at the end of each sentence refers to a rule you have just learned.

1. Neither the leading candidates nor the current dogcatcher wish to address the electorate. (19)

2. Every drummer, violinist, and tuba player want to perform on stage when the talent scouts are in the audience. (18)

3. Every boy and girl in the class plan to prepare carefully for the vocabulary quiz that will be given tomorrow. (18)

4. Either Peter or his friends are going to pop more popcorn because the last batch has already been eaten. (19)

5. Each pear and nectarine in those four boxes are rotten. (18)

6. My coach and English teacher, who coaches because he was once an Olympic frisbee medalist, is on my case about the way I handle my homework. (16)

7. Eliah and one of his classmates help every afternoon in the kindergarten. (15)

8. Sears are having a sale on garage-door openers. (17)

9. Did you know that peanut butter and jelly are actually good for you? (16)

10. Each stitch and knot in these enormous tapestries were done by hand. (18)

11. Ladies and gentlemen, the winner and still champion of the World Grammar Contest are on stage right now! (16)

12. Neither all the king's horses nor the only remaining king's man are able to glue Humpty Dumpty back together again. (19)

13. According to *The Record* every teacher and student in the school are suffering from the "I want my vacation" blues. (18)

14. Steak and eggs, always delicious and nutritious, is my favorite meal. (16)

15. Either Paula or her co-presidents is scheduled to lead the parade in honor of the veterans. (19)

16. Assault and battery are subject to criminal prosecution. (16)

17. Dombey and Sons, a company that manufactures Victorian souvenirs, are expecting a large profit this year. (17)

18. Neither the Department of Agriculture nor the farmers was sure of the correct way to grow artificial flowers. (19)

19. Agnes and her little pet canary Sybil are trying out a new brand of seed. (15)

20. Neither his hands nor his face were clean. (19)

21. Oliver Twist and his brother Chubby likes to play checkers. (15)

22. Because we all remember the last time you cooked a meal, neither your mother nor your siblings are willing to eat with you again unless you order takeout. (19)

23. Do either Cathy or Oscar have a valid dog license? (19)

24. Saks has a new line of designer toothpicks. (17)

25. Rice and beans is the dish my father always wants for his birthday meal. (16)

(Answer key on page 229.)

II B. Subject-Verb Agreement: More Practice Sentences

If the sentence is correct, write "C." If the sentence contains an error in subject-verb agreement, cross out the verb and write the correct verb at the end of the sentence.

1. Every dog and policeman automatically chase Olive.

2. Peanut butter and sardines is a combination Olive likes.

3. Have Abercrombie & Fitch opened a store in the new mall?

4. Otto and Olive like to search through dumpsters together.

5. Olive's dog and iguana are both imaginary.

6. Have each loyal brother, loving sister, and wealthy uncle finally rejected Ebenezer?

7. Every one of Olive's sons resemble a different comic strip character.

8. Has either Nastine or Boxanne paid her rent yet?

9. Neither Otto's friends nor his family are covering his taxes this year.

10. Neither the players nor their coach have any idea what went wrong in the last quarter.

11. Either the committees or the head of school are going to decide that matter.

12. Neither sickness nor lack of funds keeps Otto sober for long.

13. Burning rope or cheap cigars are creating that stink.

14. No one can guess if the whole gang or only its ringleader were caught.

15. There is always either a loud explosion or several rapid beeps when I push that button.

16. The cat next door and the dog yowling across the street is going to be in my new novel.

17. Do you believe that the shortstop and rookie-of-the-year has to have a good second season?

18. The flowers that Maisie picked and the vase that Andrew bought decorates the dining room table beautifully.

19. Do you think bacon and eggs is a healthful meal?

20. Do either the ant or the grasshoppers have enough food for the winter?

21. Every one of the table tennis serves were close to the net.

22. Bloomingdale's Department Store have nine floors of enticing merchandise.

23. Do each of the sophomore writing courses require a computer?

24. Every computer and printer in this room are going to have a new cable.

25. In the professional skateboard community, harmony and goodwill prevails.

26. How much does spelling and grammar count in life?

27. Neither Bart nor Lisa's friends is going to shoot Mr. Burns with that water pistol.

28. Over the past few days Barnes and Noble has done a brisk trade in the Cliff's Notes to *Macbeth*.

29. Rest assured that neither your parents nor your teacher are planning to stop you in your drive to get into Harvard.

30. In chemistry class this week either Erica or Joe are to do experiments in nuclear fusion.

31. Min Jae's sense of humor and her ability to get along with others win her many friends.

32. Every freshman and sophomore in this school is going to take a test in weightlifting.

33. Every Tom, Dick, and Harry has to pay taxes in April.

34. Mushrooms and pepperoni is my favorite combination when I order a pizza.

35. Russ and Daughters sells pickled herring made the old-fashioned way.

36. Neither the king nor I am perfect, but I am working on the problem.

37. The Tony and the Oscar are two of the best awards in show business.

38. How time-consuming is the class and the homework in that subject?

39. Neither the students nor the head of the committee have a clue about which book we will read next for Book Day.

40. Every word in Emily Dickinson's poems have been used in some startling way.

41. Every family and business in the affected area have been asked to purchase flood insurance.

42. The pie-eating contest and the giant pumpkin raffle have been postponed because of lack of interest.

43. Either Kermit or the other Muppets are going to get Miss Piggy's attention.

44. Every one of my friends seems fascinated by the idea of interstellar travel.

45. Do Brooks Brothers have a department that sells sportswear?

46. Chicken and rice is the most fattening dish Herbert cooks, but he likes to eat it four times per week anyway.

47. David, Lisa, and I are going to watch the next *Seinfeld* rerun together.

48. *CBS Reports* are going to feature Tom Brokaw on the next broadcast.

49. On some fruit and vegetable farms, harvesting and weeding is done by machines.

50. Every student in this class and in the other English classes is glad to finish these boring sentences.

II A and B Cumulative Exercise

If the sentence is correct, write "C." If the sentence contains an error in subject-verb agreement, cross out the verb and write the correct verb at the end of the sentence.

1. Otto's smallest problem is taxes, for that scofflaw never pays them.

2. The only thing Olive spends money on is shoes.

3. Olive's favorite possession are her Old Master paintings.

4. The pavement of all the streets in the city need repair.

5. The dogs that chase Otto around the stadium knows that he is afraid of them.

6. Otto, followed by a regiment of barking dogs, go running down the street.

7. The general, not his officers, take responsibility for that defeat.

8. Olive's children, excluding her daughter Boxanne, has never gotten past fifth grade.

9. Every one of the trombonists need lip gloss before performing.

10. Each senator and representative has to decide the issue solely on the merits of the bill.

11. Either Wendy or the lost boys has to take responsibility for Tinkerbell's twinkle.

12. Holden thinks his best quality is his ability to see insincerity and to reject it totally.

13. Baldwin's essay, not the novels, were assigned to the ninth grade.

14. Ellen or Toto need to go back to Kansas too.

15. Here are fifteen reasons why you should not wear purple and black plaid shorts.

16. Many believe the law of immigration and naturalization need to be reexamined.

17. The guests at the ball, not the entertainer, were given free samples of iced tea.

18. Tallulah, along with her sisters Daisy Mae and Wilhelmina, are going to be a big hit with the type-setters.

19. According to the latest census, each canary and parakeet in America have a loving home.

20. How near to the edge of the waterfall paddles Sadie and Osavar!

21. AT&T are going to raise rates in time for the holidays.

22. There is a pimple and a scar on every square inch of that man's face.

23. Does either Mary or her little lambs like mutton stew?

24. Beancurd and mushrooms is the dish that made Pig Heaven famous in the world of Chinese cuisine.

25. Dick and Lynn, but not Don, are going to spend the weekend reading good books in a secure, undisclosed location.

26. Either the secret service or the private security guards is with her at all times.

27. Shearson and Sons are selling bonds at reduced prices since the crash.

28. Every one of those mannikins have plastic hair.

29. Leaning on the lamp, trailing his wounded foot, and nearly incoherent with rage and fright is Peter.

30. Ebert and Roeper, not the *New York Times* critic, are going to decide the fate of that picture.

31. The United States government, along with the leaders of some other friendly governments, are going to ban garlic as a terrorist weapon.

32. In that class the best student and most popular athlete is William B. Williamsberg.

33. Behind the garden at the side of the road stands a candy factory belching smoke.

34. The pitcher and star hitter of the series was injured yesterday, and the loss of that one player was devastating to the team.

35. The poodle and the hound, along with their friend the dogcatcher, is just about ready for a new type of dogfood.

36. Dreamworks have had too many successful movies this season.

37. Either Idabell or her pet rhinos has to rebel against those cruel zookeepers.

38. Does Tiny Tim and his brother believe in the Tooth Fairy?

39. Harrison Brothers sell a great home surgery course for do-it-yourselfers.

40. A certain degree of privacy and security are desirable for the most important celebrities.

41. Her problem is late arrivals and a refusal to sign in.

42. My French teacher, together with all the other teachers who had the honor of instructing me this year, are ready for a rest home.

43. How softly and sweetly in the whispering pines bellow Andrew.

44. Do Fran or Ollie really need Kukla for that show?

45. Here's the best answers to those questions.

46. Lord and Taylor are one of the best retailers in the city.

47. Bread and butter are my favorite snack when I return from mud-wrestling practice.

48. There is no problem with any of those sentences.

49. Neither the cat nor his pajamas were ready to face the veterinarian's assistant.

50. Every one of these exercises is really a test of your intelligence.

Lesson C.
Agreement when the Subject is an Indefinite Pronoun

Some indefinite pronouns are singular and some are plural, and some can be either, depending on the prepositional phrase that follows them. You need to memorize the following lists.

20. **The following indefinite pronouns are always singular and require a singular verb:** *everybody, everyone, every one, somebody, someone, some one, anybody, anyone, any one, nobody, no one, one, each, either, neither, anything, something, everything, nothing,* and *another.*

> **All the "ones," all the "things," and all the "bodies" are singular.**
> *Either* and *neither* **without their partners (***or, nor***) are always singular.**

*Each of Angela's sandwiches **is** enough for a full meal.*
*Everybody **is** afraid of Ms. Nopushova's tests.*
*Either of those computers **is** a good buy, but the Macintosh is easier to use.*

21. **When the subject is one of the "AMANS" pronouns (***all, most/more, any, none, some***) and is followed by a prepositional phrase, the verb will be singular if the noun in the phrase is singular but plural if the noun in the phrase is plural.**

*All of Salim's money **has** been spent.*
*All of my uncle's children **have** hazel eyes.*

The same holds true for fractions.

*One third of my time **is** spent doing my Biology homework.*
*Three quarters of Rancida's friends **have** had some body-part pierced.*

Sometimes the prepositional phrase will contain a singular noun and a plural one:

*Most of that rack of paperbacks **is/are** trash.*

Is or are? The writer is really commenting on the books, not the rack, so the verb will be plural. Use your good judgment!

22. **The pronouns *both, many, few, several,* and *others* always take a plural verb.**

*Few of Mr. Sober's students **think** his jokes are funny.*
*Many **respect** his command of his subject, however.*

II C. Subject-Verb Agreement: Guided Exercise

Some of the sentences below are correct, and some have an error in subject-verb agreement. If the sentence is correct, write "C." If the sentence contains an error, cross out the verb and write the correct verb at the end of the sentence. The number in parentheses at the end of each sentence refers to a rule you have just learned.

1. Either of the two cakes that Tim brought for the bake sale are acceptable for dessert today. (20)

2. Anybody Chuck knows has to laugh at his jokes. (20)

3. Both of the puppies that Nicole likes has tiny, red leather collars. (22)

4. One of Kathy's favorite soap opera stars are going to be on television tonight. (20)

5. All of the pumpkin pie was eaten by Eddie, who is always very hungry. (21)

6. Nothing about these suits lead me to believe that pinstripes are a good design. (20)

7. Anyone who breeds dogs know how easily the little furry creatures get sick. (20)

8. Everyone who want some mustard with those hotdogs should get on the Grey Poupon line. (20)

9. Most of the box of cookies have been eaten. (21)

10. Either of the two actors are able to act as acting-captain of the Acting Team. (20)

11. Otto has two sisters, and both of them, but especially Olivia, despises him. (22)

12. Neither of the candidates for the co-presidency of the Future Farmers of America wish to address the student body. (20)

13. None of the stories deals with sports. (21)

14. Someone has to take care of that kitten before it tries to bite the snake! (20)

15. All of the money in the world is not enough to buy the Yankees from George Steinbrenner unless he is ready to sell. (21)

16. All of the baseball shoes that George bought has a ripped "NY" insignia. (21)

17. Few of the clouds in the sky understands that they will bring rain to our picnic. (22)

18. Were either of the two sisters present at the Wedding of the Century? (20)

19. Nobody know the trouble I've seen. (20)

20. Are either of the boys capable of driving a standard shift? (20)

21. Neither of the spiders were ready to throw in the towel and concede the prize for best web. (20)

22. Any of the shoes with holes are to be placed in that bin over there. (21)

23. Some of the air in Los Angeles is actually clean. (21)

24. Anybody in the audience is allowed to request a special song from the band. (20)

25. All of the seniors at the prom, but not the only freshman present, are going to a club after the prom is over. (21)

(Answer key on page 230.)

II C. Subject-Verb Agreement: More Practice Sentences

If the sentence is correct, write "C." If the sentence contains an error in subject-verb agreement, cross out the verb and write the correct verb at the end of the sentence.

1. Each of these doctors have successfully operated on the brains of fleas.

2. Do either of the girls have a new tennis racket for the tournament?

3. None of the cherry pies has been eaten by George, but he did a good job on the tree.

4. Some of the velvet is soiled, and I won't be able to clean it until after the dance.

5. I hate to admit it, but a few of these sentences is stupid.

6. According to the government, nothing has been done about that pollution problem in quite a while.

7. Everyone in the orchestra need a few spare moments before tuning up.

8. Neither of the farmers know how to plant tomatoes under water.

9. Has either of the orders been sent to the manufacturer?

10. Neither of the proposed bills were accepted in its entirety, and the senate actually made many changes.

11. Biff doesn't understand why no one are laughing at his best teacher jokes.

12. Are neither of the girls absolutely certain who the mugger is?

13. A few of the students in the other class finds the grammar lessons too hard.

14. Standardized testing favors the average person, and anyone with really creative ideas don't score well on the SAT, it is sometimes said.

15. All those who don't study for the test will get lousy grades.

16. All right, everybody cheating in the last five rows are automatically suspended!

17. All the pockets in the suspect's overcoat has been searched.

18. Both of the presidents of the club was dismissed for being useless.

19. Have all of the money been spent on such trivialities?

20. Both the students in the dorm and those who rent apartments feel they pay too much.

21. Several of the bouquets that the bride threw was caught by the same desperate bridesmaid.

22. Some of Dr. Kazuki's students has decided to take the AP history test this year.

23. Another of the advertisements that you like so much are going to be shown during the Superbowl.

24. Not one of those bunnies have ever lifted a paw to help Peter Cottontail.

25. Some of the drivers wants the speed limit raised to 330 miles per hour.

26. Both of the girls have notes on that subject, but neither want to share the information.

27. Everybody in those camps know how to swim a mile underwater without surfacing for air.

28. All of Tarzan's toes was covered in banana scum.

29. On *Melrose Place* most of the stars are older than the characters they play.

30. All of the stars in the sky is enough of a view for me!

31. One of her daughters look exactly like Marge Simpson.

32. Anybody is able to pass this test with just a little knowledge.

33. Everybody want to do well on the bowling test, but only some of the students are able to bowl a strike every time.

34. Have everybody found the correct locker and locker combination?

35. Most people dislike Mr. Thumb, but most respects his ability to know exactly which seed will sprout first.

36. None of the cake is cool enough to be iced.

37. Oshkosh, which everyone think is the best city in the United States, recently tried to lure the Olympics to Wisconsin.

38. None of those New Yorkers knows that a "bubbler" is a water fountain in Wisconsin.

39. All of the notes in Segovia's most famous composition, *Granada,* is in tune with the piano.

40. Have either of the piano tuners finished working in the theater?

41. Is all of that pie for me?

42. Is all of those presents for me?

43. Several of the books that were written by that famous poet is on the best seller list right now.

44. Everyone looks forward to reading Mr. Crum's new novel.

45. None of the taxi drivers in New York City is able to drive, according to that teacher.

46. Neither of the new shows that Steven Spielberg made are ready to be aired.

47. Nothing of the gigantic castles remain after the ogre gets through with them.

48. All of Aunt Hepzibah's baseball cards are being sent to charity.

49. A few of the valuable cards, like Joe Dimaggio's rookie card, is being auctioned.

50. Have every one of these sentences been corrected?

Lesson D.
Agreement when the subject is a collective noun or noun of quantity

...When the subject is a collective noun

Collective nouns are nouns that define groups of people or things: *class, jury, group, committee, collection, team, faculty, family, workforce* are all examples of this type of noun. Collective nouns are sometimes singular and sometimes plural. The test: are the members of the group acting as a single unit, or are they acting as separate individuals? The latter will be true when there is some division or difference within the group.

23. **When a collective noun is the subject and identifies a group *acting as a single entity*, the verb is singular. But when it identifies a group whose members are acting independently or are seen as different from one another, use a plural verb.**

    Here the group is acting as one entity, an "it":

    *Jane's family **has decided** to overlook her eccentricities.*
    > [Here the whole family has made the decision as a unit.]
    *The Sexual Harassment Committee **is** very active this year.*
    *The jury **is** still out on the question of whether Eric is entirely sane.*
    > [In both sentences we are asked to think of the committee and the jury as an undivided entity.]

    But in these sentences the collective noun refers to individuals, as "they":

    *His family **quarrel** about everything.*
    > [They quarrel among themselves; we're asked to think of several individuals, not one cohesive unit.]
    *The gang **are debating** whether dancing should be an Olympic sport.*
    > [The members of the gang are debating among themselves.]
    *The congregation **have** not yet **agreed** on a new rabbi.*
    *While the prisoner smoked a last cigarette, the firing squad **were checking** the sights on their rifles.*
    > [Since each member of the squad has a different rifle, these actions are thought of as performed by individual soldiers, and the verb is plural.]

    **If you can add "individually" or "among themselves" to the verb, it's plural.
    If it makes sense to add "the members of" before the collective noun, it's plural.**

    *The congregation have not yet agreed **among themselves** on a new rabbi.*
    > [They're not agreeing with some other congregation.]
    ***The members of** the firing squad were checking the sights on their rifles.*

24. *Number* is singular when it means "the total quantity" and plural when it means "several." Nouns of quantity work like the **AMANS** pronouns.

> *The number of Ruth's friends **keeps** growing.*
> *A number of Rachel's classmates **have** read <u>Macbeth</u> before.*

> **The number is always singular. A number is always plural.**

When a noun showing quantity (*the rest, a part, the majority, an abundance,* etc.) is the subject and is followed by a prepositional phrase, it will be singular if the noun in the phrase is singular but plural if the noun in the phrase is plural; the verb must agree with it.

> *A part of Olive's capital **is invested** in lottery tickets.*
> *The majority of Moroccans **are** Berbers, not Arabs.*

25. **Plural nouns for time and money usually indicate a single amount or measure. Use a singular verb.**

> *Five dollars **is** more than Olive likes to pay for a meal.*
> *Four years **is** enough time to learn a language well.*

But:
> *More than ten thousand one-dollar bills **are** taped to the walls of the dining-room at the Cabbage Key Inn in Florida.*

Now you're counting individual singles.

II D. Subject-Verb Agreement: Guided Exercise

Some of the sentences below are correct, and some have an error in subject-verb agreement. If the sentence is correct, write "C." If the sentence contains an error, cross out the verb and write the correct verb at the end of the sentence. The number in parentheses at the end of each sentence refers to a rule you have just learned.

1. Despite the cold, the family of wrens that have made a home in the pine tree have managed to survive the winter. (23)

2. The committee, after a morning of deliberation, are now ready to offer a recommendation. (23)

3. An army of ants have built a huge mound right in the middle of the lawn. (23)

4. Frampton's family is always arguing with one another about the use of the car. (23)

5. The number of catfish that Mother caught with her bare hands is greater this year than last. (24)

6. Five dollars is too much to pay for a bag of popcorn, even a bag of gourmet popcorn! (25)

7. Twenty minutes of exercise a day are enough to keep you and your heart in good shape. (25)

8. My family always fights over who should do the dinner dishes. (23)

9. Fifteen dollars are what I owe you for that earring, not thirty. (25)

10. The number of students going on the trip reflects the amount of homework they would have to do if they did not attend. (24)

11. A number of students has expressed interest in a Dracula Anniversary Dinner. (24)

12. The Dinner Committee are in agreement that the main course should be blood sausage, without garlic. (24)

13. The faculty are not able to come to a decision about the time of the dinner, but of course it will be after dark. (24)

14. Are two hours enough for all the special events? (25)

15. Our basketball team have won all of the games this season, except for the annual teacher/student match. (23)

16. The rest of my family agree with me that I should plan an extended vacation in Iceland, where I will learn how to ski on a glacier. (24)

17. An abundance of programs offer instruction in ceramics, but I plan to get some clay and figure it out myself. (24)

18. My cousin's team are preparing a special slide show for the sports assembly. (23)

19. I like jogging, but twenty-five miles are just too much. (25)

20. For several years the Committee for Valuing Difference were asking for a coordinator of diversity. (23)

21. The Senate of the United States is in session at this very moment. (23)

22. The House of Representatives have not yet decided the fate of the tax bill. (23)

23. The hockey team is busy taping their sticks and sharpening their skates for the rematch with the Rangers. (23)

24. A number of ninth graders has recently discovered a secret nook in the basement of the gym. (24)

25. The exact count of middle school children who have vanished into that cave and never returned are greater than you may suppose. (24)

(Answer key on page 230.)

II D. Subject-Verb Agreement: More Practice Sentences

If the sentence is correct, write "C." If the sentence contains an error in subject-verb agreement, cross out the verb and write the correct verb at the end of the sentence.

1. The Amateur Surgeons' Club has just opened a new operating theater, called The Gross Theater.

2. Members of the medical profession are curious to know what goes on in that theater.

3. A number of fine musicians have given recitals there during operations.

4. Half a million dollars were not too much to pay for such a fine theater.

5. Olive's Home Surgery class meet there every Thursday.

6. Her class have never agreed about anything, particularly about the best method for finishing a fine seam.

7. Five hundred dollars are not enough to pay for Olive's bag of surgical tools.

8. Five thousand dollars, on the other hand, is enough to buy Olive's oil franchise, if you act quickly.

9. The jury was convinced that "guilty" was the appropriate decision.

10. The number of words that Otto can spell seems to be decreasing.

11. The club thinks that he will be a good president if he can ever stop hitting himself on the thumb with his gavel.

12. The Committee to Eradicate Gum Chewing on Campus have decided to install surveillance cameras in the cafeteria.

13. Fifteen minutes of Bart Simpson's pranks are quite enough.

14. A number of viewers have recently asked for an extra year of Major League Bowling, but ESPN may not give in to their wishes.

15. After such an exciting playoff round in the Stanley Cup series, my family are not speaking to each other.

16. This jury is not capable of ordering lunch without a menu.

17. The senior class is still discussing the proper farewell gift to the school.

18. A number of seniors want to buy strobe lights for the new operating theater.

19. The quantity of students who are in favor of the plan are not particularly large in comparison with the whole student body.

20. "Ten minutes are enough for this decision," declared the dean.

21. At the trial, the defense team sit on the left and the prosecution sits on the right.

22. A club in a nearby school have earned money for its trip to Alaska by knitting scarves for sale in the trendy "Penguin Boutique."

23. Although my family does not all share the same opinion on the matter, I can count on my mother's support.

24. When he heard that seven thousand dollars were needed to finance my expedition to the Ukraine, Yoshi withdrew his support.

25. Since twenty million dollars have already been invested in the project, the investors are a little worried.

26. My family hates going to the movies, even when the film has received two thumbs up.

27. The audience rises to applaud whenever Jean Claude VanDamme conducts a symphony.

28. There's a number of good reasons for buying those cookies.

29. The number of locks on her door were increasing each day, even as the national crime rate dipped.

30. Over the past few days the committee has put together a great brochure explaining how to churn butter at home.

31. The two hours given by the testing agency were not enough for Flossie to finish the milking test.

32. A number of udders were left unmilked!

33. The remainder of the cows were satisfied with Flossie's udder-handling.

34. NASA's executive board disagrees about the need for oxygen on the space station.

35. The astronauts' union, on the other hand, believes that oxygen is a non-negotiable demand.

36. How much do I owe you? Ten dollars are on the table.

37. Ten agonizing minutes have ticked by, and I still can't remember how to conjugate *avoir*.

38. The baseball team trot onto the field every day at 3:30 to practice.

39. The team simultaneously practice bunting, hitting, and catching in separate areas of the field.

40. Is four hours enough time for you to complete that essay?

41. The number of exams per marking period varies from year to year.

42. A group of students have complained about the music played by the bus driver.

43. Fifty minutes of "cool jazz" are played on one bus route, which winds around all over the place.

44. The Earth Science Club is studying volcanoes and hopes to cause an eruption in Los Angeles soon.

45. The steering committee, however, is arguing about the best place to put the volcano.

46. A number of seniors wants to blow up Hollywood.

47. Two thousand dollars are required for volcanic smoke.

48. The jury in that case have not been able to reach a decision.

49. The Survivors' Club hopes to convince each juror that "guilty" is the only possible verdict.

50. The majority of the ninth graders is extremely bored with grammar and wants to stop learning it.

I-II Cumulative Exercise

If the sentence is correct, write "C." If the sentence contains an error in punctuation with apostrophes or subject-verb agreement, cross out the incorrect form and write the correct one at the end of the sentence.

1. Here come every one of Alexander the Great's elephants, all marching in step!

2. Has all of the money been spent on potato chips, or is there enough for dip?

3. The class has spent some time debating the sincerity of Jane and Rochester's love.

4. Neither Olive's Algerian cousins nor Nastine ever know what day of the week it is.

5. Few in those girls' gang are aware of the fact that a major reptile collector is a friend of their's.

6. Otto, in company with the rest of Olive's crowd, are ignorant of this fact.

7. Everybody in this group imagines that she, like them, is reptileless.

8. Yet a blue spiny lizard and twelve iguanas share Olive's bed.

9. None of the reptiles, apart from Toto the skink, has attractive eating habits.

10. Most of the food the lizards eat are live crickets.

11. The people who work in the pet store don't let Olive come in.

12. Some of the crickets she finds in the park; the rest are stolen from the zoo.

13. When she has collected enough crickets, she frees them in the same room where she stores those spiders of her's.

14. Anybody passing her living quarters hear a frantic chirping.

15. It's most likely an escaped cricket, not Olive or the reptiles, that make this noise.

16. Each of Olive's pets have a name.

17. Her last favorite among the iguanas was called "Rover"; the new numero uno answers to "Iggy."

18. Why hasn't any of Olive's friends learned her secret?

19. Not every one of them care to know about Olive's personal life.

20. Either Nastine or Otto comes to see her every day, but neither have ever noticed the reptiles.

21. The scamperings of the lizard hasn't yet caught their attention, nor has the crickets' shrill chirping.

22. A group of Olive's wealthy relatives have decided she's insane.

23. Usually her family never agree about anything.

24. Every time an issue is raised, peoples' views for and against it are aired.

25. As a result, Olive's family rarely get any business done.

26. This time, however, they have already agreed to put Olive in a "home."

27. How has such a quarrelsome gang reached consensus?

28. Neither Olive's antisocial behavior nor her fondness for reptiles were the deciding factor.

29. Olive's extravagance with money, not her peculiarities, are what moved them to act.

30. For instance, it doesn't bother them that Lord & Taylor send Olive a new pair of shoes each month.

31. However, fifty thousand dollars, in their opinion, is just too much to pay for one pair of shoes.

32. Her glasses always seem to cost over a thousand dollars, but theirs' are cheaper.

33. The number of pairs of pants she buys are excessive, in their view.

34. Nobody among her cousins spends as much as Olive does.

35. Few in her family, famous for penny-pinching, go through a tenth of the money she spends.

36. Either of the two Tiffany lamps that Tim brought in for the Glee Club flea market are worth more than my entire contribution.

37. Either the superstitious authors or Anne is going to have to write the sequel to *Friday the Thirteenth, Part 12*.

38. A number of doors have signs that read, "No Menus."

39. Anybody Chuck knows has to laugh at his jokes, however corny they are.

40. Everything in the world loses its shape in the course of time.

41. Kyra, not the other track team members, are going to be in the Olympics in 1998.

42. One of Kathy's favorite soap opera stars are going to be on television tonight.

43. Bloomingdale's have a sale on the imported French stationery that Danielle likes.

44. None of the children's teachers were rich, but those dedicated educators didn't mind having to live in squalor.

45. In the photo that Kelly snapped, every man and woman apart from the Green twins is wearing an orange hat.

46. He got little sleep, for his grades was his biggest worry.

47. Only one of the victims is bleeding, though four others have lost consciousness from the shock of the collision.

48. Few apart from Otto have ever talked to God.

49. The reasons given in this report are sometimes absurd, sometimes simply wrong.

50. Is there any more of these pumpkin and mayonnaise sandwiches?

III. Pronoun-Antecedent Agreement

(agr / pa)

Pronouns replace nouns or other pronouns (indefinite pronouns, for instance). **The antecedent of a pronoun is the noun or pronoun that it replaces.** Normally you will find the antecedent before the pronoun that replaces it:

> *As the guests arrive, they are greeted and handed a towel.*

Guests is the antecedent of the pronoun *they*. Notice that reversing the order – *They are greeted and handed a towel as the guests arrive* – makes *they* a different set of people from the *guests*.

> *The captain of the girls' boxing team can't remember where she left her gloves.*

Captain is the antecedent of *she* and *her*. The pronouns are singular because the antecedent is singular. The pronouns are feminine because the *captain* is a woman: *captain of the girls' boxing team.*

26. A pronoun must agree with its antecedent in gender and number.

This is the basic rule. To apply it, you must identify the pronoun's antecedent and determine whether it is singular/plural and masculine/feminine/neuter.

> The **soldier** fired **his** rifle.
> My **grandmother** raised **her** children to respect literature.
> The tree lost three of **its** branches in the storm.
> The artillerymen fired **their** cannons.

27. If the pronoun's antecedent is a collective noun, the pronoun will be singular if the collective noun refers to a unit (doing the same thing or holding the same opinion), but plural if it refers to a collection of individuals (acting separately or disagreeing).

> The **team** is congratulating **it**self upon **its** victory.
> The **team** are disputing the MVP award among **them**selves.

Notice that in these sentences the verb also changes number: *is* in the first sentence, *are* in the second. When the subject of the sentence is also the antecedent of a pronoun, two separate agreements must be made.

> **To decide whether you need a singular or plural pronoun, use the same rules you used to decide whether to use a singular or plural verb.**

28. When singular antecedents are modified by *every* or *each*, or when two or more are joined by *or, nor, either-or* or *neither-nor*, they are singular, and the pronoun referring to them must also be singular.

*Either Kate or Isabelle protests the amount of work I give **her** to do.*
***Neither Ray nor Billy** has **his** book with **him**.*
*Sage notes **each rule and regulation** so that he will remember **it**.*

29. **The following indefinite pronouns are singular; if they refer to people, they are also often ambiguously masculine or feminine. When they are used as antecedents, use an appropriate pronoun or pronoun-pair:** *he or she, him or her, his or her.*

    Somebody, everybody, anybody, nobody, everyone, anyone, someone, each, either, neither.

    These are the "one/body/thing" pronouns that you studied in Rule 20.

    *Everybody knows **his or her** mother's first name. [NOT **their**]*
    *When **someone** belches, **he or she** usually apologizes. [NOT **they**]*
    *Otto didn't tell **anybody** what he would give **him or her**. [NOT **them**]*

    Note: if you find yourself using this sort of pair several times in a sentence, try to rework the sentence so as to avoid doing so:

    *Otto didn't tell **any** of his friends what he would give **them**.*

30. **The noun** *person* **works the same way as the pronouns above.**

    *When Layla dislikes **a person**, she won't speak to **him or her**.*

31. **The indefinite pronouns** *any, more/most, all, none, some* **(the "AMANS") may be either singular or plural, depending on the number of the noun in the phrase that modifies them.** *Both, few, several,* **and** *others* **are always plural.**

    Compare Rules 21 and 22.

    ***None** of those boys have tied **their** shoes.*
    ***Most** of that cheese has lost **its** flavor.*
    ***Few** can deny that **they** would rather be rich than poor.*

    In the first sentence, *None* is modified by a prepositional phrase whose noun is *boys*, plural. Therefore *None is* considered to be plural and is replaced by a plural pronoun, *their*. In the second sentence *Most* is modified by a prepositional phrase whose noun is *cheese*, singular, and *Most* is considered to be singular and is replaced by a singular pronoun, *its*. In the third, *Few* is automatically plural.

32. **When a relative pronoun –** *who, which, that* **– is the subject of its clause and refers to a singular noun or pronoun, the verb in the clause is singular.**

    *The **student who** listens best does best.*
    ***Anyone who** cares about dogs will admire that superior canine, Toby.*

    In the first sentence the antecedent of *who* is *student*, a singular noun. *Who* is the subject of the clause – *who listens best* – and therefore the verb in that clause – *listens* – is singular. In the second sentence, *who* agrees with *anyone*, which by Rule 28 is singular, and so the rest follows.

It can be hard to find the antecedent of the relative pronoun. In the following two sentences, what is it, and which is the correct form of the sentence?

Andrea is one of those girls who always speaks her mind.
Andrea is one of those girls who always speak their minds.

The *who* refers to *girls*. "There is a set of girls who always speak their minds. Andrea is one of them." Therefore:

*Andrea is one of those **girls** who always **speak their minds**.*

Notice that there are three separate words to be made plural here. How about this:

This is the only one of those keys that fit/fits the lock.

Here *that* refers to *one*, not to *keys*. Only one key *fits* the lock. Therefore:

*This is the only **one** of those keys that **fits** the lock.*

> **Just remember: "one of those who" means the verb is plural, but "the (only) one (of those) who" means the verb is singular.**

33. **When a relative pronoun – *who, which, that* – is subject of a clause, and its antecedent is a personal pronoun – *I, you, we* – the verb in the clause must have the form that would be used with the antecedent.**

*I, who **am** your teacher, tell you this.*
*It's you who **are** to be praised for understanding it.*

In the first sentence the antecedent of *who* is *I*. Plug *I* into the adjective clause, and you'll see that the verb-form must be *am*. In the second the *who* refers to *you*, and plugging *you* into the adjective clause gives *you are* for the verb.

III. Pronoun-Antecedent Agreement: Guided Exercise

Check the following sentences for errors in pronoun-antecedent agreement. If the sentence is correct, write "C." If there is an error, change the incorrect pronoun so that it agrees with the antecedent. In a few sentences you may have to change the verb. The number in parentheses refers to a rule you have just learned.

1. Did anybody do their homework or will I have to bring out the penalty box? (29)

2. We try to give everyone on the math team his or her own uniform. (29)

3. Otto is one of those men who starts to scream for no reason. (32)

4. Neither of the two men who are wearing blue uniforms is a cop. (29)

5. Is it you who claim that somebody wants to poison me? (33)

6. Captain Picard is the only one of the *StarTrek* captains who does not need a haircut. (32)

7. Has either of the two girls brought their books to class? (29)

8. She told me it's I who needs to stop mumbling. (33)

9. Every soldier is taught to scrub their rifles thoroughly with glass cleaner for that coveted never-been-fired look. (28)

10. When he heard that the vacation had been cancelled, Moises asked, "Has the faculty gone crazy?" (27)

11. Neither Olive nor Nastine will say how many nights they spent in jail for protesting the world-wide ban on pigeons. (28)

12. Neither Ada Mant nor Mrs. Ridgid are willing to compromise their position. (28)

13. Each of the waiters have been given their share of the tips. (29)

14. Has every one of those girls paid their towel fee? (29)

15. Billy Swettspeare is one of those pitchers who like hot weather. (32)

16. None of the girls asked themselves whether climbing the Empire State Building was really worth the effort. (31)

17. Either of the debaters has the opportunity to rebut his or her opponent. (29)

18. Mr. Kramp, the swimming coach, said that if anybody on the swim team was willing to spend an extra hour, he'd review the strokes with them. (29)

19. Because neither of the scriptwriters could make up their minds, the director decided that the hero would be eaten by the T. Rex just moments after the heroine had bought a jar of mustard. (29)

20. Arriving early for the preliminary logrolling tournament, some of the participants had trouble finding their logs. (31)

21. That copy of *Stocks and Bonds* belongs to Bob and Freddie, who have shared it ever since they went bankrupt. (32)

22. When the conductor raised his baton, the orchestra raised its instruments and started to play. (27)

23. A person who expects to be taken seriously must control their temper. (30)

24. Eddie, never one for taking chances, believes that everyone should bring their raincoat even if the sun is shining. (29)

25. Saks is the store where Maureen buys presents because she likes their merchandise. (26)

(Answer key on page 230.)

III. Pronoun-Antecedent Agreement: More Practice Sentences

If the sentence is correct, write "C." If the sentence contains an error in pronoun-antecedent agreement, cross out the pronoun and write the correct pronoun at the end of the sentence. In a few sentences you may have to change a verb also.

1. That chocolate cake is the only one of Otto's desserts that are worth eating.

2. Asquith is one of those students who is always daydreaming during math class.

3. Every one of the twenty-five Yankees got their World Series ring last night.

4. A mere ten days into the term, the teacher gave the class one of those pop quizzes that severely challenges the brain.

5. If these exercises seem too difficult to any particular person, they should address their complaints to the principal.

6. The science researchers, now that their team has won the Nobel Prize, is having a hard time getting through the line of reporters and into their lab.

7. I hear that anyone who fails their eye test will lose their driver's license.

8. Don't you dare ask either of my aunts where they go after church on Sunday!

9. Melody learned from her supervisor, Titus Canby, that if a salesclerk has a hang-loose attitude, they will get fired from the lingerie department.

10. After numerous rejections we learned never to ask either of the teachers about their experiences in the Sixties.

11. It is up to each individual to come to terms with their own limitations and break their own chains.

12. Each of the boys who scalped tickets outside the stadium last night should give his earnings to charity.

13. Somebody left their tray on the field and will be severely punished.

14. All of the boys who have passed their tests will receive diplomas.

15. There is no record, however, that the company will keep their promise to stockholders.

16. If there is anyone who wants to learn about Islamic culture, they should ask that history teacher.

17. Both of the graduation speakers have promised to keep his or her remarks short and to the point.

18. In the interest of nutrition, everybody among those health-conscious students has decided that he or she will boycott the cafeteria until better lettuce is provided.

19. This book is one of those weighty volumes that has more pages than facts.

20. If I were you, Piggy, I'd join one of those support groups that claims to help people control their appetites.

21. None of the middle schoolers have done their homework, and Mr. Di Cipliano is determined to find an appropriate response to this problem.

22. Every one of the students who have spent at least three trimesters at our school is eligible for the bubble gum-blowing contest.

23. Ask anybody at the party whether they caught a whiff of Albert's cologne.

24. One of the great weaknesses of this test is its failure to give every student of exceptional ability an opportunity to display their talent.

25. Parker is the only one of the competing mathematicians who were able to complete the exam in less than an hour.

26. Not a single one of the thousands of fans who came to the joust brought their lances with them.

27. Kelly is one of the players who has decided to participate in the pep rally.

28. Each boy and girl in the kindergarten must bring their lunch tomorrow.

29. Max is one of those writers who needs absolute silence when he works.

30. He gave the gavel to me, who am to preside at the meeting.

31. The army of ants brought their tiny little legs into perfect marching time.

32. My family members are arguing about my plan to become a professional torturer, but I am not involved in its dumb little quarrels.

33. Tom is only one of the many boys who is in love with Kristina.

34. Every man, woman, and child who survived Waco has sold their story to *Time* magazine.

35. We use this pen because it is the only one of the writing instruments that work under water.

36. Some would say that all college-bound students see his or her education as a means to an end.

37. A former Math teacher, Joseph Chase was one of the soldiers who was a translator for President Roosevelt at the historic Yalta conference.

38. Remember, each of these rules should be taken for what it is worth.

39. Everyone needs a few minutes to check their work after a test like this.

40. Here comes Mary and Angela with their briefcases!

41. Her fellow-potters in Ceramics class cannot agree on the type of glaze they want for their vases.

42. Colin Powell proudly presented the plaque to me, who is to represent the United States in the World Checkers Championship.

43. Every boy and girl, asked to help refugees from Liberia, did their best.

44. The box of sweaters that were sent by Parcel Post have arrived late.

45. Ms. Reed is one of the grammar police officers who really know their rules.

46. Roxie, not the other fox terriers, has to bring her food dish to the counter before she is fed.

47. The students in the Applied Biology class were just taking his or her positions when the bell rang for a fire drill.

48. Does either of the boys wish to take their spelling test again?

49. Either Mr. Bollux or Dr. DeKreppit is always complaining about the classrooms they are assigned to.

50. Derek is one of those students who thinks he knows more than the teacher.

I-III Cumulative Exercise

If the sentence is correct, write "C." If the sentence contains an error in punctuation with apostrophes, cross out the incorrect form and write the correct one at the end of the sentence. If the sentence contains an error in subject-verb agreement, cross out the verb and write the correct verb at the end of the sentence. If the sentence has an error in pronoun-antecedent agreement, cross out the incorrect pronoun and write the correct pronoun at the end of the sentence. Remember that some sentences may contain both kinds of agreement error.

1. Rehfein, not the sophomores, have tickets to the dance.

2. Every single computer program and accessory on that shelf is a mystery to Michelle, who think's she may lose her mind trying to decipher them.

3. There are no pen and pencil on Carol's desk; in fact, there are nothing besides a mirror.

4. Staples is the store with the largest stock, and its merchandise is very well priced.

5. Mr. Hadenoff is going to strangle anyone who rips up their homework.

6. Neither the kindergarten children nor Tim have remembered to bring lunch money.

7. Justin interviews a Native American weaver, while either Running Deer or her cousins takes notes.

8. The team members do not agree about the proper punishment for Ed, once its captain, now its leading absentee.

9. None of the shoes is narrow enough for Carolyn.

10. When Mr. McCutcheon fires the starting gun for the final, the ninth graders are going to swallow hard, pick up its pencils, and do some serious grammar.

11. Each of the baby boys that Kelly is minding have lost their favorite blankets.

12. Kathy is one of the few freshmen who knows karate at the brown-belt level.

13. Anne, whose your friend, plans to give you a totally disgusting story to read.

14. Antonio's track team is practicing for the next meet, when they will run farther than ever before.

15. Sears became famous for their mail order catalogue.

16. Some of the Yankees have put too much pine tar on their bats, according to analysts of the game.

17. Both of the Romulans were told not to fight Worf, the only one of the many starship crewmembers who are able to beat them.

18. Grammar sentences, not the test, is the hardest thing about school.

19. Neither Mr. Bienstock nor the deans is going to do karaoke during Music Week.

20. Anybody who wants a new copy of Lou's book must bring their old one to the bookstore.

21. Either Pietra or that other lady who is responsible for cleaning the nuclear reactor have left their gear in the doorway.

22. "Stay out of the teachers' smoking room if you like oxygen," said Karissa, who could no longer tolerate the adult's smoking.

23. Peter said that a number of staplers, the electric kind, is necessary for his office.

24. Katherine felt bad when she saw how thin the lion was getting, so she gave it a huge, meaty bone for it's afternoon snack.

25. If you spill paint on Eric's mink rug, you must pay him one years' salary.

26. Cinderella, who's shoes need new soles, has an appointment with the local glassmaker.

27. The jurors do not agree about whether Dana really took those socks from the childrens' sock drawer.

28. Much of my experience counting votes were gained when I worked for the presidential campaign in Florida.

29. Hillary's and Bill's next campaign will be different, since this time it'll be Hillary who is running.

30. "This is one of the few grammar tests that has interesting sentences," declared Dan.

31. The teacher doesn't let anyone go into the boys' lavatory when it's being cleaned, as the fumes from the cleaning fluid are sickening.

32. None of the freshmen have accepted that they must take this grammar test.

33. The Perrys' pool is not as large as our's.

34. The photographer, not the hairdressers and makeup artists, make Mike's face interesting.

35. Damian's team are going to play a game at eight o'clock sharp.

36. **Antonio: The Movie** is one of the few projects that claims Andy's complete attention.

37. Steve, as well as all of the other foreign language students, is to receive a special award from the Modern Language Association.

38. Gabe and you, who are fans of the new Student Body President, will enjoy the assemblies this year.

39. Steve or I, who am interested in parasailing, will go to the Bahamas this vacation.

40. Damian, but not one of the other students in our class, are going to Greece this summer.

41. Jamie counted, and the number of scratches on Mike's car are increasing every day.

42. Ponscomb Prep cleaned it's pool because Peter got food poisoning after swimming there.

43. The president of the Freshman Dog Appreciation Club is the only one of the students in the school who like pit bulls.

44. The injured pedestrian thinks that all taxi driver's licenses should be revoked after accidents.

45. "I am not one of the many readers who enjoys the fiction of Oliver Sayles," said Iz.

46. In their house in a secure, undisclosed location, Dick and Lynne's den has a pink carpet that some members of their family dislikes.

47. The committee do not agree about the proper award for Dana, who raised a billion dollars for charity.

48. Snow White, who's apple needed polishing, decided to take a nap.

49. Katherine is one of the few ballet dancers who have pink ribbons on they're shoes.

50. Peter believes that a number of papers are incorrectly filed.

IV. Punctuation with Quotations

(pquot)

Let's start with the most common situation: when you're quoting someone else's words, you need a way to set them apart from your own words.

34. When quoting directly, use quotation marks to enclose the exact words of the person being quoted.

> *Macbeth complains, "The time has been that when the brains were out the man would die, and there an end."*

35. When quoting a complete sentence, begin the quotation with a capital letter.

> *Macbeth complains, "The time has been that when the brains were out the man would die, and there an end."*

36. When a quotation ends with a comma or period, these marks always are placed inside the quotation marks.

> *When Godfrey said, "Spiders are crawling over my skin," his mother told him that he was hallucinating.*
> *Henry informed his girlfriend that she was "overreacting."*

37. Semi-colons and colons always are placed outside the final quotation marks.

> *Some people believe in "original sin"; Marise does not.*
> *We gain a new understanding after Ophelia's "mad scene": we see that Hamlet shares in the responsibility for her collapse.*

38. Question marks and exclamation marks go inside the quotation marks when they are a part of what is being quoted, but outside if they belong to your sentence.

> *Macbeth shouts, "The devil damn thee black, thou cream-faced loon!"*
> *Macbeth angrily demands of his servant, "Where got thou that goose look?"*

But:

> *Does Rochester really believe that Jane is "a dream or a shade"?*
> *Damn it, I won't allow anyone to call me a "cursing maniac"!*

39. When a quotation is less than a full sentence, or when it is introduced by *that*, do not set it off with a comma, and do not capitalize the first word of the quotation.

> *She declared that she was "fed up to here" with Ted's chatter.*
> *You will often hear it said that "everyone blames the victim."*

Often quotations are introduced, interrupted, or followed up by a "speaker tag," a short phrase such as "she asked," "they said," or, as above, "Macbeth angrily demands of his servant."

40. When the speaker tag precedes a full-sentence quotation, set it off with a comma.

Macbeth complains, "*The time has been that when the brains were out the man would die, and there an end.*"

41. When the speaker tag follows a full-sentence quotation whose endmark is a period, replace the period with a comma inside the quotation marks.

"*The time has been that when the brains were out the man would die, and there an end,*" *complains Macbeth.*

42. When the speaker tag follows a full-sentence quotation whose endmark is a question or exclamation mark, leave the endmark and do not add a comma.

"*Are you injured, sir?*" *Jane asks Rochester in her first words to him.*

43. When the speaker tag interrupts a full-sentence quotation, set off the tag with commas before and after it.

"*The time has been,*" *complains Macbeth,* "*that when the brains were out the man would die, and there an end.*"

Notice that the second part of the quotation does not begin with a capital letter, since no new sentence is beginning.

44. When the speaker tag interrupts a quotation and a new sentence begins after the interruption, put a period after the speaker tag and capitalize the first word in that new sentence.

"*Do you read your Bible?*" *Mr. Brocklehurst asks Jane.* "*Are you fond of it?*"

45. Use quotation marks to set off slang, technical jargon, and other expressions that you do not want considered as your own.

In journalism these are called "sanitizing quotes." They allow you to distance yourself from words that you do not want to be held accountable for.

Physicists love strange-sounding words such as "*quark.*"
Olive told Sam that she did not mean to "*dis*" *him.*

Do not overuse quotation marks! Have a reason for using them.

WRITER'S REFERENCE: HANDLING QUOTATIONS IN LITERARY ESSAYS

Use a colon to introduce a lengthy or formal quotation, or one being introduced as evidence in an argument.

Jane Eyre at one point speaks openly about the right of women to live as fully as men: "Women are supposed to be very calm generally: but women feel just as men feel; they need exercise for their faculties, and a field for their efforts as much as their brothers do; ...."

A quotation longer than three lines of prose or verse should be set off in a block, single-spaced and double-indented. Do not use quotation marks in a block quotation unless there are quotation marks in the original.

Jane Eyre speaks openly about the right of women to live as fully as men:

> *Women are supposed to be very calm generally: but women feel just as men feel; they need exercise for their faculties, and a field for their efforts as much as their brothers do; they suffer from too rigid a restraint, too absolute a stagnation, precisely as men would suffer; and it is narrow-minded in their more privileged fellow-creatures to say that they ought to confine themselves to making puddings and knitting stockings, to playing on the piano and embroidering bags.*

When quoting verse, show the line-breaks with the slash (/). Preserve all capitalization and punctuation as in the original. In a block quotation, do not use quotation marks or the slash, but quote line-for-line, just as in the original.

In "The Lie" Sir Walter Raleigh instructs his soul: "Say to the court, it glows/And shines like rotten wood;/Say to the church, it shows/What's good, and doth no good; ...."

Or, as a block quotation:

In "The Lie" Sir Walter Raleigh instructs his soul:

> *Say to the court, it glows*
> *And shines like rotten wood;*
> *Say to the church, it shows*
> *What's good and doth no good; ....*

In quoting less than a full sentence, use the ellipsis (...) to indicate that words have been left out of the original sentence. Use brackets [ ] to show changes to the original. Build a fragmentary quotation into a complete sentence of your own.

When the ellipsis comes at the end of the sentence, as in the Raleigh quotation above, notice that you need *four* dots, three for the ellipsis and one for the concluding period. Remember that the words omitted cannot be considered evidence for the claim you are making. Don't use the ellipsis as a lazy way to avoid copying out words that are important to your idea.

Use the brackets to interpolate words into what you're quoting (do this as rarely as possible), or to change a verb form, pronoun case or capitalization.

Waldo wishes he could be honest enough to say that he "want[s] to and [is] going to, write about [him]self."

The original statement read: "I want to, and am going to, write about myself." Notice how much easier it would have been to begin a word earlier, with "I." Then no changes would have been needed. Here's an example of how *not* to use brackets:

"Handsomely forgiving her [Biddy]," Pip goes up to bed.

Place context details that will make such pronoun references plain.

Do not use a fragmentary quotation as the subject of your sentence:

"Handsomely forgiving her" shows Pip's new arrogance.

Build the fragment into your sentence:

Pip shows a new arrogance when he concludes his discussion with Biddy by "[h]andsomely forgiving her" for having doubted his loyalty to Joe.

Note that in this example your replacement of a capital by a lower-case letter needed to be indicated by putting the changed character in brackets.

Use single quotation marks to enclose a quotation within another quotation.

Using a dialect word, Jane describes how "the old crone 'nichered' a laugh under her bonnet and bandage; ...."

The word "nichered" is set off by double quotation marks in the original.

Use quotation marks to set off titles of poems, stories, chapters, songs, television episodes, or any other part of a larger work. Titles of book-length works, operas, films, paintings, television series are either underlined or italicized.

Fiona's favorite poem is Stevie Smith's "Not Waving But Drowning."
Justin couldn't finish Chapter 3, "The Biochemistry of the Wart."
Wasn't "Here Comes the Sun" on the Beatles' <u>Abbey Road</u> album?
Alfred Hitchcock based his film <u>Sabotage</u> on Joseph Conrad's novel <u>The Secret Agent</u>.

IV. Punctuation with Quotations: Guided Exercise

Some of the sentences below are correct, and some have an error in punctuations with quotations. If the sentence is correct, write "C." If the sentence contains an error, cross out the incorrect punctuation and insert the correct punctuation. The number in parentheses at the end of each sentence refers you to a rule you have just learned.

1. My mother always says, You have a head like a sieve. (34)

2. I don't think that I am very forgetful, and I always reply, "you never told me anything!" (35)

3. Then she says, "I will tape everything I say to you from now on". (36)

4. "I will erase the tape", I answer when I am feeling daring. (36)

5. The argument always ends with the words "I'm sorry"; we don't like to fight. (37)

6. Did he really say, "Twinkle twinkle little star?" (38)

7. No, he asked, "Does the little star twinkle"? (38)

8. The looters' statement that it was "not against the law" to enter that appliance store was rejected by the judge. (39)

9. The judge noted, "It is never acceptable to take someone's property". (36)

10. "I will never understand what Timothy McVeigh did." said one juror. (41)

11. "Do you understand it?", asked the reporter. (42)

12. "Some Spanish truck drivers," explained the announcer, "Are seeking retirement benefits." (43)

13. "We are headed for disaster," said the Legal Aid Society representative, "deregulation of rents will immediately flood the housing court." (44)

14. Computers have given us new vocabulary, such as "soft boot" and "default." (45)

15. The statue came to life and said, "I want to live as a real, human boy". (36)

16. Pinocchio asked, "Has my nose grown longer"? (38)

17. Why have they screamed, "Surprise?" (38)

18. "Curses," exclaimed the villain, "Foiled again." (43)

19. The car's owner said that he was "angry and upset" by the parking ticket. (39)

20. "The new CD is my best," proclaimed Elvis, "I worked on it for years." (44)

21. The latest Elvis sighting, according to the *National Enquirer*, was "awesome". (36)

22. My two-year-old brother constantly asks, "Are we there yet"? (38)

23. "Not yet," explains my mother, "you must be patient." (44)

24. Tommy counters, "I am not patient. I am Tommy." (40)

25. The students yelled, "This is the last sentence"! (38)

(Answer key on page 230.)

IV. Punctuation with Quotations: More Practice Sentences

Some of the sentences below are correct, and some have an error in punctuation with quotations. If the sentence is correct, write "C." If the sentence contains an error, cross out the incorrect punctuation and insert the correct punctuation.

1. That book contains a sentence ending in "as it were"; the other book uses more modern syntax.

2. The physician told the patient, You are perfectly healthy.

3. I asked, "Are you going to do your homework or are you going to die"?

4. "No one knows," sang the blues band, "The trouble I've seen."

5. Did he really say, "The Rangers are going to win?"

6. "The winner and still champion of the log-rolling contest," exclaimed the announcer, "is Tweety McSweeny"!

7. The outstanding library book discusses the phenomenon of "extrasensory publication".

8. "You must not slide into second base with your spikes aimed upward." said Ty Cobb.

9. "I have been accused of doing just that," added Ty, "I am innocent."

10. "The little girl needs another lemon on her fruit basket," asserted the fruit vendor, "but she has quite enough oranges."

11. The best subject for your term paper is "Democracy in the Ninth Grade;" the teacher will like your arguments.

12. Musternikob, bothered by the number of people who mispronounced his name, changed it to "Tsikrkovich".

13. He says that the new name is, "easier to say."

14. "Are you sure you want to make that change"? asked his friends.

15. "Absolutely", he replied.

16. Mr. Chang proposed a bill to "take the paint off the benches in the park:" he thinks the natural look is better suited to the rustic setting.

17. Did he really say, "Paint is the enemy of all ecologists?"

18. When Mr. Chang proposed his "no paint bill", the senators laughed.

19. "I won't leave without my burger.", said the burglar who had taken six hostages.

20. The burgers "with everything," which the burglar had requested, were sent immediately.

21. "Thanks," said the burglar, "But I want fries too."

22. "Fries are out of the question"! screamed the detective in charge of the case.

23. "You can have onion rings," added the detective, "You can also have a shake."

24. The burglar countered with a statement about "The right to fries."

25. One of the hostages asked, "Are we going to sit here all day because of some potatoes"?

26. Did the burglar add, "Give me fries or give me death?"

27. No one knows if the "fries burglar" will get the death penalty.

28. Holden always thinks that people are "phony".

29. He always tells the reader that a situation "Kills" him.

30. "Cindi has never, in my opinion," commented Ellie, "Cemented her door shut."

31. "Why would she cement her door shut"? we asked.

32. "The windows become more important if they are the only means of exit, explained Cindi. However, I did not do it."

33. The reviewer discussed works of avant-garde artists whose message was, "inexplicable."

34. "I don't know much about art," said Luigi, but I know what I like.

35. "Where's my bottle?" were the baby's first words.

36. His second words told us that we should "deep-six," our Raffi tapes.

37. "Why doesn't he like Raffi?" asked the pediatrician.

38. "Who knows?" replied the mother, "We play them in the car on the way to get vaccinations."

39. Sam seems "out of touch", in the words of his supervisor.

40. Some senators were opposed to granting China the status of "most favored nation"; others argued that trade should not be linked to human rights.

41. Ollie screamed, "Don't go!"

42. Popeye the Sailor Man attributed his success to "love of spinach."

43. Popeye often asked, "Are you very tired today?".

44. "If you are," he added, "You should eat spinach."

45. Olive Oyl argued, "Broccoli is better".

46. They both suffered from "root vegetable syndrome".

47. The couple explained that, "They were afraid of potatoes and other tubers."

48. "The problem with yams" became oppressive to them.

49. Popeye's mother-in-law said that she would not cook anything, "That grew on top of dirt."

50. "Aren't you glad you have finished with all these quotation marks," asked the teacher?

I-IV Cumulative Exercise

If the sentence is correct, leave it alone. If the sentence is wrong, fix the mistake by neatly crossing out the wrong words and writing the correct word at the end of the sentence. In some cases you may have to rewrite the entire sentence.

1. The president of the club, not the members, are in charge of counting the cookies.

2. All of the air in that balloon has been pumped in by my friends Sally and Andy.

3. The members of that committee have decided to meet for an hours discussion every Tuesday.

4. "An hour's work" said Otto "should take care of all the business on the current agenda.

5. "Please do not release that boa constrictor in the small mammal house"! screamed the zookeeper.

6. Either the minister or the priest will say their prayers before the breakfast begins.

7. Give the gorillas contact lens to the veterinarian.

8. A weeks' salary is not enough to cover his gambling debts.

9. A quick look made me aware that the inside of those closets and drawers were extremely dirty.

10. "Everyone but the Einstein twins must bring their math notes to the exam," said the geometry professor, who was not accepting any excuses.

11. When Mr. Barnum barked, "See Alexander the Great"! he was referring to one of the clowns who perform in his circus, not the Macedonian conqueror.

12. Sliding through the hatch comes the eels all together in a twisting mass.

13. Here's three more reasons why you should not call your boss a "twerp."

14. Either the dancer or the singer will win the prize for their effort.

15. Mark and Mary's new notebooks are on the floor someplace, but Mary's is the only one of those books that has any notes in it.

16. The students' chief complaint about his teacher is that the grading's too hard.

17. Those statistics' errors, which no one else has noticed, were finally discovered by Dr. Berman's unique methods.

18. The number of horses in that race are greater this year than last.

19. "A number of the components of the bomb are missing," said the aide.

20. The lion licked it's paw, which had been badly hurt by the thorn, and moaned.

21. Who's responsible for using the phrase "no pay no way?"

22. Groucho's moustache is bigger than theirs'.

23. The seniors have not yet agreed where to have its prom.

24. "Saks is having a clearance sale". said the personal shopper.

25. Neither Sam nor his friends was able to eat all of the fried green tomatoes, which some of them found disgusting.

26. Every boy threw their lollipops at the candymaker when the sugary workman announced that the tour was "finito."

27. In the green box you will find the only one of the snakes that are safe to handle.

28. "The green box!" screamed the keeper, "not the red box!"

29. "Which of the boxes did you say are safe"? I inquired calmly.

30. The keeper, who had turned his attention to some other topic, replied, "see for yourself."

31. The blue box contained one of those tarantulas that has no poison sac.

32. The cheese, when cut, turned out to be crawling with small grubs, making it "inedible and totally gross," in my mother's view.

33. After the box of red pepper had spilled on the spaghetti, Mom and Dad's plates were left untouched, but my cousin ate a hearty meal.

34. "I don't mind.", my cousin said. "It's here, and I'll eat it while it's hot."

35. He added, "I like spicy food."

36. "Do you think," he mused while he was still able to speak, "This will ruin my digestive system?"

37. "The best thing to do," stated my mother, "is to scrape the sauce off the noodles".

38. Mr. Cagney is one of those podiatrists who likes toenail clipping.

39. The boys' dining room was bigger than the room assigned to the girls.

40. "We want one like their's," the girls chanted. "That's the only one of the options that pleases us."

41. There is no reason they're rooms should be unequal.

42. They're right to be annoyed, and the architect is soon to present a solution to the problem.

43. The childrens' reactions to the new carousel were surprising.

44. "We want to have more horses", they said.

45. "The paint on these horses are already peeling!" they shouted.

46. "Some of them," one little voice squeaked, "don't slide smoothly up and down their track's."

47. "My class of third graders have not come here to ride a substandard carousel," snarled the teacher.

48. "Hell, no!" screamed the kids. "We won't go."

49. Every boy and girl in that class have written a letter that trashes the carousel.

50. The mayor's office has pledged that "the designer will be shot;" however, none of the kids are convinced that the mayor will go that far.

V. Pronoun Case

(pc)

Personal pronouns – *I, you, he, she, we, they* – and the relative pronoun *who* have different forms to show their different functions in the sentence:

SUBJECT	OBJECT	POSSESSIVE
I	me	my, mine
you	you	your, yours
he	him	his
she	her	her, hers
we	us	our, ours
they	them	their, theirs
who	whom	whose

Subject case is used when the pronoun is a subject or a subject complement.
Object case is used when the pronoun is any kind of object: direct, indirect, or object of a preposition.
Possessive case is used to show possession.

LESSON A. LINKING VERBS, COMPOUNDS, GERUNDS

46. After all forms of *be*, use subject case pronouns.

> *It was **she** who stole the umbrella.*
> *Otto claims that the ablest liar in the junior class is **he**.*

You might say "It's me" in conversation, but in formal usage you need subject case.

> *When Luis answered the phone, his sister said, "It is **I**."*

47. When a pronoun is coupled with a noun or another pronoun in a compound phrase, give it the case form it would have if used alone.

> *Rudy and myself have taken charge of the project.*

Change *myself* to *I*, since you would never say, "Myself has taken charge of the project."

> *Ana waved to Julio and I.* [Would you say, "Ana waved to I"?]
> *No one understands grammar but you and me.* [Correct: both pronouns are the object of the preposition *but*.]

48. **In a clause of comparison introduced by *than* or *as*, the verb is often omitted. Give the pronoun the case it would have if the verb were there.**

Often when you make a comparison, you leave out words including the verb after the *as* or *than*.

> I'm not paid as much as she [is paid].

> **To choose the correct pronoun, supply the missing words.**

Peter told Kate that he had played worse than her.

"...worse than her did"? I don't think so!

> Peter told Kate that he had played worse than **she** [had played].
> James told Alex earlier than [he told] **me**.

49. **Put a pronoun coupled with an appositive noun in the case it would have if the noun were left out.**

> *"Us millionaires have to stick together," said Morgan to Rockefeller.*

Drop out the noun, *millionaires*. Would you say, "Us have to stick together"?

> *"**We** millionaires have to stick together," said Morgan to Rockefeller.*

50. **With a gerund, use the possessive form of a pronoun (or a noun).**

> *Kiri objects to me screaming at him.*
> *Mr. Binks has nothing but praise for the dog howling.*

Does Kiri object to the screaming or to me? Does Mr. Binks want to applaud the dog or its tuneful howling? To make it clear that it's the screaming that Kiri objects to and the howling Mr. B. wishes to praise, write:

> *Kiri objects to **my** screaming at him.*
> *Mr. Binks has nothing but praise for **the dog's** howling.*

51. **When the pronoun is an appositive, it takes the same case as the word to which it is appositive.** Such pronouns are usually in a compound phrase with a noun.

> *Both shoplifters, Harriet and her, were caught red-handed.*

Harriet and her is appositive to *shoplifters*, which is the subject of *were caught*, so ...

> *Both shoplifters, Harriet and **she**, were caught red-handed.*

V. Pronoun Case, Lesson A: Guided Exercise

Some of the sentences below are correct, and some have an error in pronoun case. If the sentence is correct, write "C." If the sentence contains an error, cross out the incorrect pronoun and write the correct pronoun at the end of the sentence. The number in parentheses at the end of each sentence refers to a rule you have just learned.

1. Mrs. Masters gave the two worst offenders, Michelle and I, a long lecture. (51)

2. Hassan thought he had seen Alexandra, but Gabe said it could not have been her. (46)

3. Teachers do not always understand the reactions us students have to them. (49)

4. The judge gave permission to us girls and to our allies to print that article about the school board. (49)

5. Otto fears that Howie Yadoon, that outgoing politician, is more popular than he. (48)

6. When you find out your grade, give Ramona or myself a call. (47)

7. The witnesses to the burglary — Velez, McCarren, and him — were questioned at length by the police. (51)

8. She objects to him ignoring her whenever he runs into her in the hall. (50)

9. Alice is a better chirper than Chester, but he is better at flying than her. (48)

10. My parents like to take Fatima and I to the opera. (47)

11. It seems to be him and me that always get caught. (47)

12. My friend Alexis hates me making fun of her name. (50)

13. Olive tells her children she knows far more about life than they. (48)

14. There has always been some unfriendliness between you and I, perhaps because of that greeting card I sent you when we first met. (47)

15. Dr. De Kreppit hates us giggling in class. (50)

16. Neither my sister nor I have any money, and I think it's unfair that my parents buy my sister more clothes than me. (48)

17. Nastine tells everyone that her heroes are the Unabomber and I. (46, 47)

18. The editor of the school newspaper gave the job of reporting on the cafeteria's cleanliness to us freshmen. (47)

19. Dr. Schiller and myself get bent out of shape by noise in the hall when we're teaching. (47)

20. Octavia says the thief could not have been him. (46)

21. When asked, the burglar returned the stolen keys to the police officer and myself. (47)

22. "No one is happier than me to see you win the award," lied the loser tearfully. (48)

23. My friends had been on line for five hours to buy powerball lottery tickets when they told reporters, "Luck is going to strike us three winners." (49)

24. You always give we English teachers grief when we use bad grammar. (49)

25. It seems that you object to us not practicing what we preach. (50)

(Answer key on page 231.)

LESSON B. WHO AND WHOM

Who and *whom* cause special problems. When do you use *who*, and when do you use *whom?* When you're unsure, here's a way to work it out.

52. **Use *who* or *whoever* if the pronoun is the subject or predicate nominative in the subordinate clause. Use *whom* or *whomever* if the pronoun is an object in the subordinate clause.**

   Hilary knows who is telling her secrets.

The pronoun *who* is the subject of the verb *is telling,* so this sentence is correct.

   She is a person who no one trusts.

Here, the pronoun is the object of the verb *trusts,* so it should be in object case:

   *She is a person **whom** no one trusts.*

How about this?

   Give the check to whomever answers the door.

Forget about the *-ever* suffix, since it doesn't affect the problem. In the clause, *whom(ever) answers the door,* the pronoun is the subject of *answers.* Therefore:

   *Give the check to **whoever** answers the door.*

> **Don't be misled by interrupting phrases like *I believe, we hope, they say.***

   She is a person whom, I have been told, no one trusts.

The subordinate clause is "whom no one trusts." *Whom* is the object of *trusts.*

Here's a good trick to know for determining whether to use *who* or *whom:*

> **Put parentheses around the clause. Put its words into normal sentence order. Turn the relative pronoun into a personal pronoun.**

   I don't remember (who/m I've told this joke). ⇒ *(I've told who/m this joke)* ⇒
   *(I've told **him** [not he] this joke)* ⇒ *I don't remember **whom** I've told this joke.*

he/him

V. Pronoun Case, Lesson B: Guided Exercise

Some of the sentences below are correct, and some have an error in pronoun case. If the sentence is correct, write "C." If the sentence contains an error, cross out the incorrect pronoun and write the correct pronoun at the end of the sentence. All of the sentences refer to rule 52.

1. Boxanne sends cards to whomever she thinks the world is treating badly.

2. Whom did she say the visitor was?

3. Bismo is one of those people who nobody believes.

4. The students who teachers give the best grades are not always the smartest ones.

5. Who do you suppose will be the first to be arrested?

6. Noah likes whomever his parents tell him he should not like.

7. Why doesn't Officer Clubb just arrest whomever he thinks stole the money?

8. Roberto is the athlete who I have been told all the players want on their side.

9. Jane Austen is one writer whom I believe everyone admires for her sparkling dialogue and amusingly snotty insults.

10. Who do you think Clinto the Magnificent should pull out of the magic hat – the rabbit or his assistant Zora?

11. The young lawyer who they say will be the next Supreme Court Chief Justice is Thomas Woods.

12. "I will give this present to whomever I wish, and you can't stop me!" screamed Bismo.

13. The Future Farmers of America managed to elect a treasurer whom no one believes is honest.

14. I am planning to take my dues money and give it to whomever needs it the most.

15. "Do you have any eggplant?" asked the man who I imagine was planning to cook that evening.

16. Jason thinks that we should tell the secret to whoever asks politely.

17. The secretary sent invitations to whomever the teachers wanted at the homework party, but no one showed up.

18. Bill Gates, whom I believe is a multibillionaire, is a Harvard dropout.

19. Any time Tai needs company, he phones whomever he finds in his school directory and shouts, "Time to party!"

20. During the last party Tai, whom the police say invited over 5000 people, ran out of hot dogs.

21. Do you know who I may call in an emergency?

22. Is this who I think it is?

23. Godzilla, who the director says wears size 55 sneakers, just signed a contract with Nike.

24. Do you think this picture looks like whoever painted it, or like me?

25. Who may I speak to about returning a few thousand extra grammar rules?

(Answer key on page 231.)

V. Pronoun Case: More Practice Sentences for Lessons A and B.

If the sentence is correct, write "C." If the sentence contains an error in pronoun case, cross out the incorrect pronoun and write the correct pronoun at the end of the sentence.

1. Bismo, who no one considers to be humble, admits that Otto can throw a ball farther than he.

2. Olive claims that the loudest screamer of all her gang is either Nastine or she.

3. Over there under the elm tree are the two women who Percy saw running out of the bank.

4. Although Pilar was madly in love with him, she couldn't tolerate him driving like a maniac on the country roads leading to their love nest in Maine.

5. The editors were always blaming we ninth graders for writing narrow, opinionated articles.

6. Flossie says Freddie was the one who snitched, but Freddie claims it was her.

7. I'm positive that those are the two uranium salesmen who Percy saw with the president of the WMD club.

8. Between you and I, she has a lot of nerve asking for help with that ice-filled freezer.

9. Don't you think the question of who should play the part of Emily is out of order?

10. Do any of you know who Clark Kent really is?

11. I was as anxious as him *he* about the canoe but calm enough to realize that the alligators were probably not that hungry.

12. Almost every year an actor who *m* everyone recognizes as a star takes a part in a Shakespearean play.

13. Ms. O'Brien was in charge, and it was her *she* who had the bright idea to sell lightbulbs as a fundraiser.

14. Sam Waterston, whom I believe is one of the most versatile actors I have ever seen, is brilliant in that film.

15. The new teacher, whom we believe has taken Mr. Green's position, is from the South.

16. Does anyone know whom Santa Claus really is when he takes off that beard?

17. I do not remember to who I lent the book.

18. He is a man who nobody trusts, perhaps because he always wears a mask and carries a gun.

19. It was ~~them~~ they who wanted to leave.

20. Nastine told Bismo that it was ~~she~~ her who, Olive had spat on.

21. He refused to allow we boys to borrow his favorite ping pong paddle.

22. Ask the co-editors, Luis and she, if the yearbook is ready.

23. He could not cook as well as her, so they hired Julia Child to prepare the meal.

24. That writer is the one who John wanted to meet.

25. It was him whistling that annoyed us.

26. A great opportunity has been given to Jill and me by the Publishers Clearing House.

27. "Who are you calling swine?" screamed Ellie right before she decked him.

28. Gary and myself are planning to string those pearls into a great necklace.

29. In the great myths, the one whom the gods select for punishment is not always the guiltiest.

30. Maybelle is so egotistical that she thinks Jack and him actually worship her.

31. Us grammar scholars are disgusted at the amount of cheating on grammar tests.

32. Jill, Elly, and myself can't help laughing at Lisa's jokes, even when they come at Bart's expense.

33. The girls were not so excited about the cookie drive as them.

34. Nancy could cook as well as him and proved it in the Pillsbury Bakeoff.

35. Give the plucked duck to whoever wants it.

36. It is her whom the committee has endorsed.

37. Jee-Hyun has a higher batting average than me.

38. The school is looking for students who it can assign to tutoring programs.

39. Kim and me have been friends for over three years.

40. Both Aaron and myself are fourteen years old, and neither of us appreciates your saying that we are children.

41. An investigation into the governor's activities proved that him taking a bribe was a real possibility.

42. In Shakespeare's *Macbeth*, the two characters who I most hate are Macbeth and his wife.

43. Rita the Metermaid is a girl who died far too soon, and when I see a star twinkling over the parking lot, I know it is her.

44. The charred meat on the grill did not tempt we vegetarians.

45. You should have seen me hopping up and down!

46. Aleksei claims that me keeping silent in the face of the protests is not acceptable.

47. Who shall I say is calling?

48. "I cannot tell a lie; it is me who is responsible for chopping up the cherry pie," said George with anguish.

49. The two shoplifters who they caught, Boxanne and she, were arrested.

50. I demand to know whom you think is the real murderer!

I-V Cumulative Exercise

If the sentence is correct, write "C." If the sentence is wrong, fix it by neatly crossing out the wrong form and writing in the correct one. Don't rewrite the entire sentence.

1. Andy says that whomever wins the Oscar should give the statue to Antonio Banderas.

2. When Karissa went into the girls' locker room, she found the lacrosse team defending its defensive strategy.

3. Bloomingdale's are having their big sale tomorrow, and Ali is planning to attend sometime before lunch.

4. Everyone who wants a copy of Lou's poem must bring their floppy disk at once.

5. Each of the computers and printers in Dr. Mullady's office are programmed to do homework automatically.

6. Neither Mr. Marshall nor the students who broke the window are going to play baseball this spring.

7. You're unbiased in this matter; whom do you consider the better actor?

8. Whom do you think would best direct Katherine in her role as Juliet?

9. Damian is one of those dancers who has rubber feet and incredible speed.

10. Everyone who thinks Gabe should sing at the concert should clap their hands right now.

11. Because they avoid danger on principle, Joel's parents are not happy about him parasailing through the Grand Canyon.

12. The activist asked Junko and us freshmen to accompany him to the protest against fur traders, because he can't stand them killing baby seals.

13. Dan thinks he might want to manufacture children's toys in the off-season.

14. Each of we freshmen is planning to give Steve a telephone call to inquire about the pet that lost its paw.

15. When asked about the stolen chicken feather, Dana pointed to Jamie and screamed, "It was him who stole the feather!"

16. Neither Brad nor his guinea pigs wants the drought to spoil the harvest from their beloved lettuce garden.

17. Andy was surprised to hear about Antonio attending the premier of *Zorro*.

18. The box, as well as the suitcases, are ready to be placed in Gordon's car.

19. The number of ninth graders who will march together in the parade is larger this year than last year.

20. "The taxi was faster than me," said Mrs. Woods. "There is nothing further to add."

21. Unanimous about the principle that grammar should be ignored, us committee members do not agree about the proper technique for doing so.

22. Few in the school besides me knows that Dr. Delanty actually wrote *Jane Eyre*.

23. Some of the material in the essays Ms. Kunde was reading weren't very original and seemed to have been copied from the encyclopedia.

24. Either Brad or the 8th graders is going to the pet store to buy Guinea Pig Treat.

25. Nastine, whom many consider annoying, thinks Boxanne is worse than she.

26. The list of all the spies, in addition to the contact words and secret code, have been carefully prepared by Gordon.

27. A number of the foreign students he met have written to Eric recently, and he feels guilty about not having answered their letters.

28. Ahmed cannot accept the fact that Kareem is taller than he.

29. The family and me are arguing about whether they should go to the movies or to prison tonight.

30. In Egbert's opinion not one of those books have a decent section on semicolons.

31. "Wake me up when its time for grammar," said Dana, who could not stay conscious when anything but participles were being discussed.

32. Jamie confessed, "It is I who stole the chicken's liver, to see what effect my action would have."

33. Every one of the freshmen are planning to give Steve a bandage for his pet's paw.

34. Has Dr. Tischler really announced that, "Today's special schedule celebrates Holland, and periods A through H have been scrambled to spell a word in Dutch"?

35. The detective wanted Maggie and us witnesses to testify at the trial.

36. Joel told Coach Duffy that everyone was worried about Jamie swimming every morning without a lifeguard.

37. Anyone who sees Marisa's outfit will raise his or her eyebrows in shock.

38. Damian is one of the few freshmen who likes to dance for hours on end; he is entering the "Tangothon."

39. Peter's mother objected on principle to him reading the sports pages before completing his homework.

40. Ilya, not his pedigreed wolfhounds, was invited to the Kremlin for an interview with Vladimir Putin, the president of Russia, who our president considers a friend.

41. Danny cannot speak Italian as well as she, but many people praise him singing in that language.

42. Be sure to give the list of Pie-Eating Contest winners to Mr. Breck and myself.

43. Mr. Lacopo, whom everyone at Horace Mann knows and admires, was once a student here himself.

44. The ninth grade is going to take a horrendous grammar test this spring, but I am sure that everyone will know the rules perfectly and come in with their minds rested and clear.

45. The radio announcer, who claims to be impartial but who we all think is biased in favor of the Mets, was ejected from the Yankee game.

46. Did you give the keys to the boy who's locker was stuck?

47. In my school the boys' bathroom was cleaned of graffiti yesterday, but today there are already six new pro-Rangers slogans on the wall.

48. When the diplomats meets today, they will issue their statement.

49. Murgatroyd, whom the committee has judged unstable, broke down and wept.

50. Everyone must accept the effects of his or her actions; it's me who have to take the rap for that broken window.

VI. Punctuation with Independent Clauses

(pcl, run-on, cs)

When you're working with **one** sentence that contains **two or more** independent clauses, each of which could stand alone as a full sentence, what sort of punctuation do you use?

First, let's look at the two most common errors that students make in this situation: the **run-on sentence (run-on)** and the **comma-splice error (cs)**. A run-on sentence is a sentence that contains two independent clauses with no conjunctions and no punctuation between them:

> *I went to look for Katya she was gone.*
> *They never told Josh they assumed he already knew.*

Where should those clauses be divided, and how? The comma-splice error tries to splice together two independent clauses with a comma, but a comma is not the right mark for this work:

> *Justine has some funny ideas, she thinks that knives are cute.*
> *Roxanne's speech is clear, it's her ideas that are cloudy.*

53. **Coordinating conjunctions join independent clauses. Punctuate with a comma before the conjunction.** The seven coordinating conjunctions: for, and, nor, but, or, yet, so.

> *I went to look for Katya,* **but** *she was gone.*
> *They never told Josh,* **for** *they assumed he already knew.*
> *They assumed Josh knew,* **so** *they never told him.*
> *Roxanne's speech is clear,* **yet** *her ideas are cloudy.*

> **Just chant: "clause–comma–conjunction–clause."**

Make sure that you choose the best conjunction to show the true logical relation of the two clauses:

additional fact :	**and**	additional negative fact:	**nor**
alternative fact :	**or**	opposing/contrasting fact:	**but, yet**
cause:	**for**	result:	**so**

> **A comma *after* the conjunction? Never!**

54. **Do not punctuate with a comma before the coordinating conjunction if it is joining something less than two independent clauses.** These conjunctions also join words, phrases, subordinate clauses or predicates. If this is the case, no comma.

> *Tiffany* **put on her boots** *and* **walked out in the mud**.

*Both **motorists** and **pedestrians** need to be careful at crosswalks.*
*The bottle-rocket **made a loud bang** but **never climbed into the air**.*
*Pam left her shoes **under the bed** or **in the bookcase**.*

Avoid a common error and chant: "Subject–verb–conjunction–verb." No comma.

55. A semicolon may join independent clauses. The semicolon tells the reader: "There is a connection between these clauses; you find it."

There are three shot-put champions among Olympia's children; two are girls.
Justine has some funny ideas; she thinks that knives are cute.

Don't overuse the semicolon. Used in moderation, it lends your writing elegance.

56. The semi-colon joining independent clauses may be followed by a transitional adverb. You may put a comma after the adverb, except for the adverbs of time.
The words below are transitional adverbs. These are not conjunctions and may not by themselves join independent clauses; use them after the semi-colon. They are very useful in expressing the logical relation of your two clauses. Placing a comma after a transitional adverb, while not mandatory, distinguishes it from ordinary adverbs and sets it off as indicating a turn in the thought.

additional fact:	moreover, besides, furthermore, likewise, also
opposing/contrasting:	however, nevertheless, still, nonetheless, really, in truth, in reality, in fact
resulting fact:	accordingly, therefore, consequently, hence, as a result, thus, if so, in that case
alternative fact:	otherwise, if not, on the other hand, at the same time
time:	then, now, later, earlier, once, at present, finally, in the end, at last, next, thereafter, previously
example:	for example, for instance
emphasis:	indeed, truly, surely, to be sure

*Natasha hates furs; **moreover,** she hates the people who wear them.*
*Bob has not worked for years; **nevertheless,** he always seems to have money.*
*Adam is extremely afraid of falling; **accordingly,** he won't go down stairs.*
*Nora has to change her socks; **otherwise,** her sisters will begin to complain.*
*Vera worked for hours on her Latin; **finally** she completed one problem.*
*George used to fail every Latin quiz; **now** he aces them all.*
*Adolf has few redeeming qualities; **indeed,** you could say he has none.*

Wake-up call about *however*: this adverb is sometimes used transitionally, sometimes parenthetically, and sometimes as an essential adverb of extent-to-which:

> *Jeff has no shoes;* **however,** *he doesn't care.*
> *Most people consider mice to be vermin; Ella,* **however,** *makes pets of them.*
> *Bismo will never learn to use a handkerchief,* **however** *hard he tries.*

It is only in the second situation that you will find *however* between two commas.

A note on semicolons: sometimes it makes sense to use a semicolon between two independent clauses if there are other commas elsewhere in the sentence, especially in the first of the two clauses. It's important to show your readers where the first clause ends and the second starts. That place is harder to pick out when those clauses contain a number of other commas.

> *When Leon is angry, his eyes grow red, large, and tearful, and he starts to curse.*

In this case you can upgrade the comma you would normally use to a semicolon:

> *When Leon is angry, his eyes grow red, large, and tearful; and he starts to curse.*

Writer's Reference: THREE GOOD WAYS TO FIX A COMMA-SPLICE ERROR

Remember, you make this error when you put a comma between two independent clauses, like this:

> *Julie is not happy, she keeps her feelings hidden.*

It's not obvious what the connection between the clauses is. Show the connection.

Method 1: add the right coordinating conjunction:

> *Julie is not happy,* **yet** *she keeps her feelings hidden.* [So might work here too.]

Method 2: change the comma to a semicolon and add the right transitional adverb:

> *Julie is not happy;* **still,** *she keeps her feelings hidden.*

Method 3: subordinate one clause to the other with the right subordinating conjunction:

> ***Although*** *Julie is not happy, she keeps her feelings hidden.*

VI. Punctuation with Independent Clauses: Guided Exercise

Some of the sentences below are correct, and some have an error in punctuation. If the sentence is correct, write "C." If the sentence contains an error, correct the punctuation. The number in parentheses at the end of each sentence refers you to a rule you have just learned.

1. The renowned physicist spoke at great length and in great detail to the undergraduates, however, despite her careful notes, Rita was confused. (56)

2. Ellen knew everybody at the party, but the boy standing near the band. (54)

3. Apologizing over and over again, Magda picked the fuzz balls off the clean clothes, and then put the clothes in the basket. (54)

4. Bagelina, though grumpier that anyone else on the team, is by far the best tennis player, furthermore she has a degree from Cal Tech. (56)

5. Borzoi has very bad breath, unfortunately neither Magda nor his fellow Siberian chefs have the courage to present him with a bottle of mouthwash. (56)

6. He's a well educated man, however he has no common sense. (56)

7. Maria ran from the cafeteria into the field, and watched the lunch table smolder. (54)

8. According to Pachydermia, a credit card is valuable it pays the bills. (55)

9. Rahma did everything for her mother was very permissive. (53)

10. The rattlesnake bit her; the botanist was soon searching wildly for anti-venom. (55)

11. I have no idea whose diesel powered loom this is; nevertheless, I will return it to the garage as soon as I have finished weaving. (56)

12. He found a pie on top of the refrigerator but his wife was not the baker. (53)

13. It could be that he is yelling at the spectators, and limping with pain at the same time. (54)

14. Harriet hasn't had trouble with the car yet when I drove it, I could barely turn the steering wheel. (53)

15. The pizza festival was a gigantic success, no fewer than 500 kids participated. (55)

16. Life suddenly seems very bleak to Nelson but Howard will soon cheer him up. (53)

17. Don't blame everything on me; it was Jake, not I, who spilled the beans. (55)

18. Email has greatly improved the quality of homework, now students can copy from each other in the privacy of their own rooms. (56)

19. Adam could not concentrate on the baseball game, he was too excited about doing grammar with Charlie and me. (55)

20. Dr. Madmed examined my uncle, and said that a quick course in Zen meditation would cure him. (54)

21. He did not, however, believe a word that the doctor said. (56)

22. I really hate the way my parents always compare me to my big sister, according to them she's the best student and the best athlete in the family. (55)

23. Malibou washed the dishes with that new anti-bacterial rock powder, and dried them with heat from the underground geyser. (54)

24. You saw him I can't believe it! (55)

25. She breaks out in hives whenever she takes a test, moreover she sweats. (56)

(Answer key on page 231.)

VI. Punctuation With Independent Clauses: More Practice Sentences

If the sentence is correct, write "C." If the sentence contains an error in punctuation, correct the punctuation as needed.

1. None of the actors have reported for rehearsal and the director is frantic with worry.

2. Catherine is the editor of our school paper and Martin is the editor of the literary magazine.

3. Because we did not have much time to spend in North Dakota, we saw only one burial ground, the next time we have a little vacation time, in two years or so, we plan to live in the state for at least a month.

4. The astronomy program was cancelled, however we are still going to build our own space shuttle.

5. The Amtrak train was about an hour late the conductor had no idea what was going on.

6. Van Gulik's *The Chinese Bell Murders* is set in ancient China and the hero is a district magistrate named Judge Dee.

7. Does either of you really know the way to San Jose or to Los Angeles?

8. Their two daughters' choosing to stay in Paris surprised Elinor and Jim, and hurt them a little.

9. Bouncing Babcock likes the movies on HBO but he does wish that they would broadcast more John Wayne epics.

10. Mr. Sludgewater was angry his wife had to put up with his grouchy silence for two days.

11. The teacher corrected the essay in red pen but she corrected the research paper in a lovely violet shade.

12. Rippie is sure that her book is the one with the torn cover, nevertheless she checked the name inside before taking it home.

13. All of us seniors felt sad about Kildare's getting expelled, he was our valedictorian, we felt humiliated.

14. Pop's old car runs fine, nevertheless Marguerite wants to change the oil at least once before the trip.

15. Puny failed every single spelling test we had this year; consequently, she had to buy a spell-checker for her future depended on her excelling in English.

16. Uncle Wiggly, and Peter Rabbit are two of my favorite characters.

17. Olive went for a walk for she was restless.

18. Otto studied the beer can at last he saw how it opened.

19. Nastine fell down four flights of stairs but did not hurt herself.

20. Boxanne feeds the pigs on weekdays Rancida takes over on the weekend.

21. Life is long and stupid grammar tests only add to its nastiness.

22. Olive dislikes all her children however, Bismo is her least favorite.

23. Nastine didn't answer she was too angry to speak.

24. Because Otto is bald, he likes to wear a hat, but he can rarely find one that fits him, since his head is so large.

25. Fistula isn't mute she just doesn't like to talk.

26. You'll find my pet turtle in his bowl or under the leaky pipe.

27. When you buy a car, and it's not a new one, be sure to check the lights and the tires, which are often in poor shape.

28. Morgan likes animals, still, she could do without large bugs.

29. Don't leave your present for my mother may never see it.

30. There are many Elmers in my family, most wish they had a different name.

31. In the morning I split the bagel carefully with my Swiss Army knife, and buttered the delicious, doughy treat.

32. Oscar badly wanted to play football on the first-string varsity team but hated having to wear all that padding.

33. They had not told anyone but Belinda already knew.

34. As I walked to school, I saw a woman whose shopping bags had burst, and helped her pick up her groceries.

35. Amelia likes to fight her brother Zebediah, however, is a physical coward.

36. A quiz is just a quiz, a test is torture.

37. Junco has some bad habits, for instance, he cracks his knuckles during tests.

38. There was a check for everyone who had not quit yet Alex got nothing.

39. Oksana searched the Ukraine for a pair of ballet slippers, but wound up dancing in army boots.

40. Ingrid rarely showers now once she was a clean girl.

41. Kelly visited the coastal cities of Africa, however she never reached the interior.

42. Takeshi is descended from samurai, and wants to study his heritage.

43. The Justice Department sent a letter to Senator Thompson, consequently the hearings were not convened.

44. Maria, and Alfonso went to the pizzeria to ask that pineapple be banned as a topping.

45. The Egyptian plaque shows a young man holding a goose and the farmer looks more dignified than some of the pharaohs on other plaques.

46. I need cookies, milk, a remote, and a good cable connection, but I don't need popcorn to make me happy.

47. I think, therefore I am, according to some philosophers.

48. Next week on our annual vacation to the Bahamas, we are going fishing for sharks, and snails.

49. The teacher told my parents that I have a good grasp of grammar, consequently they asked me to edit their correspondence.

50. I am good at grammar I never make a mistake unless I want to make one.

I-VI Cumulative Exercise

If the sentence is correct, write "C."   If the sentence contains any errors, cross out the incorrect form(s) and write in the correct one(s). Some types of errors may require you to make more than one correction. Edit as needed, but don't rewrite the entire sentence.

1. Needing to raise money, Otto offered to sell his clothes, for his collection of odd socks alone were worth the price of a beer.

2. Some of the disciplinary council are growing impatient, but neither the chairperson nor Mr. Lipsmacher are willing to compromise their position.

3. Each of the waiters have been given their share of the tips.

4. The grammar room is with the other English classrooms, once it was in the torture center.

5. The cast is celebrating the success of their production.

6. Someone or other has been leaving their litter in this room.

7. The students' use of these rooms are probably to blame.

8. Edna bought the only one of the workbooks that have the answer key in the back; the others in her class have to solve the problems by referring to general principles.

9. Neither Jeff nor his brother know how to refill their pens.

10. Do the boys know whom they're asking?

11. Was it he who was telling the players that they have to agree on a strategy?

12. Every mutt and mongrel in the pound is going to be adopted by Mrs. Lee.

13. He's one of those actors who doesn't know how to project his voice farther than the front of the stage.

14. Can each of those candidates explain what changes his program will accomplish?

15. Most of the people whom Otto insults resent him glaring at them and muttering, "Pond scum!"

16. Leah is the only one of the set-builders who knows how to hammer a nail.

17. Neither of my uncles is going to leave any money to me, who am their only nephew.

18. Beethoven's and Bach's passion for music is evident in their compositions.

19. The childrens' nurse wants one of those radios that play underwater.

20. Property upstate, including resorts and hotels, have been losing their value.

21. Ludmilla told Mr. McCutcheon that it was indeed her whom he had spotted playing goalie for the Rangers.

22. The two students who I believe they caught using preprogrammed calculators during a math test were severely punished.

23. Olive's son Mungo makes a racket when awake, she would rather he slept all the time.

24. Boxanne sends cards to whomever she thinks the world is treating badly, urging him or her to cheer up, and eat a bowl of stewed prunes.

25. Otto thinks Bismo, whom no one else likes, is more popular than him.

26. He told his interrogators – Officer Chubb and I – to speak to Bismo, with whom he had spent the afternoon.

27. "Who's jingling coins are making all that noise?" he asked.

28. She said, "It's just one of those things that are always happening to me."

29. "It wasn't me! It was Andreas whom they convicted of the theft!" said Olaf.

30. "The world is too much with us," said Wordsworth, "getting and spending, we lay waste our powers."

31. Mr. Swanyea hates us sniffling and runs over with a tissue when he hears the slightest sneeze.

32. Dr. De Kreppit, on the other hand, doesn't mind our sniffling, but is ready with a box of lozenges when he hears the slightest cough.

33. Greg called me a "dingbat," however, he's hardly the one to talk.

34. One of the words that most annoy Iliana is "cute".

35. Who did Boxanne last kiss, Bismo or Thelhim?

36. Bismo, who no one considers to be humble, admits that Otto can throw a ball farther than he.

37. Because he uses Sweetfeet, Fernando is one of the few members of the hiking club who never gets blisters.

38. The artists, not their teacher, left their crayons on the radiator for three days and are quite upset about the melted wax.

39. "Do I wake, or sleep?" the poet wanted to know.

40. Not one of the people in the house knows Finnish but my Finnish aunt is out back, chopping wood for the sauna and singing Finnish folksongs.

41. I want to go home I am tired!

42. He is possessed by the delusion that he is a remarkably successful man, and has eminent friends in every state in the Union.

43. *Great Expectations* is the only one of Dickens's novels that has been read during the summer school term.

44. The little kitten missed it's mother, the cat.

45. My instructor in sky-diving objected to me holding the rip cord with both hands.

46. Some of Alfie's G.I. Joe collection is stuck together with Superglue.

47. I answered the telephone promptly, and hung up just as fast.

48. At the doughnut exchange I traded a cream-filled for a jelly-filled and then ate maple-twists until I was sick.

49. Between you and I, this is an excruciatingly boring exercise.

50. I learned much about grammar, consequently I will ace the test.

VII. Pronoun Reference

(ref)

Clear reference requires that the reader be able, without hesitation, to **find a one-word antecedent to which the pronoun refers**.

> *After Olive counts her money, **she** hides **it**.*

The antecedent for *she* is *Olive* and for *it* is *money*. *She* "refers to" *Olive*, *it* to *money*. Problems arise when there is more than one word to which the pronoun could refer (**ambiguous reference**), or when the antecedent is implied but cannot be located (**vague reference**).

57. **Avoid ambiguous reference, where more than one possible antecedent is present.**

Here are some examples of **ambiguous reference**:

> *When teachers have to fail students, they are not happy.*

Does *they* refer to teachers or students? The statement would make sense either way. What we need now is an elegant cure for this problem. There is an easy, clumsy cure:

> *When teachers have to fail students, the students are not happy.*

The repetition sounds terrible. Try rearranging the clauses:

> *Students are not happy when teachers have to fail them.*
> *Having to fail students does not make teachers happy.*

You need to try out a few possibilities to get the best one. How about this?

> *Martha told Laura that she was going to ace the history test.*

Which *she*? The wrong way to fix this is: *Martha told Laura that she (Martha) was going ....* One solution is to make the indirect quotation direct:

> *Martha told Laura, "I'm going to ace the history test."*

If you don't want to put words into Martha's mouth, you could do something like this:

> *Martha was confident that she would ace the history test and told Laura so.*
> *Martha was sure that Laura would ace the history test and told her so.*

58. **A pronoun cannot be used to refer vaguely to an entire phrase or clause or to a possessive adjective.**

There are several different kinds of **vague reference**. The most common takes a whole clause as antecedent for the pronouns *which*, *this*, and *that*.

> *He said he had gone to see the nurse, **which** was an outright lie.*
> *Liz suddenly shrieked, and **that** made everyone jump.*

In both examples, the pronoun refers to the whole main clause. Such a construction is acceptable in conversation but not in formal writing. One solution is to put in a word that would act as antecedent:

Liz let out a sudden shriek, and that made everyone jump.

Now *that* refers to *shriek*. But there's a shorter way: eliminate the pronoun:

Liz's sudden shriek made everyone jump.
His claim that he had gone to see the nurse was an outright lie.
He lied outright when he said ...

The expletive construction can help:

It made everyone jump when Liz suddenly shrieked.

There are a number of other ways to restructure the sentence. Any will do as long as it preserves the intended meaning and emphasis. Just remember:

Which, this, and *that* must have specific single-word antecedents.

Here's another very common error of vague reference:

In Shakespeare's sonnets he explores the many different sides of love.
The posters on Jason's walls display his love of large reptiles.

You may want to say that *Shakespeare* acts as antecedent to *he*, but the word in the sentence is *Shakespeare's*, a possessive and therefore an adjective. So is *Jason's*. The antecedent for a pronoun has to be a noun or another pronoun.

In his sonnets Shakespeare explores ....
By the posters on his walls Jason displays his ....

In both erroneous forms the false antecedents, *Shakespeare's* and *Jason's*, were in a prepositional phrase. In other situations the vague reference is more acceptable:

Julie's right eye is blue, but her left eye is brown.

Technically incorrect, but there's no real risk of confusion. Use common sense.

Often the solution is to get rid of the pronoun.

In today's Times it says that the President is in trouble again.
In my biology textbook they use too many technical terms.

What is *it*? Who are *they*? No clear answer. Get rid of the pronoun:

An article in today's Times says that ...
My biology textbook uses too many technical terms.

It all comes down to this: **Either make the reference clear and unambiguous by supplying a single, one-word antecedent, or else get rid of the pronoun.** Always reread your new sentence to be sure that it makes sense.

VII. Pronoun Reference: Guided Exercise

Correct the errors in pronoun reference in the following sentences. Where possible, cross out the incorrect form and write in the correct one above it. In some cases you will need to rewrite the sentence. Be careful to keep close to the intended meaning; try for the most elegant solution. Avoid repeating nouns. At the end of each sentence is the number of the appropriate rule.

1. Otto plagiarizes his English papers, which is a shameful action. (58)

2. To be sure that her children read her poems, Olive nails them to the door. (57)

3. In Olive's diary she tells of her love affairs with world leaders. (58)

4. Otto asked Billy to stop tying knots in his hair. (57)

5. A policewoman was lecturing Olive when she grew angry and bit her. (57)

6. Otto often screams, "Down with the republic!" which annoys everyone. (58)

7. Olive always cleans the guts out of fish before eating them. (57)

8. People are not supposed to lie, but Otto tells several a day. (58)

9. Olive named her third and eighth daughters Nastine, and this shows her fondness for that name. (58)

10. In Otto's regular bar they don't tolerate nonsmokers. (58)

11. Olive truly loves Otto, but it doesn't stop her from trying to burn him. (58)

12. In Otto's fistfight with Bismo Borderline, he was seriously injured. (58)

13. Otto is a dedicated bowler, but Olive doesn't care for that sort of thing. (58)

14. Olive's father was a professional hairdresser, but she refused to enter that profession. (58)

15. Otto was walking his dog, when he started to howl. (57)

16. At the police station they have many stories to tell about Olive. (58)

17. Otto lies about Olive, and it makes her furious. (58)

18. Olive noticed that the judge was smiling as she came into court. (57)

19. Otto told his brother to clean up his room, and that started a fight. (57, 58)

20. In *Macbeth* it says that he hears a voice saying, "Sleep no more!" (58)

21. Olive's mother always calls her "Olivia," which infuriates her. (58)

22. After tenant activists released rats in City Hall, they were arrested. (57)

23. Olive loves olives, and this explains why she puts nine of them in her martini. (58)

24. When Margot compares herself to Ms. Citrus, it is clear that she knows more about grammar. (57)

25. Does it say in the directions that you are allowed to rewrite the sentence? (58)

(Answer key on page 232.)

VII. Pronoun Reference: More Practice Exercises

Some of the following sentences are correct; mark those with a "C." Some contain errors in pronoun reference. Where possible, cross out the incorrect form and write the correct pronoun above it. In many cases you will need to rewrite the sentence. Keep close to the intended meaning. Avoid repeating nouns.

1. Eddie sent me a letter with that package, which is illegal unless he paid first-class postage.

2. I read Raji's composition, and it said that our school was becoming very dirty.

3. Emily appointed Kay as head of the committee because she knew how important the job was.

4. I bought an orange at the store, which should improve my health.

5. The chair was next to the piano; I wasn't sure if I should move it.

6. The president of the company appointed his son as vice-president because he felt that family was all-important.

7. The girls did not wear their uniforms to gym class, which inspired the teacher to give five days of detention.

8. Jack punched Salim, and he could not be restrained for at least an hour.

9. He has wealth, fame, and every advantage in life; however, that does not make him likable.

10. We spent three hours fishing for shark, but it was not worth it.

11. She is a great believer in witchcraft, but she doubts they really ride on broomsticks.

12. In *Time* it shows hungry children in refugee camps around the world.

13. I know many Irish writers, but I have never met any of them.

14. The government is very pleased with the design of the new currency, which is supposed to prevent counterfeiting.

15. When one sees *Gone With the Wind*, in which Clark Gable plays Rhett Butler, one immediately understands that he is a romantic fool.

16. One also understands how racist their portrayal of black people is.

17. When it was made, the movie was not seen as biased, but now this is obvious.

18. The mastery of housework is not worth either my elbow grease or my time; nevertheless, I give it my best.

19. *Heaven's Gate*, which cost $32 million to film, earned very little, which disappointed its investors.

20. McMouses are better tasting than McRibs, which is why I prefer them.

21. At the final performance Pavarotti was absent, and that caused much critical comment.

22. The understudy did a wonderful job filling in, which earned him a regular contract.

23. The understudy's father loved opera, and little Marco always wanted to be one.

24. In Shakespeare's *Macbeth* he is preoccupied with the notion of power.

25. I devote an hour a day to exercising my major muscle groups, for I feel that it improves my mind and senses as well as my health.

26. My mother is a dance instructor, but I know nothing about it.

27. In Len Deighton's *Ipcress File* they show a suspenseful spy situation.

28. The boy whom Magda stole from Ellie often called her names.

29. While Pilar was brushing the dog, hair fell all over the couch, which annoyed her mother and sent her running for the dustbuster.

30. Babe Ruth was a better hitter, but they say Ty Cobb was the best all-around player in baseball.

31. I dropped a bottle of vinegar on my toe and broke it.

32. The reasons for Hitler's failure have been discussed at great length, but it is still not clearly understood.

33. I stuck my head out the window, and my mother told me not to do it.

34. The president of the school announced that we are not bankrupt, but the school paper says we are.

35. Pat wants to be a lawyer because it has always interested her.

36. There's one picture I love in the library's copy of *Michelangelo*, but I can't take it out.

37. My opinion, if you can trust it, is that Jerry is not reliable.

38. Essex led an uprising against the Queen; this resulted in his being beheaded.

39. My young cousin is greatly frightened by young dogs, which resulted from an early encounter with a biting collie not at all like Lassie.

40. I almost fainted when they told me it was true, but I still believed that your story had been fabricated.

41. Sheila just read "The Tell-Tale Heart," and she liked it very much.

42. The roller coaster frightens me, even though it is supposed to be safe.

43. My cat Fibonacci is frightened of her own shadow, which is not removable.

44. Liz commanded Isabella to do her homework.

45. Gloria's mother studied nursing when she was a girl in Aberdeen, and therefore Glorietta is interested in becoming one.

46. At the party last night, Dave ate more cake than he should have, which made him slightly sick to his stomach.

47. Do you think Rogers will pitch on Friday even if it rains?

48. While Odysseus was sleeping, his crew ate the cows, which was forbidden.

49. Once the movie was over, the audience began to boo. That annoyed the director.

50. It says in my grammar sheet that no sentence has more than one error. Hah!

I-VII Cumulative Exercise

In the following sentence you may find any of the errors you have studied so far. Make all necessary changes in the incorrect sentences, and write "C" next to any sentence that is already correct.

1. Here is my wallet, keys, and briefcase.

2. Aunt Winnifred told her cousin that the next mud-wrestling contest would be her last.

3. The fact that Homer, my little canary, could not open his cage door, was unacceptable to him.

4. The bookbag in the cubby beside the cafeteria has a little peanut butter on it's zipper.

5. Bart ate Homer's favorite shirt, therefore Marge bought a new one at the mall.

6. If anyone wants tickets to the Yankee game, they should see Mrs. Woods today.

7. Sliding into second, the baserunner screamed at whomever was in his way.

8. Shakespeare's play *Macbeth* is difficult, and its meaning in some places is obscure, the students usually like it anyway.

9. As if aware of my "math anxiety," the poltergeist appeared in time for every math test, and scared me.

10. Bill Clinton was taller than any previous President of the United States, which was an advantage in the media.

11. Mr. Williams, who everyone says was a great football player, likes soccer too.

12. The astronomer explained to we girls that Jupiter has a giant red spot.

13. The seniors lead us to believe they know everything, however the freshmen do not agree.

14. *Annie John* is the only one of Jamaica Kincaid's novels that have been assigned to the 8th grade.

15. Herbert and myself are constructing a glass table, but every time we try to hammer a nail, the glass breaks.

16. The only one of the planets that have visible rings is Saturn.

17. Grandma rides her bike faster than I; indeed, she pedals like Lance Armstrong in the Tour de France.

18. Our school, who's noted intellectual students, world famous alumni, and great bagels have been much praised, is building a new tanning salon.

19. Jane Austen and her sister read her writing aloud every evening.

20. Its not too late to give the parakeet its seed.

21. We agreed to prepare the sandwiches and the beverages, consequently the work was completed quickly.

22. Was it Mark Twain who said, "Everyone always talks about the weather, but no one ever does anything about it?"

23. The number of *Star Trek* episodes I have recorded is surprisingly large.

24. A number of ninth graders are going to prepare a good dinner for the homeless.

25. Elvis is the only one of the dead rock stars who still appears in shopping centers.

26. Tell me who you want for sophomore class president.

27. Fill out your identification card carefully; Mr. Alexander will give you one.

28. Bo could not understand why everyone brought their lunch to the SAT.

29. "You stole my calculator," Ernst told Scott, "my sister saw you."

30. Citing the government report, Dr. DeFective explained that every television and VCR that are made in the United States emit mind-altering radiation.

31. Neither of the doctors is certain about the best solution to the hangnail that so troubled Larry, and disrupted his exercise program.

32. Neither of Mr. Lacopo's star players has reported that he could not find a new tennis racket.

33. Mrs. Reed and myself went over the assignment until I understood it.

34. Caribbean writers in the Twenties coined the term "negritude".

35. After the terrorist had been sighted entering the boy's locker room, the entire football team decided to leave.

36. Between you and I, I hate the owner of that store; however, I am always polite when I go in there.

37. Neither her cats nor Alice are ready to walk through that looking glass.

38. The relatives have been arguing for hours about me going to Egypt.

39. There was much fuss when Trustfunda lost all her money but she could care less.

40. Through the railroad crossing, and down the widest avenues in the city roars the getaway car, followed by the police cruiser.

41. I heard an odd weather report on WNYC; it said that, "An unknown event will take place in Suffolk County this weekend."

42. What in the world do either of them want with a rotten banana?

43. Daisy picked a flower for her sister Rose, and she liked the present very much.

44. The number of deer tick's is high this year.

45. There was a little tension during Ben's and Jen's first date after Ben had his little adventure in the strip joint.

46. Some of the new puppies have rejected the puppy chow because it is too salty.

47. My parents were not happy about me quoting Melville's story "Bartleby the Scrivener" and saying, "I would prefer not to," when they asked me to walk the dog.

48. The very best basketball player on the court is him.

49. Horace is short, fat, and pimply, which doesn't bother him at all.

50. Everyone should do as well on their grammar test as you.

VIII. Modifying Errors

(mod, dm)

Modifiers are adjectives and adverbs, or phrases and clauses acting as such:

Bertha Mason is a <u>violent</u> woman. She howls <u>madly</u>.	[adjective, adverb]
Bertha is a violent woman <u>who howls madly</u>.	[adjective clause]
Bertha howls <u>because she is filled with evil energy</u>.	[adverb clause]
Bertha howls <u>at the moon</u>.	[adverb phrase]
Bertha howls at the man <u>in the moon</u>.	[adjective phrase]
Bertha is a woman <u>to avoid</u>.	[infinitive phrase acting as adjective]
Bertha howls <u>to ease her longings</u>.	[infinitive phrase acting as an adverb]
<u>*Locked in her attic*</u>*, Bertha howls.*	[participial phrase]

A modifier needs to attach itself clearly and unambiguously to the word it modifies.

59. Be sure that a modifier is placed so that it modifies the word intended and not another word. Sometimes a misplaced modifier **(mod)** will attach to the wrong word:

Mr. Green tells the story of how he married Eleanor to his mother.

Oh, he married Eleanor to his mother? *To his mother* was supposed to modify *tells*.

> **Modifiers must be close to the word they modify.**

In the example you can make Mr. Green's mother an indirect object:

*Mr. Green **tells his mother** the story of how he married Eleanor.*

Be careful with adverbs such as *even, only, almost, not, ever, never, again, often, nearly, hardly,* and *just*. Consider the following sentence:

Olive only buys bagels on Sunday.

This should mean that Sunday is the only day she buys bagels, right? In ordinary speech, maybe. But now look at the next four sentences, where *only* and the word it modifies are both in boldface. Notice that words like *only* usually modify what follows.

Only Olive *buys bagels on Sunday.*	[No one but Olive does.]
*Olive **only buys** bagels on Sunday.*	[She doesn't eat them until Monday.]
*Olive buys **only bagels** on Sunday.*	[She buys nothing but bagels.]
*Olive buys bagels **only on Sunday***.	[Never on Monday through Saturday.]

The last sentence is the way to express, in formal writing, the idea we started with, that Sunday is the only day Olive buys bagels.

60. Avoid placing a modifier where it might modify one of two different words. An ambiguous modifier (also marked *mod*) is like an ambiguous pronoun reference: it isn't clear which of two words is to be modified.

> *The man driving recklessly swigged at his bottle.*

What does *recklessly* modify, *driving* or *swigged*? Move it:

> *The reckless driver swigged at his bottle.*
> *The man driving swigged recklessly at his bottle.*

61. Avoid placing a modifier where it "dangles" (*dm*) without a clear single word to modify.

> ***When only eight years old****, Martine's temper was already uncontrollable.*

What does the phrase modify? Not *temper*; it's meant to modify *Martine*, but she's not in the sentence as a noun. (*Martine's* is an adjective.) So, let's make her a noun.

> *When only eight years old, Martine already couldn't control her temper.*
> *When she was only eight years old, Martine...*
> *When Martine was only eight years old, her temper...*

Many dangling modifiers are created by passive constructions, especially after an introductory infinitive phrase:

> *To outshout Bruno, strong lungs are needed.*

Who or what is *to outshout Bruno*? We're not told. Can we fix it by reversing the elements?

> *Strong lungs are needed to outshout Bruno.*

No. This may sound better, but the problem isn't solved. Although infinitive phrases normally can serve as both adjectives and adverbs, when they introduce the sentence, they are always adjectives and need a noun or pronoun to modify:

> *To outshout Bruno, **you** need strong lungs.*

Note: Imperative sentences (commands) contain an "understood" *you*, since commands are always directly addressed to a person or persons: "Go to your room, young lady!" means "*You* go ...." The following sentence is therefore correct:

> *To make chicken pot pie, buy a chicken and put it in a pot with a pie.*

VIII. Modifying Errors: Guided Exercise

Some of the sentences below are correct, and some have an error in modifiers. If the sentence is correct, write "C." If the sentence contains an error, rewrite the sentence as needed. The number in parentheses at the end of each sentence refers to a rule you have just learned.

1. Olive only knows one doctor, but her friend Mary knows at least twelve. (59)

2. Otto found the book under the bed that he had been looking for. (59)

3. To make friends with Olive, considerable tact is required on your part. (61)

4. Otto is weird enough even to interest advanced students of weirdness. (59)

5. The policeman who arrested Olive yesterday was ordered to release her. (60)

6. Otto is just interested in one thing, designer bubble gum. (59)

7. He nearly wrote a whole book on the subject. (59)

8. When living in a tiny New York apartment, it is important to keep your things in order. (61)

9. Singing in Grand Central Station, Otto's voice drove many people away. (61)

10. Olive dropped the hat in the sewer that Otto was going to wear that night. (59)

11. Otto drove to the bar where he was going to drink in Bismo's car. (59)

12. All people cannot easily accept Olive's table manners. (59)

13. Olive found some clothes in the street that she put on. (59)

14. While standing in front of a bar, a truck splashed Otto. (61)

15. Olive even curses when she's happy; when she's sad, she gets violent. (59)

16. To improve your grammar scores, some studying is helpful. (61)

17. Those who read quickly forget what they've read. (60)

18. Olive nearly knows everything about Otto. (60)

19. Otto corrected the letter that Bismo had written in several places. (59)

20. When completely loaded, the bus-driver stood up and yelled at the children. (61)

21. Sliding down a cliff-face, Otto's suspenders luckily caught on an out-cropping. (61)

22. Olive slipped the bottle in her purse that she'd stolen from the perfume store. (59)

23. When exposed daily to germ-carrying students, the flu is easy to catch. (61)

24. The teacher that Tommy angered frequently made the boy's life miserable. (60)

25. Providing a self-addressed, stamped envelope, the letter to the publisher will look more profes-sional. (61)

(Answer key on page 232.)

VIII. Modifying Errors: More Practice Sentences

Some of the sentences below are correct, and some have an error in modifiers. If the sentence is correct, write "C." If the sentence contains an error, rewrite the sentence as needed.

1. While trying on a new pair of sandals in the store that my sister likes, a fire truck roared by.

2. After hiking all day in the mountains of Laos, Chou said that he only wanted a sandwich, not a three-course meal.

3. To write a good essay, analysis is needed.

4. The car that hit the pole last summer was involved in at least fifteen accidents.

5. After dressing in his costume, Harold rushed from the locker room.

6. Knowing little about chemistry, what he had hoped would be the formula to cure baldness blew up in Henry's face.

7. Dr. Schiller almost ran the whole marathon but walked the last four miles.

8. The box of chocolates even melted in the heated room, and chocolate has a higher melting point than most people think.

9. Although not fully recovered from the mumps, Andy's mother sent him to school.

10. Sitting on the park bench, the plane flew right above us.

11. Eric went to Paris and just bought one postcard.

12. Only Evelyn sang at the concert; everyone else was far too shy.

13. I almost wrote half of the detective novel, but before I write any more, I have to decide who the murderer is.

14. Knowing our plans for the reunion, the cafeteria was decorated with old photos.

15. Hiking barefoot, the sharp stones cut our feet.

16. The eagle is endangered only because it is losing its natural habitat.

17. Kosmos has such difficulty with language that he cannot even imagine clearly articulating an idea.

18. To beat the Polgar twins at chess, good strategy is essential.

19. The new tax bill only guarantees protection for the rich.

20. To form a lasting union, the colonial legislators had to put aside some of their differences.

21. Squinting into the sun from behind the special polymer, an eclipse is a beautiful sight.

22. He was only absent from school for about three days so he does not have much make-up work to do.

23. While lounging and singing old camp songs, the hot dogs were roasting on the fire.

24. Mother was passing refreshments to the many guests in the form of ice cream and cake.

25. Thinking quickly clears up your doubts.

26. Sitting on the dock we could see Spotty, our pet goose, waiting for us as we rowed to shore.

27. He sold a necklace to the man with a fine diamond clasp.

28. Being made of stone, the builder expected his work to last for centuries.

29. Driving through the mountains, several bears were seen by the tourists.

30. The boys bought an old car from the dealer that had no fenders.

31. Titiana was cleaning her window one day when she decided to look outside.

32. That boy Magda dated often stood her up.

33. Because Elmer is on another strange diet, he mainly eats pineapples and sardines.

34. To beat "Deep Blue" at chess, you have to think like a machine.

35. I said when I bought the house I would save money.

36. Mother gave the steak to the dog that was too tough to eat.

37. While competing in the Seventh Annual Pie-Eating Contest, a cherry pit stuck in Egbert's throat.

38. Being an adolescent, pimples are a problem.

39. When told to stand still, Kelly didn't even blink.

40. As a Russian, communism is part of my history.

41. She assigned us five hours of homework with a smile.

42. While writing the Bible, the pen leaked ink all over Moses' parchment.

43. To pass English, illiteracy helps.

44. She only eats peas when she has a knife coated with sticky honey.

45. I had considered carefully resting up for the dance.

46. A battered man's hat was hanging on the peg.

47. At the age of five, Naomi's grandfather took her to her first Yankee game.

48. When playing the piano, the waiter brought me the phone.

49. Lauren wants to go just to the party, not to the dinner.

50. Trying to put his fist through the wall, the angry soldier broke a bone.

I-VIII Cumulative Exercise

If the sentence is correct, mark it "C." If the sentence is wrong, fix the mistake by neatly crossing out the wrong words and writing the correct one(s). In some cases you may have to rewrite the entire sentence.

1. Didn't Emily and her ensemble altogether butcher that song "Make 'Em Laugh?"

2. Waiting on the sidewalk patiently, the nursemaid hurried to her little toddler to help him cross the street.

3. Bismo has learned that shouting frequently can damage your vocal cords.

4. Because he hates my writing poems, Otto chases me all day long with spiked shoes but I am too fast for him!

5. Either my guinea pig Porkchop or my dog Sam love to eat snacks of lettuce and carrots.

6. In fact, each of them eat everything they can get their paws on.

7. The mathematicians, after meeting for three days and nights, still have not made any progress towards settling how to teach it.

8. Most canaries only eat birdseed, but Homer likes spaghetti, eggs, pizza, and anything else he can find.

9. "How many *a*'s are there in 'separate'"? asked Sonji.

10. In *The Catcher in the Rye* there's a passage that is often quoted; it says that Holden hates "phonies," all of those who lie to appear better than they really are.

11. Holden goes to Central Park to look at ducks whose beauty moves him, he also watches some skaters.

12. Dinah flew around Tom and him, and then tried to talk to some robins in the nearest tree.

13. Each of the new initiates has sworn, "Never will I reveal the club's rituals or its members' secrets", but Otto had his fingers crossed.

14. The reason for Agatha's wishing you to ignore all the false clues in the story is that they accidentally reveal the solution to her next mystery.

15. Yes, you can go to the store to buy jelly beans, and to pick up a lotto ticket besides.

16. When Mr. Di Cipliano asked Olive why she had flung her biology textbook through the cafeteria window, she shouted that she was, "Sick and tired of this nonsense about organelles."

17. My cat Spot jumping on the table is due to his overwhelming desire for a taste of Mom's tuna casserole.

18. The announcer on WFMU praised a song called, "Socks, Rugs, and Pocket Hole."

19. The number of people willing to pay one hundred dollars for those tickets is not small.

20. Since you have led many other secret spy missions, you may choose whoever you think is the most effective operative for this one.

21. On the screen, Kato just tried to knock off the Pink Panthers head with a giant bamboo pole.

22. Annie left the cat she had rescued from the dumpster in a box beneath her bed.

23. Mary, along with Tom and his brothers, are going to sing in the glee club next year.

24. She put glue into the toothpaste tube, which made me talk as if I had lockjaw for at least a week.

25. No, you can't go to the movies with that creature whom I believe wears fifteen earrings in the same lobe.

26. The list of those selected to meet with the aliens from Venus is posted on the bulletin board located outside the principals office.

27. The candidate, who you all know is the most honest man in Sing Sing, will only speak about his platform to minor felons, not those convicted of major crimes.

28. The team is practicing for its next game, but we believe that it will have no effect at all.

29. Sears is having a gigantic sale on wallpaper printed with Homer Simpson's picture in its Young Republican Style section.

30. The coach only gave new uniforms to players who had scored at least 17 points.

31. My parents objected to me using the new supercomputer to play SuperMario because they needed the machine for national defense work.

32. Woven by ancient artists, the museum displayed the beautiful textile next to a portrait by Rembrandt.

33. The number of videos shown on MTV are falling every year; however, the station seems to show more commercials than ever.

34. Each of the circus performers, along with all of the clowns, are going to wear red noses in the parade.

35. At the age of ten, my father told me that I was old enough to begin skydiving.

36. Every one of those boys has told Mr. Somma that he is a genius.

37. I am only one of the many teachers who, for environmental reasons, uses recycled paper for quizzes.

38. The only one of the boa constrictors that I like is curled up in the corner of that tank over there.

39. The son of respectable parents, a cave was the home where Mr. Pithakus preferred to live.

40. I don't like smelly vegetables like cabbage; nevertheless I will compliment that awful casserole to avoid hurting my mother's feelings.

41. The jurors have not reached a verdict in the libel suit about the mayor's slandering his ex-wife.

42. Every girl threw their lollipop at the coach when she announced extra laps.

43. Although he had majored in math, David worried because he knew less about plane geometry than me.

44. Olive almost ate seven of those dozen donuts; there are five and a quarter left.

45. Threatened with immediate execution, the raven was ready to swear never more will I say, "Nevermore."

46. All of the air in those balloons has been pumped in by my friends Sally and Andy.

47. Discovered in the attic just last week, the servant scrubbed the grime from the picture.

48. The telephone company has hardly added a single mile of fiber-optic wires to its network, although its clientele is clamoring for new phone and DSL lines.

49. The lion's paw is hurt, so he cannot eat you right now.

50. I have come to the end of another section of grammar, which makes me very happy.

IX. Punctuation with Essential and Nonessential Elements

(pen)

ADJECTIVE CLAUSES, PARTICIPIAL PHRASES, APPOSITIVES

Modifying phrases and clauses can be seen as either **essential** to the sentence or as **nonessential**. If nonessential, they merely add information and can be cut without loss of meaning. If essential, however, deleting them radically changes the meaning of the sentence. The test to apply is simple:

> **Remove the modifying phrase or clause and check what you have left.**

If your sentence still makes the same basic statement, the element was nonessential; if it now leaves you with important questions unanswered or says something markedly different, the element was essential.

> **Set off nonessential phrases and clauses with commas.**

62. Set off nonessential adjective clauses with commas.

> *The pilots, who want higher pay, are threatening to strike.*
> *The pilots who want higher pay are threatening to strike.*

The first sentence tells us that all the pilots are threatening to strike, and we are told, as additional information, that they want higher pay. If you were to take out the *who*-clause, the basic statement would remain unchanged: "The pilots are threatening to strike." The clause in the first sentence is nonessential and set off by commas.

In the second sentence the *who*-clause limits the pilots under discussion to those who want higher pay. Now it is only they and not all the pilots who are threatening to strike. The clause in the second sentence is essential to showing this; it is not set off.

> *Barney's, **where Richie Gotrox buys his shirts,** is very expensive.*
> *The store **where Richie Gotrox buys his shirts** is very expensive.*

The clause in the second sentence is essential because without it the sentence would read: *The store is very expensive.* The reader can't know which store is meant; in the first sentence, the store is identified by its name, and therefore the clause isn't needed and is set off by commas.

> *The day **when I have fewest classes** is Tuesday.*

Omitting the clause would give you the sentence, "The day is Tuesday." Which day?

> **When an object is modified by an adjective clause, it is common to begin the clause with *that* if it's essential but *which* if it's nonessential.**

*The watch **that** Jared stole from a store doesn't work.*
*That watch Jared is wearing, **which** he stole from a store, doesn't work.*

63. Set off nonessential participial phrases with commas.

Luisa, wearing a straw hat, strolled through the park.
The woman wearing a straw hat strolled through the park.

In the second sentence the phrase identifies the woman, who is sufficiently identified by her name in the first.

Note that all infinitive phrases that work as adjectives are essential, and all that work as adverbs are nonessential:

The dog to watch out for is that insane Airedale. [adjective]
The dog, to gain some private ends, went mad and bit the man. [adverb]

64. Set off nonessential appositives or appositive phrases with commas.

Beethoven, the famous composer, wrote music even after he went deaf.
The composer Beethoven wrote music even after he went deaf.

In the first sentence Beethoven is sufficiently identified by his own name. In the second it's his name that's appositive; if left out, the sentence reads: *The composer wrote music even after he went deaf,* leaving the reader to ask: *Which composer?*

Otto's uncle Adolf was a famous shoplifter.
Otto's uncle, Adolf, was a famous shoplifter.

Both sentences are possible, but in the first, Otto must have more than one uncle for the name to become essential for identifying which one is the famous shoplifter. In the second, we are expected to know (from context) that Otto has only one uncle, whose name then becomes additional information.

Limestone, or calcium carbonate, has nothing to do with the citrus fruit.

Calcium carbonate is another name for limestone. To leave out the commas would imply that they were different things being considered separately.

> **Do you and your reader already know who or what is being discussed? If so, the phrase or clause is nonessential and is set off by commas.**

WRITER'S REFERENCE: A NOTE ON ADVERB CLAUSES AND PREPOSITIONAL PHRASES

Adverb clauses are introduced by subordinating conjunctions such as *because, although, if, when, whereas, before, after,* and many others.

> Rachel always screams **if she wants attention.** [She doesn't always scream.]
> Rachel is going to scream**, if I read the signs right.** [She is going to scream.]
> Dimitri didn't curse at you **because he dislikes you.** [He did curse at you, but he had another reason.]
> Dimitri didn't curse at you**, because he likes you.** [He didn't curse at you.]

The difference in meaning is not always as clear-cut as in these examples, and in most cases it isn't worth your while to sweat the commas. But here are some principles that a careful writer observes:

Set off a nonessential adverb clause with a comma.

> George has not eaten any meat, since he is a strict vegetarian. [Compare to:
> George has not eaten any meat since he was twelve.]

When an adverb clause introduces a sentence, it is *always* set off by a comma, whether essential or not.

> Before Ms. Fierfel comes into class, she kicks open the door and makes sure that there are no terrorists in the room

When a prepositional phrase introduces a sentence, it is *never* set off, unless it is very long or includes another prepositional phrase inside it.

> After the game we went out to eat pizza and criticize the referees. [Simple phrase, no comma.]
> At the end of the third shelf down from the top, Harry Potter found a booklet entitled, "Spells For Selling Millions of Books." [This introductory phrase has two other phrases "nesting" inside it: *of the third shelf down, from the top.* Set it off with a comma.]

A few helpful conventions to let you know whether a clause is essential or nonessential:

1. Clauses stating an opposing or contrasting fact are usually nonessential and are set off by commas:

> Jenni loves mangoes, **though she rarely buys them**.
> Bill, **however dishonest he may be**, never lies to his mother.
> Maria brews up a pot of strong coffee, **no matter how late it is**.
> Carl never gets colds, **whereas Will is constantly snuffling**.

Clauses introduced by *when* and *while* are nonessential when used to state an opposing or contrasting fact, as above:

> Sara insists that Gordon is a genius, **when everyone knows he's not.**
> Dave is in and out of the shower every hour, **while his sister rarely bathes.**

2. But clauses that name a time, including clauses introduced by *when* and *while*, are usually essential.

> *My mother never uses the right glasses* **when she's driving.**
> *Clarice looks both ways* **before she crosses the street.**

3. Clauses that begin with *as* or *since* are essential when they name a time, as above:

> *Mr. Falkstein wept* **as he told the story.**
> *Helga has never been the same* **since she left Iceland.**

4. But when clauses that begin with *as* or *since* explain a reason, they are nonessential.

> *Raymond wept,* **as he had never heard such a sad story.**
> *Jamie never tries to sing,* **since her voice is harsh.**

5. Clauses beginning with *so that* are essential when they define a purpose but nonessential when they define a result.

> *Isabella sat up all night* **so that she could see the Hale-Bopp comet.** [purpose]
> *The comet never appeared,* **so that she was disappointed.** [result]

6. Finally, adverb clauses of comparison are always essential.

> *Otto has never been able to afford as much beer* **as he can hold.**
> *Olive sings far louder* **than anyone else can.**

IX. Essential / Nonessential Elements: Guided Exercise

Some of the sentences below are correct, and some contain errors in punctuation with essential and nonessential elements (but not adverb clauses). If the sentence is correct, write "C." If the sentence contains errors, add or delete commas in the proper places. The number in parentheses at the end of each sentence refers you to a rule you have just learned.

1. The collection of tales known as *The Arabian Nights* is the best-known work of fiction from the Arab world. (63)

2. The tales, that make up *The Arabian Nights*, were not all composed by a single author. (62)

3. The men and women, who tried out for the position of dogcatcher, live inside the city limits and close to the animal shelter. (62)

4. In front of the museum many mimes, who perform without words, contribute to the party atmosphere of the city. (62)

5. Folk legends are often turned into musicals, composed by professionally trained musicians. (63)

6. *World Leader Wrestling* televised by CNN will now be used to decide international conflicts. (63)

7. The cartoon character, Archie, was drawn by a graduate of the Horace Mann School in Riverdale, NY. (64)

8. Riverdale his high school is a common setting, along with two other important places, the malt shop and Veronica's house. (64)

9. The principal's office, the second most frequently seen location, is drawn in the kind of loving detail that lets you know that the cartoonist spent much time there. (64)

10. The 19th century novel, *Great Expectations,* illustrates many of the customs that Dickens observed in London. (64)

11. Places, named in *Great Expectations*, can today be found unchanged from Dickens' day. (63)

12. The 17th century Puritan colony, Salem, executed twenty people for the crime of witchcraft. (64)

13. Nathaniel Hawthorne who was descended from one of the witch trial judges was so ashamed of his ancestor's actions that he changed the spelling of his name from "Hathorne" to "Hawthorne." (62)

14. Some of the spells, that Hathorne claimed to have discovered, were probably fabricated by villagers anxious to seize land from the accused witches. (62)

15. Gertrude's favorite pet a guinea pig named Lettuce loves to eat green vegetables. (64)

16. My great-grandmother Galla is the only one in the family who lives in New Jersey; my other great-grandmother lives in Florida. (64)

17. Otto to make a political point dropped his pants in the auditorium. (63)

18. Any athlete, who is dumb enough to smoke, will learn a hard lesson about halfway through any competition that he or she has entered. (62)

19. Most of the skits on *Saturday Night Live* that were written by David are based on experiences in his own life that he considered funny. (62)

20. I can't understand half the words, that Shakespeare puts in his plays. (62)

21. The famous explorer and scholar, Sir Richard Burton, traveled to many countries, which he described in several books. (64)

22. Burton, co-discoverer of the source of the Nile, was also famous as the first Christian, who had successfully made a pilgrimage to Mecca. (62)

23. None of the faithful in Mecca guessed that the bronzed figure wearing full Arab dress was really British. (63)

24. Some scholars trace the origin of *Seinfeld* back to ancient India which many people consider the origin of all story-telling. (62)

25. Mr. Flint is too cheap to repair the chair, purchased at the thrift shop for under four dollars. (63)

(Answer key on page 233.)

IX. Essential / Nonessential Elements: More Practice Sentences

Some of the sentences below are correct, and some have an error in punctuation of essential and nonessential elements. If the sentence is correct, write "C." If the sentence contains an error, add or delete commas as needed. There may be more than one error of this kind in any given sentence.

1. A person who is good at shopping should be rewarded for this skill.

2. Travel is faster on the express trains which stop only at certain stations.

3. The teacher wearing the apron is Mr. Somma.

4. Spending money which helps the economy but decreases my bank balance is my favorite hobby.

5. Olive's daughter Nastine takes care of two other daughters Boxanne and Rancida.

6. The poet Burns raised as a shepherd taught himself to write verse.

7. Olive is angry at Fang her dog who howls when she sings.

8. Rancida who owns no shoes always says a prayer as she walks out on the street.

9. Apart from Nastine and Rancida whom you have met Olive, a forgetful mother, has two daughters named Imbecille and Vaselina.

10. The elder daughter, nicknamed "Cilly," always answers when someone calls.

11. Vaselina who keeps silent is actually as verbally gifted as her elder sister is.

12. She fears that her fifteen siblings not one of whom she trusts might misinterpret her words.

13. She fears that they'll betray her to her mother who doesn't believe in gentle speech.

14. Cilly, quick and agile, does not fear Olive who is a slower runner than she is.

15. Olive looking her children in the eye tells them the truths they least wish to hear.

16. The children who enjoy this treatment stick around for it; Vaselina who is quite timid gets out of her mother's way.

17. The packing crate where Olive and her children all live together is too small.

18. I pledge not to raise any taxes that will cause inflation.

19. The new taxes which all raised inflation were quickly enacted.

20. The book, that Marian Anderson wrote, tells of her confrontation with the Daughters of the American Revolution.

21. A gentleman, who drinks a cocktail in the morning, will be ready for a nap by two and for the grave by seventy.

22. Black Forest cake which was featured in a recent issue of *Gourmet* isn't hard to make.

23. Students who are artistically challenged may take doodling for credit.

24. Austen's novel *Emma* is much better than the movie of the same name.

25. The film *Persuasion* based on Jane Austen's work is much better than the other movies that have been made from Austen's novels.

26. Finns who are used to long, dark winters adjust quickly to climates where the sun rarely shines.

27. In medieval Baghdad, a city of thieves, it was common for thieves, who had retired from their trade, to join the ranks of the police.

28. Those of Otto's brothers, who disapprove of his lifestyle, haven't yet made up their minds to complain to their father, Blotto.

29. Gorillas, supposed to be fierce, are actually as nonviolent as any species that animal behaviorists have studied.

30. The prophet, Mohammed, who was a merchant, received the Qur'an from the archangel Gabriel.

31. The team, to keep its members from getting rusty, shuffled them into positions that none of them had ever played.

32. The scene, in which Macbeth returns from killing Duncan, is very chilling.

33. Lady Macbeth's saying, that "a little water clears us of this deed," does not reveal much sensitivity.

34. However, she later suffers from a torture, sleep deprivation, that any high-school student can relate to.

35. The website to get uncensored news from is Alternet.com.

36. Frankfurters or hot dogs are eaten with pleasure by anyone who doesn't have a delicate stomach.

37. The month when hurricanes are commonest is September, the month when I was born.

38. Amelie a little girl brought up by her youngest uncle Marcus is someone who likes to dress in strange costumes.

39. The students in my class, who write the best essays, always let a day go by between the time when they write a draft and the time when they revise it.

40. The novelist Nella Larsen is best known for one book, *Passing*.

41. The firemen, who arrived first at the fire, had it under control before the rest of their unit could get there.

42. A male native of Marrakesh an old Moroccan city is known as a "Marrakshi"; a female who is from that city is called a "Marrakshia."

43. Anyone hailing from New York man or woman is called a "Noo Yawka."

44. "Ecstasy," or "E," is a drug, that is widely abused by people who enjoy large crowds and elaborate hand movements.

45. "No man, but a blockhead, ever wrote, except for money," said Dr. Johnson.

46. Dr. Johnson also replied to the thinker, who claimed that you couldn't prove things really exist, by kicking a stone, which happened to be nearby, and shouting, "Thus I refute him!"

47. Trekkers in the Himalayas who drink water from streams without first boiling it are asking for a case of bilharzia a nasty species of parasite.

48. The world's most dangerous animals, to judge by the number of human fatalities they cause, are the elephants, beloved by visitors to zoos.

49. Jane Austen's early novel *Northanger Abbey* was actually one of the last of her books published.

50. The Senegalese group, known as Orchestra Baobab, plays African tunes that have crossed the Atlantic to become part of the Afro-Cuban musical tradition but which then were brought back to Africa in the 70s by Cuban soldiers.

I-IX Cumulative Exercise

If the sentence is correct, mark it "C." If the sentence contains errors, fix them as neatly and economically as possible. Rewrite the entire sentence only if necessary.

1. The committee nominated Mel Gibson for the award because he played his character Hamlet exactly the same way he had played the role that made him famous, Mad Max.

2. There is a museum called the Museum of Headache Art, a fact I learned from the newsletter, *Headache*.

3. The museum exists only on the Internet, although one of the "real-world" museums I know qualifies for the name that this one has.

4. To see the digital reproductions of forty-four paintings by migraine patients, www.achenet.org is a website you can visit.

5. Having seen how little neurology can do to help, Ygraine, whose head aches constantly, has abandoned her plan to become one.

6. Hiro only has three dollars, and five dollars is the price of the magazine.

7. Many people avoid the famous psychiatrist Dr. Mindfinder, but it is he whom you should call if you ever lose your mind.

8. Four thousand dollars are too much to pay for that baseball card, even if it is signed by Don Mattingly.

9. Pete said when he retired from baseball he would give up gambling.

10. Olive locked the door of the men's bathroom, where many of her ex-boyfriends were grooming in front of the mirror.

11. Although there was a meeting scheduled for today, the French Fries Appreciation Society has not in fact met since Tuesday is a much more convenient day for most members, than Monday.

12. Many of the baseballs that Tom sewed are ripping at the seams.

13. A number of students believe that Abdul is the one who should be called the Shakespeare of the 90s.

14. The book I bought with parchment pages was very expensive.

15. Lydia threw her gymnastics record book at the girl whom she believed had screamed at Ms. Balletta.

16. We Mets haters, Brian and I, are planning to boycott Shea Stadium, where there are too much inferior pitching and too many raucous fans.

17. The umpire said that Winfield was safe, however Jimmy thought that the ump was blind.

18. Heran sewed the seam under the light of a strong lamp that had ripped during the football game.

19. Allison almost received cards from all her friends, but two were out of the country.

20. Give that hotdog roll to the people it belongs to – Pete and she.

21. Since Renee dislikes visiting a country, whose language she can't speak, she wants to go to Paris with someone who she thinks is fluent in French.

22. I wrote the answers to all of the grammar questions on the test with blue ink.

23. Any of those dog-lovers, who bring their hounds to my party, will be in the doghouse.

24. Beavers gnaw trees with their teeth to keep them from growing too long and getting cavities.

25. Emma asked Maria if she would receive complimentary seats to "Rent."

26. The whole game depended on the next throw and Mighty Casey, who until then had led the league in home runs, struck out.

27. Geoffrey is always commenting that, "Teachers don't get penalized for returning papers late, while we do get penalized for handing our papers in late."

28. As the schoolchildren were guided by the polar-bear keeper, their eating habits and exercise regimen were explained further.

29. Daria complained, "My teacher never let's us criticize her because she gets to class late."

30. Neither the Madonna backup singers nor the only one of the boys who play the organ is going to perform.

31. Otto stopped by Fidget Rent-a-Car, but he was unable to rent a tank, equipped with a rocket launcher, because of the high demand.

32. Ian Banks's novels are written in a style that's sometimes called "gnarly", if you know what that means.

33. Gorman loved candy, moreover, he adored icing.

34. When iced, Gorman ate the entire cake.

35. To ice a cake efficaciously, use a broad knife.

36. Michelangelo's *Pieta* a statue known throughout the world is due to be polished soon.

37. Did you feel bad that it was her who picked up when you phoned?

38. Neither Newt nor Charles will ever use his cell phone again, which is a shame.

39. The first two chapters of the book, the only one she ever wrote, was exciting.

40. "I can't memorize vocabulary words, however many tricks I'm taught," wailed Maria, "my Latin class is hell."

41. The candidate waved to an empty field, no one except the camera crew was there, but his father had told him, "That's the right thing to do, George, and you must always do the right thing."

42. A student, concerned only with grades, cannot be considered a true learner.

43. Part of Octavia's lab group knows what it's doing; Octavia, on the other hand, is clueless.

44. She wants to study psychology because her mother was one.

45. Tooth powder, that is gritty, injures even healthy teeth.

46. The bellhop stopped me and handed me my bill, which was printed neatly on the hotel stationery, and informed me I owed seventeen thousand dollars for two nights' stay.

47. To operate a car in low gear, the gearshift must be moved to the left.

48. He read Shakespeare because it allowed him to make literary allusions.

49. I cleaned the window with the rag that had two panes of glass in it.

50. Its a good thing this exercise has come to an end, because I am tired.

X. Verb Forms

(vb)

Lesson A. Verb Tense

Verbs change their form, most importantly when they show the time at which an action took place. The form that shows time is called *tense*. Here are the most important tenses and their forms and uses. Below the tense name in the first column you'll find the helping verb used and what it's used with: infinitive or participle.

Present (is + present participle)	She *is doing* me a favor. He *eats* an apple a day. She knew that the dodo *is* extinct.	Shows an action going on or a habitual action or a general truth.
Past (did + infinitive)	I *took* my dog to the vet. *Did* she *tell* the truth?	Shows an action occurring at some definite moment in the past.
Future will + infinitive	We *will* not *give* up.	Shows an action yet to occur.
Present Perfect have/has + past participle or + been + present participle	You *have lost* your mind. Jo *has lived* in New York for twenty-eight years, *or* We *have been living* in ...	Shows an action that happened in the past at an undefined time. Shows an action begun in the past and continuing into the present.
Past Perfect had + past participle	By the time summer came, he *had spent* all his vacation money.	Used to show an action that occurred before another action in the past.
Future Perfect will have + past participle	By the time summer comes, he *will have spent* all his vacation money.	Shows an action that will be completed by some specified future moment.

Notice that most tenses, including all the "perfects," require one or more helping verb.

65. Keep your verb tenses consistent; don't shift tense without reason in the middle of an account.

It is normal to narrate events, fact or fiction, in the past tense, since they must have already happened before they can be told. Sometimes for narrative impact it works to tell a story in present tense. But stick to the one you choose.

> *Percy worshipped Mary, followed her around, laughed at her jokes, and fetched her pizza; but when at last he's alone with her, he doesn't know how to talk to her.*

The sentence shifts from past to present at the semi-colon. The verbs should be all present or all past tense.

66. **Summaries of events in literary works are usually given in present tense.** This is sometimes called the "historical present." The plot of the work extends over a span of time; in focussing on a particular event, you take it as the "present moment":

    *Macbeth **imagines** that he **sees** a dagger in the air before him.*

    Then earlier or later moments in the story will be put in relation to this present:

    *Macbeth **realizes** that all his friends **have abandoned** him.*
    *He **sees** suddenly that his old age **will be** loveless.*

67. **It's usually best to use past tense when reporting what someone said:**

    *David explained that he **could** not pay his rent this month.*
    ***not** David explained that he **can**not pay his rent this month.*

68. **But when an indirect statement asserts a generally accepted truth, the verb in the statement is in present tense.**

    *Fritz never learned that the world **is** round,*
    *not Fritz never learned that the world **was** round.*

    The world still is round!

69. **Use the present perfect tense to show an action begun in the past but continuing into the present. (Helping verb: *has, have*.)**

    This tense is used to set a present state of affairs in relation to its origins in the past.

    *Jesse, William, and Henry James, **have been** robbing banks and holding up trains for fourteen years now.*

    The present perfect verb *have been robbing ...and holding ...* fills in the span between fourteen years ago and now and lets you know that the James boys are still at it.

    *Dr. La Farge's chameleons were born in a Moroccan forest, but they **have adapted** very well to living in the northeastern U.S.*

70. **Use past perfect tense to show the earlier of two past actions. (Helping verb: *had*.)**

    A careless sentence:

    When the James brothers were hanged, they robbed more than three hundred trains and a couple of dozen buses.

    You can see the problem: the use of simple past tense for both events makes them seem to happen at the same time, yet three hundred is an enormous number of trains to rob while being hanged, to say nothing of those anachronistic buses.

*By the time the James boys were hanged, they **had** held up more than three hundred trains and a couple of dozen buses.*

Some judgment is needed when you apply this rule. If I say, "I went to the pet shop and bought two dozen crickets," one of these actions must have been performed first, yet it's not important to sort them out carefully. It's really a single event I'm describing.

The doctor removed the pear from Bolta's throat, and then she could breathe again.

And *then* and *again* act as time markers that make use of the past perfect unnecessary. Past perfect tense is most often used in an adverb clause, as here:

*After we **had filed** our teeth to sharp points, we gathered to eat dinner.*

Even though *after* is a clear time marker, it is still best to use the past perfect.

71. Use the future perfect tense to set a future action in relation to another action still further in the future. (Helping verb: *will have*.)

With the use of the future perfect tense, you are transferring your point of view from now to some moment yet to come, and from there looking back on an action to be performed in the interim.

*By the time they take their SATs, the students **will have** learned many points of usage useful to them in their writing.*

The *will* jumps you forward to that dreaded moment of the SATs, while the *have* jumps you back, not all the way to now, but to the span of time between now and then and shows you the actions in that span.

X A. Verb Tense: Guided Exercise

Correct errors in verb tense where they occur in the following sentences. Some sentences may contain no error; mark them with "C." The number in parentheses following each sentence refers to a rule you have just learned.

1. In Act IV of *Macbeth* the title character seemed bloodthirsty when he decided to kill Macduff's entire family. (66)

2. Olive never told a lie before she turned two. (70)

3. Otto met Boxanne, he became her friend and learned all about her habits, and then she turns around and tells him, "You don't know me!" (65)

4. Nastine never understood that tomatoes didn't grow on trees. (68)

5. Bismo claimed that losing that game didn't bother him. (67)

6. Otto explained that spelling is not his strong point. (67)

7. At the beginning of the novel *Jane Eyre*, Jane is sent to a dreadful school, which Charlotte Brontë modeled on a real place. (65, 66)

8. Otto said that amoebas were one-celled animals. (68)

9. Mrs. Klein is living in the same apartment on Essex Street for the last 64 years. (69)

10. When Beverly finishes washing the dishes, studying chemistry, and slopping the hogs, she may tune into "The WB." (69)

11. Believing that she fed her children already, Olive prepared no dinner. (70)

12. When she finished high school, Amy learned to play poker so that she could pay her way through college. (70)

13. Jack told the reporters that he will not apologize to Mrs. Beanstock. (67)

14. Imus did not apologize to the court, even though he clearly insulted the judge. (70)

15. When John sterilized the milk for the baby, he poured the milk into the bottle. (70)

16. By the time Telemachus returns home from Sparta, his father already landed on Ithaca and is waiting in the swineherd's hut. (66, 69)

17. Where the superpharmacy stood, a gas station operated till its tanks exploded. (70)

18. The bags were packed, the tickets were purchased, and all they had to do was to board the *Titanic* and relax. (70)

19. Mr. Hellman himself assured me that mayonnaise did not have many calories as everyone thinks. (68)

20. Olive looks forward to her children's graduation, when she will complete twenty-nine years of parenting and begin to enjoy the "empty nest" syndrome. (71)

21. By the time the tilers finish laying the marble in Mr. Blowbucks' bathroom, he will blow five thousand bucks. (71)

22. Mrs. Kraus lectured me on my ignorance and informed me that Andromeda is a constellation, not a planet. (68)

23. In *The Catcher in the Rye*, Holden is often unsure of his own motives, but he always thought he understood the motives of others. (65, 66)

24. By the sound of the tone, you will finish your breakfast. (71)

25. When Katherine danced for fifteen hours, she was a little tired, and her toes throbbed. (70)

(Answer key on p. 233.)

LESSON B. SUBJUNCTIVE MOOD

Happily, unlike French and German, English makes little use of the subjunctive mood and has dropped most of its forms. Where *indicative mood* is used to make statements and ask questions — the usual business of sentences — the subjunctive may express a request or a wish, or imagine a situation that is not actual ("a condition contrary to fact").

72. In a noun clause expressing a request, the verb takes the form of the infinitive without "to."

Such a noun clause will always begin with "that" and will be either the direct object of a verb like "request" or appositive to a noun meaning the same thing.

> *Mr. Singer has asked that every senior **see** him as soon as possible.*

In an indicative sentence, the verb after "every senior" (singular) would be "sees."

> *The terrorists posted their demand that the grammar final **be** cancelled.*
> *Of Olive I ask only that she **take** some care about what she says.*

Do not use the helping verbs *would* or *should* in this situation. Another form of request, using *if*, calls for their use:

> *The interviewer asked Olive **if she would** mind working fifteen hours a day.*

73. In a noun clause expressing a wish, substitute the following forms:

FACT	WISH
I am; he/ she/ it is	I were; he/ she/ it were
I/ he/ she/ it was	I/ he/ she/ it had been
I have; he/ she/ it has	I had; he/ she/ it had
I/ he/ she/ it had	I had had; he/ she/ it had had
I go; he/ she/ it goes [or any other verb]	I would go; he/ she/ it would go
I/ he/ she/ it went	I/ he/ she/ it had gone

You would normally, in an indicative sentence, use *am* and *is* for first and third persons singular:

> *I **am** on my way to see the Wizard of Oz..*
> ***Is** your room clean?*

But in expressing a wish, use *were* or the form appropriate to the verb you're using:

> *I wish I **were** on the way to San Jose instead of here in class.*
> *She inspected her car and wished that it **were** cleaner.*
> *Angel wishes that he **had** a better computer.*
> *Gabrielle wishes that her little brother **would vanish** in a puff of smoke.*

As with requests, these clauses are always noun clauses starting with *that*, either stated or implied. These clauses may function as either direct objects or appositives.

74. In an adverb clause that expresses a situation contrary to fact, use *were* instead of *was* for first and third persons singular. When the clause begins with "if," use *would* as the helping verb for the verb in the main clause, never in the adverb clause.

Contrary-to-fact clauses normally begin with *if, as if,* or *as though*. Be careful, since some "if" clauses describe real possibilities:

> If I **am** not careful in my investments, I will lose my savings.
> Anita looks as though she **is** going to burst out laughing.
> The buzzards are circling, but it looks as if Pete **is** going to make it to the saloon.

The time to use *If I were, If he were, If she were, If it were* is when you can say at once, *But I am not, But he/she/it is not.* In these sentences, the verb in the main clause will have *would* or its contraction *'d* as its helping verb.

> I'd wear my hair long if I **were** she. [But I am not she.]
> She looked at Phil as though he **were** something found under a rotting log.
> Queen Victoria complained, "Mr. Gladstone addresses me as though I **were** a public meeting."

One very common error in this situation is the use of *would have* in the adverb clause:

> If Mr. Scofflaw **would have** paid cash, he could have avoided the sales tax.

The correct verb in this case is always *had*:

> If Mr. Scofflaw **had** paid cash, ...

> **Never use *would have* as helping verbs in an adverb clause beginning with if.**

X B. Subjunctive Mood: Guided Exercise

If the sentence is correct, write "C." If there is an error in verb form, correct it. The number at the end of each sentence refers you to the relevant rule.

1. Monsieur Martinet treats Laurie as though she was an utter airhead, but she's not. (74)

2. There are a number of people who inhabit a space as though nobody but they were living there. (74)

3. The hen was blunt in her insistence that I should be careful not to break eggs when making an omelette. (72)

4. Nathalie blithely picked up a hammer and a handful of nails as though it was the easiest thing in the world to build a set representing the front of Notre Dame Cathedral. (74)

5. By its struggling the cricket expressed a wish that it were not about to be fed to the chameleon. (73)

6. The chameleon, for her part, wished that the cricket hold still. (73)

7. Does Alfred still wish that he would be fluent in Latin? (73)

8. If somebody would have told me the meeting was cancelled, I wouldn't have had to travel fifty miles on icy roads. (74)

9. Joao told his parents that he would not object if someone was to give him a new CD player and about a thousand bucks to buy CD's for it. (74)

10. If I was given a dollar for every homework excuse I've listened to, I'd be a millionaire. (74)

11. His aunt wanted to know if Otto would be staying in her guest-room much longer. (74)

12. The Governing Council has passed a bill that demands that all students should be allowed to wear baseball caps and chew gum at all times. (72)

13. I insist that Greg pays me for the frisbee and that he settles the business of the scalped seventh-grader on his own. (72)

14. Stan would be happier if his little brother would not have told their parents how the lawnmower came to burst into flames. (73)

15. Nick wishes that this exercise will be done soon. (73)

(Answer key on p. 234.)

LESSON C. Tense of participles

The present active participle, *swallowing*, has a past tense, *having swallowed*.
[Note that *having swallowed* is not the same as the past passive participle, *swallowed*.]
This form is useful in relating two actions correctly in time.

75. Use the past active participle to show action that happened earlier than the action named in the verb. Use the present participle to show action happening at the same time as the action named in the verb.

What difference in meaning can you see between the following sentences?

> *Taking care of his business, Mr. Trump met with several friends.*
> *Having taken care of his business, Mr. Trump met with several friends.*

In the first sentence the actions of taking care of business and meeting are simultaneous, and Mr. Trump's friendly meetings are actually his way of taking care of business. In the second sentence he meets his friends after he has finished taking care of business, and the mood should therefore be more congenial. Use the right sequence!

WRITER'S REFERENCE: THE USE OF PASSIVE VOICE

Verbs that take a direct object ("transitive" verbs) are said to be in active voice when the subject performs the action named by the verb. But transitive verbs can be made passive by using a form of the helping verb *be* plus the past participle. In this case the action is performed upon the subject.

Active:	*The mouse **ate** the cheese.*
Passive:	*The cheese **was eaten** by the mouse.*

Both are good English sentences. But notice that the second uses more words to express exactly the same idea. Hence the following recommendation:

Avoid passive voice, except when the performer of an action is unknown, unimportant, or not information you wish to divulge. Use passive voice to place special emphasis on what was done.

You may not know who or what did it:

> *Several stores **were looted** overnight in Djakarta.*

You may not care who or what did it:

> *The 23rd Street subway station **is being** redecorated.*

No doubt by the Transit Authority, but so what.

You may want to be tactful:

> *The costumes that **will be worn** on Halloween will expose an unusual expanse of skin.*

Politer than saying that trick-or-treaters will be flashing more flesh than usual.

*The Detestation Society is protesting the policy on testing that **has been implemented**.*

You know very well which sadists implement testing policy in this school, but you feel it's more diplomatic not to point the finger at them. But don't use passive voice just to avoid responsibility, as a recent president famously did by admitting, "Mistakes **have been made**" when his administration was involved in scandal.

Finally, you may want to stress the act and not the agent, as Shakespeare does here:

*"When the battle**'s lost and won**," cackle <u>Macbeth</u>'s witches, showing how little they care who wins or loses but emphasizing the idea that life is a battle that can be lost, as they hope to make Macbeth lose it.*

X C. Tense of participles: Guided Exercise

If the sentence is correct, write "C." If there is an error in participial form, correct it. Refer to rule 75 in doubtful cases.

1. Sharpening his axe, the executioner swiftly beheaded the condemned grammarian.

2. Brushing his hair and examining the results in the men's room mirror, Billy carefully slid his base-ball cap back on.

3. Not having brought a cape, Jim wasn't prepared to cover the puddle for the queen.

4. Confessing his crime, Raskolnikov awaited punishment patiently.

5. Sitting for twenty minutes in silence, Chatsworth is glad to be allowed to speak.

(Answer key on p. 234.)

Some optional practice sentences on passive voice:

Determine whether the passive forms should be left as they are. If not, change the sentences to active sentences.

1. The stream was stopped by beavers with dams that were made of gnawed logs.

The beavers stopped the stream w/ logs

2. A new Fun 'n' Games Center is being built where the Student Detention Facility stood.

3. I am sorry to report that a wallet has been stolen from someone in this room.

4. When the cells of the hive have been built by the bees, the nectar and pollen are brought in, to be made into honey.

when the bees built the cells.....

5. Considerable excitement is being expressed by the editors on account of the number of good poems that have been submitted by younger students this year.

submitted poems tha ... editor ? trent.

(Answer key on p. 234.)

X. Verb Forms: More Practice Sentences

If the sentence is correct, mark it with "C." If there is an error in verb form, correct it.

1. Today Arthur celebrated his one hundredth birthday; he lived a whole century!

2. If Shakespeare was alive today to see the new Shakespeare Garden at our school, he'd be very proud.

3. If those boys were to join the wrestling team, they will have to add muscle and lose flab.

4. Adrian behaves in Home Surgery class as though he is the only one of the students there who knows how to do a tonsillectomy, but in fact Tina and Gina do also.

5. General Nollidge insists he always knew that Iran was in Asia.

6. By the time the Nazis came close to discovering how to build nuclear weapons, they already lost the war.

7. Paula would have tried out for the part of Hamlet if she would have remembered the long and rich tradition of female Hamlets.

8. Mr. Lewis has often complained that Zach plays his oboe as if it was a trombone.

9. Cleopatra insisted Mark Antony love her more than he loved Rome.

10. Mr. Warriner on his deathbed had but one request of Ms. Woods: that she puts together a usage workbook far easier to use than his "Complete Course."

11. Courtney wished, since wishing doesn't cost anything, that she went with the orchestra to San Francisco instead of babysitting in Dobbs Ferry.

12. When the judge got his hand stuck in the cookie jar, his wife laughed as if it was the funniest thing in the world.

13. I suggest that the new cafeteria is furnished with chairs designed to look as if they were already stained with food.

14. By next April many a student will have asked that exams should be abolished.

15. Houria Aichi, an Algerian-born singer very popular now in the North African community, sang since she was a young girl.

16. Another Algerian singer, who calls herself Djur Djura after a range of mountains, described in an interview how her brother tried to kill her for singing in public.

17. Mr. Recollet can tell you what stores have occupied any given site in Hartford, where he is living since 1957.

18. Walking down the length of Fifth Avenue, we turned east on Waverley Place.

19. Napoleon demanded of his marshals that they march their troops at nearly impossible speeds to the place he had chosen for battle.

20. By the time Jaime takes his SAT's he will learn why a love of words is a useful taste.

21. If the end of the world is coming, then I wish it will come when I am asleep.

22. If you insist that I speak truthfully, I must say that no one yet enforced the attendance policy consistently.

23. Broadcasting for Mussolini during the war, in 1945 the poet Ezra Pound was locked in a cage by American troops.

24. Traveling in new places, I often wish that I were able to recall the geography I learned over the course of my life.

25. Staring at the useless underwater phone, Mr. Fallfort wishes that he had better sense than to buy it.

26. As we speak, the incoming tide just flattened the sand castle.

27. Margot wished that she would be able to comply with Monsieur Martinet's demand that she rise and sing "La Marseillaise," but she found that she had forgotten all the words it had taken her so long to learn.

28. The novel it took Abdelkrim so many years to write would by now have been read by millions if he wouldn't have forgotten the typescript in the luggage rack on the train.

29. If Helga were smart, she will not open the door whose bell has just been pushed by a maniac's finger.

30. Mrs. Jimmy Abreak ignored her husband's request that she add chocolate to the chicken soup, having had to listen to equally stupid ideas since her wedding day.

31. So many students hurried to join the Detestation Society that it now has a triple-digit membership.

32. The Detestation Society has circulated a demand that no tests are to be given without four weeks' prior notice.

33. Agreeing without dissent that a "test" may not consist of more than three problems nor last longer than fifteen minutes, the Detestation Society now takes up the knotty question of what a "quiz" is.

34. Many students, learning of the Detestation Society's program, regret not having such a good idea long ago themselves.

35. "By the time we will have abolished all grammar tests, our teachers will learn to respect us!" shouted a disgruntled sophomore.

36. "Teachers should punish themselves," the Detestation Society protested at an all-school assembly, "for giving us impossible tests ever since the school was founded."

37. If the principal was angry, he gave no sign of it but politely asked the president of the Detestation Society that she should keep her remarks brief.

38. The assembly was in danger of running overtime, he said, for the French Fries Appreciation Club already put on a long skit promoting their activities.

39. Tess Malatesta, who had won an uncontested election for the presidency of the Detestation Society, testily replied, "By the time they graduate, students will swallow as many frightful French tests as tasty french fries."

40. By this time some guys in the front row raised placards reading "Testosterone, ¡sí! Testing, ¡no!" and were waving them in front of the network cameras.

41. The placards caught everyone's eye, being hand-lettered over the course of the preceding week by the AP Political Agitation class.

42. "I wish I was still an anchorman in Anchorage," sighed the principal, who had switched jobs, wanting to work with adolescents.

43. Never finding out that Jesse James was a bank robber and no relation whatsoever to the famous writers Henry and William James, Professor Futtenmauth was startled by his colleagues' response to his paper on the James brothers.

44. By the time of his retirement, Professor Futtenmauth of Dunsinane College will commit more blunders than will be made by any fifty other scholars.

45. For example, it was the professor who, tricked into believing that William Shakespit had written a novel called *Great Expectorations*, wrote a note to the librarian requesting that he should order a copy.

46. *Jane Eyre* was falsely attributed to Jane Austen by Professor Futtenmauth, who just weeks before claimed Emily Faulkner as the author of *As I Lay Wuthering*.

47. The chairman of the department has privately expressed his wish that Professor Futtenmauth quickly retires or, even better, croaks.

48. "If I would ever have guessed that Bacon wrote *Hamlet*," grunted Professor Futtenmauth, "I would have denounced that Shakespig as a thieving swine."

49. His colleagues are pointing out to the dean of faculty that an honest review of Professor Futtenmauth's performance was not made in the last ten years.

50. Having considered the matter carefully, I think that if I was Professor Futtenmauth, I would not wait to be fired but grab the early-retirement offer.

I-X Cumulative Exercise

If the sentence is correct, write "C." If there is an error, correct it.

1. By the end of the year, who in this class will fall in love with whom?

2. Olive discovered that Skoolya took a test for her identical twin, Foolya, whom everyone thinks can't be told apart from her.

3. Eric often wished that he were not the sort of guy, who raised his hand and then forgot what he had been going to say.

4. Before she set out to cross the Sahara, not only had Ms. Luni made out her will, but she also found a good home for her turtles.

5. Male teachers think that no one among the students object to their continually popping into the boys' bathroom, but they're mistaken to think they're welcome there.

6. Lying for several centuries on the ocean floor, divers will soon recover the ship that was wrecked off Cape Cod.

7. Having tunneled through granite, the vein of gold was a welcome sight to the miners.

8. During some periods it was said that the Pope even outranked the Holy Roman Emperor.

9. Otto wishes that less of his English homework was grammar, which he has never properly understood.

10. Emma Bezzle submitted the accounts to Ms. Steel, the club's advisor, before she properly falsified them.

11. Al Urchik has requested that the sheepskin be removed from the bed, where he is to sleep.

12. If caviar were cheap, you could eat it without thinking for a second helping would be within your means.

13. Werner Werkard can hardly wait for the SATs, by which time he will master even the finer points of English grammar.

14. Mr. O'Shure wishes that his student Otto was either a more consistent worker or else a better liar.

15. Every poem and play and novel read at our school have been carefully selected for their literary value.

16. "When you have handed in the essays you were supposed to have written last night," said Monsieur Martinet. "You may begin to study for the test that I will give you."

17. When Monica Mapsentz told her geography teacher, Mr. Di Sorriento, that Ireland was situated to the west of England, he demanded that she no longer participate in class discussions.

18. My uncle Fred, a bank president, buried a fortune in gold before he died, but neglected to tell his children where it was.

19. Much of the gold that he buried were in ingots, but the rest were minted in South African gold coins.

20. No one among the wedding guests had proposed a toast, but the stranger who raised his glass suddenly burst into tears.

21. Towards the end of the winter, the members of the Freudian Club looked back to see what mental illnesses they found among themselves and were pleased to learn that they were all sane.

22. "You are not the only one of my student's who is going to have wept by the time this course is over," chuckled Monsieur Martinet.

23. I can tell you now that if I was you, I would read as many books as I could before the SAT's.

24. Sigrid often wishes that her conscience were not so active, for most of her pleasures are illegal.

25. Odysseus isn't the only one of the epic heroes who have ever suffered, but his troubles are increased by him taking those ill-timed naps.

26. One of the shepherds who shovel out the sheep's shed has issued a shrill statement requesting that the sheep should do their business out of doors.

27. The majority of Sigrid's co-workers admire her efficiency.

28. The composer, best known for his use of unique instruments that he himself invented, is Harry Partch.

29. If Perry Francis would not have spoken so ambiguously, we would not now be struggling to guess his meaning.

30. Each of those boys, especially Otto, have a good deal of catching up to do if they wish to pass the grammar test.

31. In the medieval Arab city criminals were so powerful that their violence and trickery forms the material of many stories.

32. Housebreakers first sent in a turtle with a candle on its back; in that way they would learn if anyone were home by their exclamations of surprise.

33. A woman named Ghazia lured many a man to their deaths by enticing them into dark alleys.

34. Ghazia, who most of her contemporaries considered irresistible, was as cunning as she was beautiful.

35. Her victims were strangled by her henchmen as they gazed in awe at her beauty.

36. Judging by the accounts of disinterested witnesses, al-Uqab was a master thief.

37. Al-Uqab once bet that he could steal a large sum of money from a doctor's house while guards were watching it.

38. The guards were taken by surprise, they were not expecting al-Uqab to turn up as an apparition of Jesus.

39. The *ayyarun* of Baghdad were gangs armed with clubs, which few people had the courage to criticize publically.

40. The *ayyarun* collected protection money from merchants, a practice that went on from the time Cain tried to shake down Abel till today.

41. These gangsters only avoided fights when they were seriously outnumbered..

42. A number of beggars in Cairo were apt to crash prosperous citizen's parties, where there was an abundance of good food.

43. Contract killers always brought a dog along to a strangling, if he lived in a respectable neighborhood.

44. One man beat the dog, which caused it to bark deafeningly, while the other villain was strangling the victim.

45. No neighbor ever heard the victim's cries, the dog's barking drowned them out.

46. "Ahmad the Sickness" a criminal from Cairo was sawn in half on account of the severity of his crimes.

47. In studies of folklore they say that Arabs prefer urban criminals, while Europeans like pirates and highwaymen better.

48. It seems that everyone enjoys hearing about a crime that doesn't affect them personally.

49. Perhaps we all wish we would have a bit more of the crook in us.

50. Having said that, it's probably a good thing that we aren't more crooked.

XI. Parallelism and Comparisons

(paral, comp)

Lesson A. Parallelism *(paral)*

The rules for parallelism stem from the need for order and balance in the sentence. In writing, symmetry of expression improves the clarity of the ideas being compared or contrasted. A sentence's structure is *parallel* when ideas that are equal in placement, importance, or function *match*. That is, they have the same grammatical identity; they are all adjectives or prepositional phrases or clauses, for example. Most of the time your "ear" will tell you whether or not a sentence is parallel. Sentences with errors in parallelism sound "off" or unbalanced.

76. Elements of the sentence with the same function must have the same grammatical identity.

For example, if a sentence has a compound subject, all the parts of the compound must match.

Swimming, skiing, and scuba-diving were her favorite pastimes.

The above sentence is parallel because the three subjects (swimming, skiing, and scuba-diving) are all gerunds. Here's one with a problem:

Winning the lottery, climbing Everest, and to go to the moon were her dreams.

This sentence is *not* parallel, since two of the subjects are gerunds and the last an infinitive.

Here's another example of a sentence with an error in parallelism:

He was famous for his smile, his fortune, and because of his ability to predict earthquakes.

Why was he famous? The sentence offers three reasons: a prepositional phrase (for his smile), a noun (his fortune), and another prepositional phrase (because of his ability to predict earthquakes). To be parallel, the reasons must match grammatically. Here's one possible correction:

He was famous for his smile, his fortune, and his ability to predict earthquakes.

Now we have one prepositional phrase with *for* and its three parallel objects (*smile, fortune, and ability*), all nouns.

Voice matters also. Shifting from one voice to another is awkward:

The artist painted thirty separate shades, and then varnish was applied by her.

If you begin with active voice, stay with active voice:

The artist painted thirty separate shades and then applied varnish.

77. Pairs of conjunctions must join equal elements.

Several conjunctions are used as pairs:

not only ... but (also)   both ... and
either ... or   neither ... nor

[Note: In "not only ... but also" it is not always necessary to include the "also."]

These conjunctions must join *matched* elements:

He gave an A+ not only <u>to Oliver</u> but also <u>to Alexa</u>.

The conjunction pair (not only ... but also) connects two prepositional phrases. Now look at this sentence:

He ordered Not only <s>did he order</s> <u>pizza and tacos with all the trimmings</u> but also <u>a ten-liter bottle of soda</u>!

Compare the underlined elements. The first is a clause containing a subject (he) and a verb (did order). The second is simply a noun (bottle) and its modifiers. To make the sentence parallel, move the first part of the conjunction:

He ordered not only <u>pizza and tacos with all the trimmings</u> but <u>also a ten-liter bottle of soda</u>.

Now the conjunction pair joins only nouns (pizza, tacos, bottle). The sentence is parallel. Here's one without "also":

Jane not only pilots gliders but builds them.

78. When making a comparison, be sure the items being compared are parallel.

The same issues of matching come up with comparisons as with parallelism. Again, symmetry is the goal. Here are two sentences with errors in parallelism:

(1) *The critic praised the new musical <u>for its sprightly melodies</u> as well as <u>what the actors said when they were not singing</u>.* *for its dialouge*

(2) *The critic liked <u>the sprightly melodies</u> but not <u>that the actors spouted clichés</u>.*

In the first sentence, the first element of the comparison is a prepositional phrase (for its sprightly melodies) and the second is a clause (what the actors said when they were not singing). In the second sentence, the first element of the comparison is a noun (melodies) and the second is a clause (that the actors spoke). Here are the correct versions:

(1) *The critic praised the new musical for its sprightly melodies as well as for its spoken dialogue.*

(2) *The critic liked the sprightly melodies but not the hackneyed dialogue.*

Notice the saving in words and the gain in elegance!

XI A Parallelism: Guided Exercise

If the sentence is correct, write "C." If there is an error in parallelism, correct it by choosing the best way to make the forms parallel. The number at the end of each sentence refers you to the relevant rule.

1. Sewing the costumes was not difficult, but to clean [ing] them after the mudwrestling match was another story. (76)

2. Hot, humid weather makes people irritable and behave impatiently. (76)

3. The boy who had eaten the last cookie apologized frequently and with contrition [contritly]. (76)

4. The guide told us the Pentagon has [about] five sides and about its miles of corridors. (76)

5. Joshua is not only [Not only is Joshua] president of the Future Flea Trainers of America, but he also plans [But Also that plans] to join the circus. (77)

6. Both climbing the walls and to go [going] on a fifty-mile hike are recommended ways to relieve pre-grammar-test tension. (77)

7. Teachers love their profession because of the high salaries, the exciting field trips, and helping [paying] young people to understand the fine points of grammar. (76)

8. Neither the Christians nor did the lions sleep well before the morning they were to appear together in the Roman arena. (77)

9. Carlita was overjoyed not only because she had won the Gold Medal but also because of having been chosen for the Olympic team. (77)

10. Archie threw the ball, and the window was broken by him. (76)

11. After his speech Leo was criticized for mumbling, that he didn't stand up straight, looking at the ceiling instead of at his audience, and that he spoke in a monotone. (76)

12. Academic success depends on three things: keeping alert in the classroom, to study without a radio, and one must be very nice to the teacher. (76)

13. Either John cooks the supper or washes the dishes. (77)

14. Britt not only toasted marshmallows but she also ate them by the dozens. (77)

15. After finishing this grammar exercise I plan to play video games, to eat a healthful snack, and party hearty. (76)

16. Jamie was tall, rich, smart and thought a lot of himself. (76)

17. The Chinese government neither acknowledges the mistakes of Tienanmen Square nor do they apologize for the massacre. (77)

18. Both the errors in logic and that Yuka made several careless mistakes doomed her math grade. (77)

19. Rogers likes to go fishing, but Agnes chooses sidewalk-surfing. (78)

20. Either Amy and Jennifer must finish the assignment within a week or report to the grammar police. (77)

21. Les is not only famous for his musical talent but also for his sweet singing voice. (77)

22. Costa Rican coffee is smoother, but there's more spicy flavor to Ethiopian coffee. (78)

23. Silvia assured us that cotton candy will both be sold on the day of the carnival and during the following week. (77)

24. As the weather becomes warmer, tiny insects not only swarm but they land on Olive's neck as well. (77)

25. Igor plans to go into politics, but Boris wants archaeology. (78)

(Answer key on page 234.)

LESSON B. COMPARISONS *(comp)*

Adjectives and adverbs have two degrees besides the ordinary, "positive" one. These degrees are the comparative (including the idea of "more") and the superlative (including the idea of "most"). Regular comparative forms end in "er." Regular superlative forms end in "est." Of course, many comparisons are irregular. Here are a few samples:

POSITIVE FORM	COMPARATIVE	SUPERLATIVE
happy	happier	happiest
slow	slower	slowest
quickly	more quickly	most quickly
bad, badly	worse	worst
good, well	better	best
beautiful	more beautiful	most beautiful
smart	smarter	smartest

While some grammar rules are simply customs, those governing comparisons rely on logic and order.

79. Be sure that the sentence clearly expresses the comparison you want to make.

Look at the following sentence:

Patrick is smarter than any boy in the class.

The above sentence makes sense if Patrick is *not* in the class. But if he *is* a student in the class, the sentence must be phrased this way:

*Patrick is smarter than any **other** boy in the class.*

Here's another example:

Mark Twain's novels are easier than James Joyce.

What are you comparing? Books to books, right? But the above sentence compares novels to an author. The correct version compares books to books:

Mark Twain's novels are easier than James Joyce's.

(The word "novels" is understood.)

80. All comparisons must be complete.

Finish one comparison before you begin another. Have you ever heard a politician claim, "My plan is better"? Better than what? Better than doing nothing? Better than the plan supported by my rival in the other party? Better than allowing King Kong to eat the world's entire supply of bananas? The sentence gives us no way to determine the meaning of the politician's claim. Here's another type of incomplete comparison:

The boss paid me more than Alfred.

So what does the sentence mean? Did the boss pay me $50 while he paid Alfred $25? Or did the boss pay me $50 while stingy Alfred paid me only $25? To make the meaning clear, finish the comparison:

The boss paid me more than he paid Alfred.
                    or
The boss paid me more than Alfred paid me.

When two comparisons are in the same sentence, each should be able to stand on its own. There are two comparisons in the following sentence, but only one is complete:

She is as smart, if not smarter than, her sister.

The first comparison ends too soon. Right now, all we have is "she is as smart ...her sister." We need the second "as." Here are two ways to fix the sentence:

She is as smart as, if not smarter than, her sister.
She is as smart as her sister, if not smarter.

The second version is shorter and more elegant.

81. **Use the comparative form when comparing two elements, and use the superlative form when comparing more than two elements.**

Incorrect: *Shawna is the best of the two poets in that issue.*
Correct: *Shawna is the better of the two poets in that issue.*

Incorrect: *Of the fifty thousand runners in the New York City Marathon, he is faster.*
Correct: *Of the fifty thousand runners in the New York City Marathon, he is fastest.*

XI B. Comparisons: Guided Exercise

If the sentence is correct, write "C." If there is an error in comparison, correct it. The number at the end of the sentence refers you to the relevant rule.

1. Babe Ruth was better than any baseball player of the 1920s. (79)

2. Of the three yachts in that regatta, *The Landlubber* is faster. (81)

3. When I cut salami, I want a knife that is as sharp, if not sharper than, a samurai sword. (80)

4. After reading 400 pages of Dickens' great novel *Bleak House*, I think that Jane Austen is better. (79)

5. The bird with the best sense of direction is more important to the annual migration than any bird in the flock. (79)

6. In the Soapbox Derby Harold's entry will be the best racer in the field of thirteen. (81)

7. Aunt Hortensia has a command of hiphop lyrics that is as good as, if not better than, her command of rap lyrics. (80)

8. Shaquille's slam-dunk strategy for winning that chess game is more effective. (79)

9. Hot shot accountants save me more money than my lawyer. (80)

10. When offered a choice of red or green, I found that I like that red, chewy Juicy Gum the most. (81)

11. Wily Coyote is sneakier than Donald Duck, if not the sneakiest cartoon character ever. (80)

12. Bill Clinton is taller than any ex-president in United States history. (79)

13. Having failed to win at table tennis and unable to face the agony of defeat, Marco demanded that the match be decided by his best score in two additional games. (81)

14. Wing flaps to slow the plane are as efficient, if not more efficient than, having the passengers drag their feet on the runway. (80)

15. In speaking about his role as a hippie in the Sixties, Oliver was the most reticent of the two teachers in his age group. (81)

16. Langston Hughes' poetry is more expressive of life during the Harlem Renaissance than Countee Cullen, another important African American writer. (79)

17. In the poetry slam William Wordsworth won as many prizes, if not more prizes than, Percy Bysshe Shelley. (80)

18. Zeus, who still has a few shrines in Greece, was more powerful than the gods of ancient Greece. (79)

19. Hercules was stronger but not more intelligent. (80)

20. The two competency tests are difficult, but the reading test is the hardest. (81)

21. During that hugely popular series, the Yankees scored more runs. (80)

22. This weekend I want to attend the Knicks' playoff, the Mets/Yankee game, and the Belmont Stakes race; but if I can't attend all three, the race is most important to me, for I have more money on that than on either of the games. (81)

23. The short green bush has little purple berries that are tastier. (80)

24. The new chancellor is as critical of the City University, if not more critical than, the mayor. (80)

25. Elizabeth Taylor has been in more movies than any actress of her generation. (79)

(Answer key on page 235.)

XI. Parallelism and Comparisons: More Practice Sentences

If the sentence is correct, mark it with "C." If there is an error in parallelism or comparisons, correct it.

1. It was clear that either Hilary would have to buy ice cream for everyone or Ignacio, for they were the only two with money. *[or Ignacio]*

2. Of the three explanations Frank's was the clearer. *[clearest]*

3. The Egyptian section of the museum is comprehensive, educational, and it has a lot of mummies. *[that]*

4. Some pet lovers admire dogs that are trained to perform tricks, cute, and lovable.

5. Elizabeth assured me that this grammar will not only come in handy but impress my romantic partners as well.

6. In his day Michael Jordan shot more accurately than any basketball player. *[other]*

7. Ralph is as fast if not faster than I am. *[as I am]*

8. Andy received honorable mention for his singing, and because he danced well.

9. In the world of competitive eating, the hotdog-eating contest at Coney Island is as famous as the Fort Worth Chili Festival, if not more famous.

10. *C* Compared with his three siblings, Lance, who thinks that closets look better with nothing in them, is certainly the messiest. *[b/c he]*

11. The perfect reading-group selection should be interesting, well written, and not take too long to read. *[short]*

12. Dr. Schiller's moustache looks like Groucho Marx. *[c]*

13. Our grammar coach was not only angry at our run-on sentences but our misplaced modifiers as well. *[also at]*

14. Dr. Cilli impressed us by falling on the banana peel, screaming in French, and then he made an emotional speech. *[making]*

15. Steffie had a better waltz step than anyone in her dance production. *[else]*

16. Egbert gave me more points for a partial right answer than Mary. *[gave me]*

17. Chubby's reading was better than Alexei. *['s]*

18. Rodney, the champion of the spelling bee, has three main talents: his ability to distinguish letters, his love for vowels, and that he could [his ability to] memorize the dictionary.

19. Aunt Hildegarde is better at solving quadratic equations than the [other] women on her task force.

20. Carlos likes both oil painting and to sculpt [sculpting] with partially melted M&M candies.

21. When serious television critics compare *The Simpsons* to *Futurama*, they all agree that *The Simpsons* is best. [better]

22. Restricting calories is more effective than if exercises are performed. [exercising]

23. I neither knew what I was supposed to do on the grammar test nor how to do it!

24. The tango is harder to learn than all the [other] dances.

25. Rick threw Bernie a curvier curve ball than David. [had thrown]

26. The prom committee realized that it either had to buy more decorations or shrink the dance floor.

27. Both the Chinese government and the American government plan rallies, protests, and to negotiate a secret treaty. [negotiations for]

28. My parakeet Alice's final approach to the cage after a wild flight across the living room is steeper than the canary. ['s]

29. Bart is as likely to "dis" his teacher, if not more likely, than Nelson. [as] [is]

30. The Outing Club members hiked into the forest, took the tents out of the backpacks, and the tents were [them] raised within an hour.

31. Brad chooses to study Mozambique, but Gordon elects sewing. [to study]

32. My romantic partner has sent me 150 valentines so far, but the one with the yellow roses is prettier. [than the rest]

33. After reading all 234 provisions in that treaty, the Secretary General decided that #34 was the least practical.

34. To err is human, but forgiving is divine.

35. Either the mugger demands your money or your life.

36. Jerry Seinfeld's latest comedy routine sounds like Jerry Springer.

37. I gave my canary Homer more birdseed than my parakeet Dinah.

38. I don't know about you, but I think these sentences are the dumbest in the entire book.

39. To be or the possibility of not being was the question bothering Hamlet.

40. In planting philodendrons, be sure to place as much fertilizer as, if not more fertilizer than, you used for the hibiscus bush.

41. Constantino was annoyed not so much by the umpire's decision as that the crowd booed unmercifully.

42. The grammar test checked our ability to identify verbs, choose correct pronouns, and to punctuate properly.

43. The former military dictatorship in Nigeria was more restrictive than China.

44. Ally McBeal wins more cases than any lawyer on the show.

45. Derek not only fielded the ball with ease but also style.

46. What a dog eats costs far more than taking it to the vet.

47. Elvis Presley owned more blue suede shoes than any singer.

48. The new Dogcatcher-in-Chief proved capable and that he could swing a wild leash.

49. Dr. Lipsmacher, the vet, gave Melanie more attention than her dog, who went home and howled.

50. The mud for the wrestling contest should be sticky, wet, and you need a lot of it.

I-XI Cumulative Exercise

If the sentence is correct, write "C." If there is an error, correct it. Fix all the errors you find.

1. Writing the best poem of the 21st Century and to live long enough to get paid for it are Marmaduke's main goals for the new millennium.

2. Bismo refused to go see *The Matrix Reloaded*, condemning it as "fascist" and "it's way overproduced, man."

3. Archibald hates his name because it is, in his opinion, corny, overly long, and he can't always remember how to spell it.

4. Not only have Proctor and Gamble created a new fuel, made from soapsuds, but also another from laundry starch.

5. Opening Bismo's wallet, the pickpocket was impressed by the amount of money there, but it's being so dirty startled him.

6. Only three things matter to me when I buy new jeans: how well they are made, if they fit tightly, and did a celebrity endorse the brand.

7. Marmaduke wished he had better sense than to slap Bismo with a dead fish, which was the act of a clown.

8. Sawing with firm, even strokes, the pile of timber was soon reduced to logs that would easily fit in the wood-burning stove.

9. Does either of the two candidates for political office have the faintest idea how to compute a budget, let alone a tax cut?

10. Elva nearly finished half her history test when the teacher called "time"!

11. Annoyed by her punishment – writing "I will not talk during filmstrips" fifty times and mopping the cafeteria – Claudia put her pencil down, and sat motionless.

12. Lying beside the lake, Mr. Keene contemplated either a fishing trip or going to Kenya on a photo-safari instead.

13. The children's babysitter is in trouble for they only behaved for ten minutes out of the three hours they were supervised.

14. The coach asked a number of people to try out, but none of them were picked by him.

15. "This pool will not only give you pleasure now but in twenty year's time!" shouted the salesman who clearly thought that volume would make him more persuasive.

16. "I have just received rather disquieting information about Fogg", said the inspector, who was met with cries of "Balderdash!" and "Rot!"

17. *Winged Migration*, which has footage of migrating birds shot in flight, was more dramatic than any movie I saw in the last decade.

18. The birds were filmed by cameras, carried on radio-controlled "ultralite" aircraft.

19. If Otto would have listened in class, he both would have learned what the test will cover and its date.

20. Neither the *Venezuela* nor the other yachts in that fleet are going to reach London on time, despite all our efforts we are going to lose the race.

21. Someone read Phineas Fogg's *London Times* before he did, the worst social error ever witnessed in the gentleman's club to which Fogg belongs.

22. Anyone who is willing to cook and clean for Fogg must be able to adapt their behavior to the man's whims.

23. "He is a cold-hearted, implacable fiend", said the valet as he quit Fogg's employ.

24. The fellow whose stomach was growling noisily demanded another helping of the same chili, that he was already having trouble digesting.

25. Fogg is as difficult, if not more difficult, an employer than you can possibly imagine.

26. Fogg traveled hundreds of miles by balloon yet he neither noticed any migrating birds nor any ultralite aircraft.

27. Fogg insists that his toast should be 83 degrees, no more and no less, and the butter should be fresher than a farmer.

28. Passepartout agreed to act as valet for Fogg, and of the three duties he performed during the first afternoon of his employ, cutting the butter in 1.75 inch pats was the more difficult.

29. Otto reached his hands towards the chocolates before he noticed they were gone.

30. When he heard that someone robbed the Bank of England, Fogg said that the theft might have been predicted.

31. Attempting to circle the globe in only 80 days, the trip nearly killed Fogg and Passepartout.

32. Fogg accepted a wager of 5000 pounds, the bet was that he could complete his trip within the stated time.

33. Fogg treated the rats in his house better than his valet.

34. Passepartout, not his many admirers and friends, were sure that the trip would be a failure.

35. Fogg carefully placed the frog he had rescued from the soggy bog in the bathtub.

36. The officers of the committee overseeing Fogg's club was in agreement that Fogg's ideas were as crazy as anything they had ever heard.

37. Fogg is a character in Jules Verne's novel, however, he was also the subject of a movie and many other theatrical interpretations.

38. In Jules Verne's novel it says that Passepartout was French, but in Michael Todd's movie he was played by the Mexican star, Cantinflas, who was better known than any Mexican actor.

39. "We are not migrating birds, but we will fly in a hot air balloon, they will photograph us anyway," said Phineas Fogg.

40. "To lose weight, eat whatever you like but small helpings are the key," the doctor told Fogg, who wanted his balloon to rise.

41. Did Fogg really say that he eats breakfast at "8:34, not 8:33 or 8:35?"

42. As the balloon floated slowly over the Pyrenees to Spain, which is an unusual way to travel, the French countryside looked like a green and tan carpet below them.

43. The summer has been so hot that the air conditioner has nearly been running continuously, not stopping for an hour even in the middle of the night.

44. Passepartout's manner is not as dignified as his employer, nor his clothes as elegant, but he commands respect.

45. The migrating birds not only thought that Fogg's balloon looked showy but his top hat was silly, but flew past without a comment.

46. The manager at Cook's Travel Services, like everyone else who come into contact with Fogg, considers the eccentric millionaire foolish but someone you have to love.

47. "Fogg is the one who we all consider the frontrunner for the 'One Doughnut Short of a Dozen' award." said the manager of the Bank of England.

48. Before Fogg had won his bet, everyone was sure that he would lose it.

49. The guitar as played in Flamenco music is as melodic, if not more melodic, than classic rock guitar.

50. Cante Jondo which is the haunting Flamenco song of pain is derived from African, Spanish, and Hebrew traditions.

XII. Double Negatives

(2-)

82. A double negative makes an affirmative statement.

In some languages, a double negative simply emphasizes the negative meaning of the sentence, but in formal English usage, the rules of logic prevail. So if you say:

> *I did not see nobody in the park.*
> *He declined to make no comment on the matter.*
> *I can't hardly wait for summer vacation.*

you are really saying:

> *I saw somebody in the park.*
> *He agreed to comment on the matter.*
> *I can wait for summer vacation.*

Note that we are speaking of *formal* English usage. In slang, a double negative is often taken as emphasis:

> *I didn't do nothing!*

Most double negatives will be obvious to you, but one particular construction causes problems. The adverb "but" (meaning *only*) creates a negative. The following sentence violates the double-negative rule:

> *I can't help but think that you are a traitor.*

A correct though somewhat old-fashioned use of adverbial *but* would remove the negative from the verb: *I* **can** *but think that you are a traitor.* Here is a more up-to-date form:

> *I can't help thinking that you are a traitor.*

WRITER'S REFERENCE: REDUNDANCY *(red)*

Would you rather attend ~~a twenty-minute~~ lecture or a forty-minute lecture that gave you the same information? Most students would prefer the shorter session. So would most readers. Especially now, when time is at a premium and readers have lots of other claims on their time, it is important to be concise in writing.

Don't repeat words or ideas unnecessarily.

The easiest way to trim your "word budget" is to avoid repeating yourself. Look at the sentences below:

> ~~Tense and nervous, Mohammadou walked around the water cooler several times. The water cooler was filled with cool, refreshing water.~~ Mohammadou circled the cooler until he felt less anxious.

water

Tense,

Those 29 words say very little. "Tense" and "nervous" actually have different meanings, but in the above sentence they are used as filler. The writer is not using them to distinguish separate feelings. Sentence two adds nothing. The cooler was full; well, why would you have an empty water cooler, and what else would be in a water cooler but water? A cooler doesn't *heat* the water; a cooler *cools* the water to make it *refreshing*. One whole sentence bites the dust. Sentence three repeats two ideas – "circled" (we know Mohammadou walked around the cooler) and "anxious" (we know he's "tense and nervous"). The only new idea is the time concept, implied by "until." Here's a better version:

Tense, Mohammadou circled the water cooler until he felt calmer.

Now we have 10 words – a savings of 19 words!

One common redundancy involves adding an adverb, especially an adverb of direction, to a verb where that direction is already a part of the meaning. Now look at these sentences:

Before I left for vacation, I returned all the borrowed books back to the library.
The porters lifted my trunks and suitcases up onto the train.

In the first sentence, *return* means *bring back*. Would you say, "I brought back back the books I'd borrowed"? In the second, can you *lift* something anywhere but *up*? If so, please contact Ripley's; you have a career waiting for you.

Of course, sometimes a writer repeats words in order to emphasize the meaning:

You may not have the car keys, oh no, not tonight!
I myself will take care of the problem; I won't pass it along to a subordinate.

However, repetition should be deliberate and rare – a break from the pattern, not the pattern itself.

Repetition may also be a problem not within one sentence but within the essay as a whole. Concluding paragraphs are often a problem. Some students see the conclusion as a *summary* and simply reword the introduction. Bad idea! The conclusion should extend the meaning, not restate it.

XII. Double Negatives: Guided Exercise

If the sentence is correct, write "C." If there is a double negative in the sentence, correct the sentence. Consult Rule 82 in cases of doubt.

1. When the king, died, the prince could not help crying like a baby.

2. The sound that Melverina made when the ketchup bottle hit her big toe was so soft that we couldn't hardly hear her.

3. Joey was so in love with football that he couldn't help but wear his football uniform to the party.

4. Monica hardly cannot bear Janice's laugh, and she always tells Janice sad stories to avoid hearing that shrill braying.

5. When asked about her favorite pizza topping, the President didn't say nothing.

6. The African statue was so beautifully carved that the museum couldn't help but place it in the most prominent display.

7. Sophie was not the first to deny that she wouldn't hardly obey Edward.

8. Niles was so upset when he heard about the Yankees' loss that he couldn't hardly speak.

9. When I heard the first three notes of the song, I could not but think of the last time I saw Paris.

10. Otto doesn't know hardly any songs but "The Yellow Rose of Texas."

Optional problems on redundancy

Eliminate all unneeded words from the following sentences. Consult the Writer's Reference section above in cases of doubt.

1. When the tenth-grade tiling competition was over, Julie had laid more tiles down on the floor than any other sophomore.

2. Around his neck Herman, the little orange cat, wears a flea collar to kill fleas.

3. The police officer is now at this present time walking up to the thief.

4. My knees were stiff after hours of running on streets and roads around town.

5. The block-and-tackle with which the workers raise buckets of pitch up to the roof looks as if it's ready to break.

6. When Mambo King Tito Puente plays at the Puerto Rican Day Parade, the marchers take a "dance break" and dance.

7. The official school calligrapher wrote the names of all the seniors on the diplomas, one for each 12th grader.

8. In the urban city the huge number of people who live in apartments have few or no lawn-mowing chores.

9. Way out in the country in rural areas, especially on the banks of Dawson's Creek, the mosquitoes are biting.

10. Arranged in a round circle, the fifteen inhabitants of that dormitory prepared for a tug-of-war with the other dormitory.

11. At the present time the school now has two new buildings that were just built.

12. "Uh oh, here comes every one of the Capulets," thought Romeo, searching everywhere for an exit out from the disco.

13. The barber who cuts hair has become a millionaire since the fad for short hair has become trendy.

14. My four-year-old little sister, tired and exhausted, screamed all the way down the street until my mother picked her up and carried her.

15. The ocean of salt water was buoyant and helped the leaky boat that was filling with water to float.

16. Many people don't know that Gerlsrock Academy began as a co-ed school, educating both boys and girls.

17. Clarabell the Cow, weary and exhausted after winning the Milk Producer of the Year Award, mooed only a few minutes instead of making a long acceptance speech.

18. Agatha wants to become a veterinarian and cure sick animals.

19. To get to the Yankee game on time, take the subway train that runs underground.

20. In my opinion I think that Shakespeare made his plays difficult so that students would have to spend more time reading them.

21. Hip Hop music is the anthem of modern teenagers of today, just as rock and roll was the anthem of previous generations of teenagers of yesterday.

22. The rugs that carpeted the living room floor felt soft underfoot to Walker's tired feet.

23. At the present time there are currently over two hundred grammar rules left to learn.

(Answer key on page 235.)

XII. Double Negatives: More Practice Sentences

If the sentence is correct, write "C." If there is a double negative, correct the sentence.

1. Now that my brother does not work there, 2005 is the first year since 1930 that no member of my family has not worked at Con Ed.

2. I could but lament that he had eaten the very last chocolate chip cookie, since further action would clearly be against the law.

3. Augie, called yet again for jury duty, could not help but yawn as the training movie, *So you want to be a Juror,* played overhead.

4. Selfless as Mugatroyd is, she can but ask for absolutely nothing for her birthday.

5. "Edgar did not do nothing to help write that short story," claimed Allan.

6. Roger never said that he would not go to the dance, so Monica tried to find another date.

7. I couldn't help but overhear your comment about eavesdropping.

8. She was asked to pay the check but declined because she did not have nothing in her wallet.

9. The cheap jacket did not cost barely a cent but was quite fashionable anyway.

10. Recently explorers have begun to question whether or not Sir Edmund Hillary wasn't actually the first person to ascend Mount Everest.

11. Elmer and Osceola hadn't but three acres left when the bank finished its foreclosure on their property.

12. Osceola could not but think that the decision to plant champagne grapes instead of soy beans was a mistake.

13. Jack "The Giant" Alexander could not hardly believe the size of the boxer facing him.

14. "I can but try my best," concluded Teeny Meany, "and if I fail, I will descend to the mat with honor."

15. Fred "The Fair" Farnum, the referee, couldn't do nothing to help Teeny Meany, despite his thoughts about the appropriateness of the match.

16. "I couldn't hit nothing," Teeny later told Sportlines, the cable network.

I-XII Cumulative Exercise

If the sentence is correct, write "C." Correct any errors you find.

1. Manufacturers fill light bulbs with "noble gases" such as argon because they are more stable.

2. Olive could not but halfway believe her eyes when she saw a bald eagle, wearing a wig.

3. In 1944 one of France's most beautiful and historic cities St. Malo was bombed into rubble by the very Americans who were supposed to be liberating it.

4. Elmer's painting is not so much exceptional for its subject as for his delicate handling of winter light.

5. If the Royal Air Force wouldn't have bombed the German city of Lübeck during the war, Hitler would not have ordered the Luftwaffe to hit towns such as Exeter which had no military value.

6. Hitler ordered Exeter to be bombed when he consulted his Baedeker, a well-known guidebook.

7. They call these raids the "Baedeker raids" in history books.

8. Arnie's voyage proceeded uneventfully when the plane, that he was traveling in, hit an air pocket and dropped twenty feet, sending his champagne splashing against the overhead bin.

9. The police officer told the motorist, whose speedometer had topped 120 miles per hour, that a speeding ticket wasn't a badge of honor.

10. "I didn't hardly do anything!" screamed Bart as Homer rounded the corner of the garage with a look of annoyance.

11. Olive wishes heartily that she didn't stay up all night to study for the grammar test.

12. Writing out all the answers to these exercises is sure to increase your use of paper, if not how clearly you express yourself.

13. Although Marie spent the better part of an hour fishing, she could not even catch one trout.

14. My uncle who is a farmer told his brothers that pears are as good for you as, if not much better than, any other fruit.

15. My favorite old movie, *The Thin Man*, is as funny, if not funnier, than any movie ever made in America.

16. On the hard-to-reach shelf above Margot's desk is the only one of the books that is relevant to her essay topic.

17. Bismo may look like a monkey, but even Einstein sometimes looked as if he just came down from the trees.

18. By next Wednesday, only a week from today, the giant comet will hit the United States, but until then James' mother is still insisting that he cleans his room.

19. Stuck on the bedpost overnight, Nat found that his chewing gum lost its flavor.

20. The soldier in the front rank, wearing the pink fatigue cap and silver combat boots, certainly stood out from the soldiers in the regiment, who were dressed in camouflage suits.

21. Alice's flight through the living room was smoother than any other parakeet in the entire world.

22. "Waiter, will you please ask whoever is smoking to put it out"? asked Reina.

23. Any fish would be acceptable to Marie but a trout called "Old Walleye" is the one she can't help but wish to catch.

24. The Yankee game was postponed on account of the large number of Mets fans who even refused to leave the field after the national anthem.

25. Each reporter and camera technician contribute to the evening news in their own way.

26. There is an understanding among we juniors not to respect the principal's request that we should remove our baseball caps during assemblies.

27. The roofer, like all the other workers, are working twenty hours a day to complete the vacation home early for the generous billionaire.

28. Eating over twenty hotdogs in the annual Fourth of July Hotdog Eating Contest, Marmaduke exclaimed when the final bell rang, "I cannot help but wish that french fries are served to complete my meal."

29. The number of kinds of flower that grows in the desert are larger than you'd guess.

30. Olives make a salad salty, but even more salt is added to it by anchovies.

31. Everyone should bring their book to class; I cannot excuse those, who claim to have lost it, for they should have known better.

32. During the recent bubblegum war, Lorna objected to Myrna criticizing Big Pink brand, because she owned stock in it.

33. In *Their Eyes Were Watching God* Janie found that taking risks brings more rewards than if she'd stayed home.

34. How she dances the tango is nothing compared to his way of dancing the tango.

35. The majority of those meteorologists agree that the weather here in the summer of 2003 was better than Europe.

36. The forgetful father accused a man of killing his son who was his son.

37. Every fashion model and hiphop star wear their hair less elegantly than Annie and I.

38. Karl told Dick that the power failure meant profits for his company as large, if not larger, than the war.

38. The compulsive gambler loses both his gold and he doesn't get sympathy either.

39. Rafael and he and the rest of we sophomores are angry at these authors putting multiple errors in the same sentence.

40. When Spencer read the paper, he gave it to Tracy to look over.

41. Because of his intensely fearful reaction to that close call with the rocket, everyone should be careful when they are lighting matches in the area around Horace.

42. Seeing what grief drunk driving can cause, Rachel and myself insisted that Blotto should let someone else take the wheel.

43. Olive wiped the tears from her daughter's eye, and the gasoline from the floor that had spilled when the Molotov cocktail broke.

44. Strangely, the several species of chameleon that inhabits the north of Africa, a region more famous for deserts than forests, are arboreal or tree-dwelling.

45. In the nineteenth century European painters nearly copied all the Japanese artists but Hokusai the great Japanese printmaker sometimes used Western compositions.

46. Otto is amazed at the number of people, who's understanding of psychology does not go not much further than Freud's, "Oedipus complex."

47. Olive leaving soon depressed Otto, who hadn't gotten around to borrowing the money he needed to get liquor from her.

48. A number of the shops in London is no different from any mall in America.

49. When you look at the sticker in a London shop, you can't hardly believe that the price in London is half again as expensive as New York.

50. Barnes and Noble tries to be one of those cool stores a person wishes they live in.

Words to Watch Out For

The following section introduces fifty sets of words or expressions that are often misused in writing. Which errors do you make? Here's your chance to find out what they are and how to edit them out of your essays.

Besides your interest in improving your writing, you have another motive for mastering these words: word-usage problems of these kinds are featured on the new SAT. You're preparing yourself for that test by studying what follows.

Words to Watch Out For 1-4

The following pairs of words look or sound like one another, but they are used as different parts of speech and usually have very different meanings.

W.1 Accept and Except

Accept is a verb meaning *receive, take, permit*; its opposite is *refuse, deny*.

> *Professor Offgard **accepted** the package from the Unabomber.*
> *A true saint **accepts** the hardships that life sends.*

Except can be a verb meaning *leave out, make an exception for*; its opposite is *include*.

> *Dr. Nopushova gave almost no one an extension on the research paper, but she **excepted** those who were facing the dreaded Chemistry test.*

Except is more commonly used as a preposition meaning *with the exception of*:

> *Everyone in my family has brown hair **except** me; I have red hair.*

W.2 Badly and Bad

Badly is the adverb, the opposite of *well*; *bad* is the adjective, the opposite of *good*:

> *Little pig #1 built his house **badly**, for it collapsed at the wolf's first huff.*
> *It is a **bad** builder who blames his or her tools.*

Remember that after a linking verb the word that describes the subject must be a predicate adjective:

> *When Chondita heard of Julian's trouble, she felt very **bad** for him.*

Not "badly": "felt" is a linking verb, and the predicate adjective "bad" modifies the subject, "she" not the verb. To say that she "felt badly" would be to say that she was not very good at feeling, and this meaning is not the intended one.

> *That cheese smells **foul**.*

Here again, "foul" describes the cheese, not the manner or extent of its smelling.

W.3 Beside and Besides

Beside is a preposition of location, meaning *alongside, next to*:

Always keep a wastepaper basket **beside** your writing desk.

Besides can also be used as a preposition meaning *as well as* or *apart from*:

Olive cannot cook many dishes **besides** liver and onions.
Three students have done well **besides** Brainard, who always gets A's.

Besides is sometimes used as a transitional adverb, the kind that follows a semi-colon and makes a logical transition to the second of two independent clauses. In this usage it means *additionally, moreover*:

Reggie doesn't use computers, because he thinks they're soul-destroying; **besides,** he's never been able to make one work.

W.4 Conscious and Conscience

Conscious is always an adjective meaning *awake, aware, taking knowledge of*:

Monsieur Martinet was not only **conscious** of his students' unhappiness but indeed secretly pleased by it.

It is never used as a noun, although you will hear a variant form, *subconscious*, used as a shorthand expression of the psychological phrase *subconscious mind*:

What appalling violence lay buried in little Adolf's **subconscious**!

Conscience is a noun meaning *a sense of right and wrong*. Its adjective form is *conscientious*, meaning *obedient to conscience*:

His **conscience** told him not to, but Otto switched the salt and sugar anyway.
Mr. Y. Reedham Givanay was **conscientious** about returning papers a half hour after receiving them.

Words to Watch Out For 1-4: Exercise

If the sentence is correct, write "C." If there is an error in word usage, correct the error.

1. Although the students in the Fear of Flying class felt bad about their first takeoff, everyone beside Tim was ready when the pilot announced that it was time to fasten seatbelts.

2. All people of good conscience contributed to help the earthquake victims, putting their change in the box situated besides the cash register.

3. Brendan made a conscious decision to allot some time each day to the study of Celtic pottery, but besides that effort, he spent the summer as a total vegetable.

4. Waltzing badly to the beat of a Johann Strauss tune, everyone in the dance club (accept Gerard) was told to leave the competition and take additional classes in rhythm.

5. Informed that he had won the coveted "Clown Prince of America" trophy, Horace stood beside the podium and exclaimed, "I except."

6. With a stuffed nose, teary eyes, and sweating brow, Margaret assured the crowd waiting for her speech that she felt "badly but not to the point of losing consciousness."

7. The entire soccer team, excepting Alphonse, commented that the safest driver, beside Nicole, was Otto Bahn.

8. Gordon explained that he had scored so badly on the test because he had not been conscious of taking one, but his teacher could not except this excuse.

9. The golfers, lined up beside each other at the practice tees, consciously practiced their swings and other skills besides.

10. Troubled by her conscious, Mariaelena refused to accept a bribe to perform bad on the Physics test and so lower the curve.

11. Boxanne was surprised to learn how badly she had frightened everyone by losing consciousness on the eighth-floor balcony.

12. My conscience is troubling me, and I feel badly about the tricks in this sentence and others besides; I beg you to accept this apology in the spirit in which it is offered.

Words to Watch Out For 5-8

W.5 Lose, Loose, and Loosen

Lose is a verb meaning the opposite of *gain, find,* or *win.* Its past tense is *lost.*

> We *win* some and we **lose** some, and when we **lose** some, we fuss.
> Once the "it" in "to **lose** it" meant one's virginity; now it means mental balance.

Loose is an adjective meaning *not tight;* it can also mean *free, unconfined.*

> Andrew's pants are so **loose** that it's a wonder they stay up.
> Mother Goose opened the gate and let the goslings **loose** in the yard.

Loose can be used as a verb only to mean *set free* (past tense *loosed*):

> We opened the bag and **loosed** the crickets into the snake's cage.

The verb that means *make loose, untighten* is *loosen* (past tense *loosened*):

> To **loosen** his tie or let it strangle him: this was the question for Steve.

W.6 All ready and Already

All ready is an adjective phrase that means *ready without exception* or *entirely ready.* It can modify either a singular or plural noun or pronoun:

> When the trumpet sounded for the dead to arise, they were **all ready**.
> After the mechanic had replaced the engine, the car was **all ready** to go.

Already is an adverb meaning *by that time:*

> By nine o'clock in the morning the temperature was **already** eighty degrees.

W.7 All together and Altogether

The situation here is similar to W.6. *All together* is an adverb phrase used when a number of entities are acting in unison or simultaneously.

> "When troubles come, they come not single spies but **all together**."
> **All together**, with one single voice, students cheered the publication of a usage workbook with hundreds of entertaining problems.

Altogether is an adverb of emphasis that means *entirely, absolutely:*

> There is **altogether** too much importance attached to getting into Ivy League colleges.

W.8 Some time, Some place and Sometime, Sometimes, Someplace

The two-word phrase *some time* is the noun *time* modified by the adjective *some.* Likewise for *some place.* The phrases mean *a certain quantity of time* or *a certain location.*

*I would like **some time** to think about this tricky usage issue.*
*Joel wanted a room, a closet, **some place** where he could be alone.*

Sometime and *someplace* are adverbs that will modify a verb and express its action as taking place *at some time* or *in some place*. *Someplace* means *somewhere*. *Sometimes* means *upon occasion, from time to time:*

*Otto said he'd pay me back **sometime**, but I'm not holding my breath.*
*Ann Minisia knew that the exam was being given **someplace**, but she had forgotten exactly where.*
*"**Sometimes** I take a great notion to jump in the river and drown," sang Leadbelly.*

The adjective *sometime* means *former*, not *occasional:*

*Edwin O. Reischauer, the **sometime** U.S. ambassador to Japan, has written extensively on the history of Japan.*

> **Wake-up call:**
> "**Although**" is one word. "**Even though**" is two words. They mean the same.

Words to Watch Out For 5-8: Exercise

If the sentence is correct, write "C." If there is an error in word usage, correct the error.

1. When Brock complained that he was the only one in the entire Glee Club to sing in tune, he was not all together wrong.

2. "All together now!" said the orchestra director as he placed the baton beside the score on the music stand and loosed his tie.

3. Wanda said that she would visit sometime, but even as she spoke we knew that she was altogether too busy to travel all the way to the other side of town.

4. ~~Loosing~~ *Losing* little sleep over the election she had rigged, Marla was already planning her first major abuses of power.

5. "Loosen your hair clip, lose the knee socks, and find someplace new to shop," said the director to the aspiring star.

6. Now that Zack has packed the tooth polish, he is all ready for his big weekend visit to his first choice college, located some place near Boston.

7. I need someplace to work, but the barn is altogether too smelly for the delicate maneuvers of hula-hoop repair.

8. His best friend and sometime volleyball coach, Penelope, believes that Odysseus can't ~~loose~~ *lose* his bid for election to the Athletic Board.

9. Charlie has all ready tried three times to loosen the top of the pickle jar with his fingers, but he keeps losing his grip and his temper.

10. The Bongo Bangers rehearsed altogether too hard for the Big Bongo Banging Bash, and they were already exhausted when the bash began.

11. "Some times my little brother makes me so mad," exclaimed Drusilla, "that I'm all ready to loose my trained pack of hamsters on him and let them nibble him to bits!"

12. Piero asked sarcastically if we planned to leave sometime soon, but Della had chosen that moment to lose her watch someplace in the hotel room, and Francesca couldn't loosen the strap of her sandals, so we were altogether disorganized and not at all ready to go.

Words to Watch Out 9-12

The words in these pairs are often mistaken for one another. Learn the difference!

W.9 Disinterested and Uninterested

Both of these adjectives express a lack or absence of interest, but the kinds of interest meant are different. To be *disinterested* means *to have nothing to gain or lose, to be neutral or unbiased*:

> They ruled out Mr. Byce as an arbitrator in the dispute because he was not completely **disinterested** in its outcome.

To be *uninterested* means *to find the matter uninteresting, simply not to care*:

> Meg started to tell her father about her brush with death, but he was so **uninterested** that he actually yawned.

W.10 Unique and Unusual

The adjective *unique* means *one of a kind, incomparable* while the adjective *unusual* means *rare, uncommon*. Only *unusual* can be found in comparative or superlative forms: *so unusual that, more unusual, very unusual, most unusual*. There are no degrees of uniqueness.

> My recording of James Brown's "Papa's Got a Brand New Valise" is **unique**, since only one copy was printed before Mr. Brown decided to change the title.
> Venice is **unusual** among cities for having canals instead of streets.

Venice is not unique in this regard; Amsterdam also has many canals.

W.11 Farther and Further

Farther is an adjective or adverb, the comparative form of *far*. Use it to measure physical distance. *Further* was once the comparative form of the archaic adverb *forth*, meaning *forward towards some goal*; it is now used as an adjective or an adverb to extend a logical train of thought. It also expresses movement forward in time.

> It is **farther** from New York to New Jersey than the map shows.
> We traveled **farther** than we had ever gone before.
> **Further**, it is important to note that usage errors will lower your grade.
> The speaker went on to make ten **further** points that no one could understand.

W.12 Nauseated and Nauseous

Both *nauseated* and *nauseous* are adjectives derived from the noun *nausea* meaning *a state of disgust, disequilibrium, or gastric distress in which one is apt to vomit*. But *nauseous* means *causing a feeling of nausea*, while *nauseated* means *made to feel nausea by something*; it indicates a response.

> Driving by the factory, Sonia held her breath to avoid inhaling the **nauseous** fumes.
> Josie was so **nauseated** by the recipe that explained how to cook fetal lambs that she very nearly barfed on the cookbook.

Words to Watch Out 9-12:   Exercise

If the sentence is correct, write "C." If there is an error in word usage, correct the error.

1. It is hard to tell when Kermit is nauseous because he is green all the time.

2. Klarise was certain that she had come up with a unique reform – eliminating the useless letter C and replacing it with either K or S – but the National Academy of Language Correctness was disinterested in her proposal.

3. Blind Pew stopped just in time, for two steps further would have carried him into the nauseous pit.

4. Every English teacher judges grammatical correctness by his or her own practice, so that it is hard to find an uninterested arbiter in any grammar dispute.

5. The magician's next trick, which was to saw a lady in half while she screamed and blood flowed from the box, was more unusual than any other trick we had ever seen, and it left us feeling more than a little nauseous.

6. The details of that murder case were so nauseating that the defense lawyers tried to cut off any further discussion of them.

7. Rover was so disinterested in serving as a watchdog that he chased the burglar no farther than the gate to the yard.

8. The view from the Hubble Space Telescope is unique, since you can see ~~further~~ *farther* into New Jersey from there than from anywhere else.   C

9. Mrs. Grooly listened to the two teams debate whether Donna Karan or Karl Lagerfeld designs a more ~~unique~~ style of clothing, but she was so uninterested a judge that she fell asleep.
   Unusual

10. Even the most disinterested film critics expressed a strong response to *Night of the Disemboweled,* an unusually nauseous variation on the gory horror flick.

11. How much ~~farther~~ *further* can these candidates go in reducing *unusual* unique human situations into generic campaign issues?

12. Most parents tell their children, "You're unique," but Mr. Huryew was so disinterested a father that he could not tell his daughters apart.

Words to Watch Out For 13-16

The words in the following groups are often mistakenly used for one another. Learn the difference!

W.13 Allusion, illusion, delusion

Allusion is a noun meaning *a reference to something outside the immediate context*. Its adjective form is *allusive* and its verb form *allude* (see next item). *Illusion* is a noun meaning *something seen or imagined to exist that is not in fact real*. Its adjective form is *illusory*. *Delusion* is a noun close in meaning to *illusion* but adding the idea of deception by self or others; *delusions* are more serious as an indicator of mental illness than *illusions*. The adjectives *delusive* or *delusory* describe something that is deceptive or that exists only in delusions; *delusional*, which means "proper to delusion," is also used to describe someone subject to delusion. The verb form is *delude* and gives as a past participle (often used as an adjective) *deluded*.

> When English teachers get into <u>Hamlet</u>, they can hardly speak without making an **allusion** to that too too famous play.
> Mr. Hartstein's speech was so indirect and **allusive** that few could understand it.
> Well into her fifties, Wandine held on to the **illusion** that she could yodel.
> The candidate's plan to provide housing for everyone turned out to be **illusory**.
> My uncle Johnny is the victim of the **delusion** that he is Tina Turner.
> How could anyone be so **deluded** as to imagine that computers will solve all the problems in American education?

W.14 Allude and Elude

For *allude*, see above, number W.13. *Elude* is a verb meaning *escape, get away from*.

> "Perhaps it would be best if Mr. Jerry Biltmore did not build the new library," the committee concluded, **alluding** delicately to the collapse of the gym he had put up.
> "I know your face, but your name is **eluding** me, dear," Olive told her son.

W.15 Healthful and Healthy

Both adjectives are derived from the noun *health*, but the first means *bestowing health, good for you* while the second means *being in a state of good health*. Thus to call a food "healthy" asserts that the food is enjoying good health but does not mean that you will be the healthier for eating it.

> Unsalted nuts are a **healthful** snack, but I prefer those salty pistachios.
> Was it really spinach that made Popeye so **healthy**?

W.16 Continual and Continuous

Both adjectives are derived from the verb *to continue*, but *continual* means *repeated often* while *continuous* means *without stopping*.

> The **continual** thumping of the compressor is bad enough, but the **continuous** screeching of the power saw is altogether maddening.

Words to Watch Out For 13-16: Exercise

If the sentence is correct, write "C." If there is an error in word usage, correct the error.

1. Every twenty minutes the cafeteria erupted into cheers for the victorious soccer teams and then subsided into relative quiet, but the continuous noise gave the staff a headache.

2. Your continual nagging is driving us all insane; and to be perfectly honest, we would all be grateful for even a moment of quiet. [*continuous*]

3. The speeding car alluded the police by zooming across the drawbridge and settling into a continuous 100-mile-per-hour pace.

4. When the obese dietician instructed us to "eat a healthful diet," the irony of his advice did not elude us.

5. Many students suffer from the illusion that continuous bouts of work with the least possible rest will win them high grades and keep them healthy. [*Continual*]

6. The illusion that everything has a sinister meaning specific to oneself is the classic symptom of paranoia.

7. The continuous shouting of the hecklers made it impossible to hear a single word of the speaker's eloquent illusions to Plato, Cato, and Mr. Potatohead. C

8. The British have apparently deluded themselves into thinking a "chip butty" – french fries between two slices of bread – is a healthful and delicious lunch.

9. It eludes me how anyone can be under the illusion that continual allusions to Shakespeare will make a point stronger.

10. The healthful juices that Herb is continually drinking have turned his skin bright orange.

11. Are you truly in a healthful emotional state when you have lost all your illusions about your friends?

12. Mr. DiPlomazzi used the phrase "frequent fryers" to elude delicately to his wife's continual fried-chicken dinners. C

Words to Watch Out For 17-20

Here are some more words that are often confused.

W.17 Principle and Principal

Principle is always a noun; *principal* is usually an adjective but has some noun uses including one very well known in schools. They share the idea "first in importance." A *principle* is some conviction held to be so important that it determines a whole code of conduct or belief. From the noun is derived an adjective *principled* meaning *having strong principles and guiding one's actions by them*. The adjective *principal* means *most important*, and the officer in a school who is so called is the most important administrator that directly oversees the education of students; he or she is the "principal" teacher. In a deal or contract, the *principals* are the individuals directly involved. In finance, your *principal* is the capital on which you earn interest.

> The most basic **principle** of a republic is the freedom, not the equality, of its citizens.
> Honoria is so **principled** that she will not even look at a classmate's homework before she has completed her own.
> Many points of Emma Biscious' program disturb me, but my **principal** concern is about her plan to make herself Glee Club President-for-life.
> The head of school is responsible for all aspects of school life, but it's the **principal** to whom the teachers must answer.
> The lawyers negotiating the merger refused to deal with Mr. Ventura on the grounds that he was not a **principal** in the matter.
> Aunt Julia lives off her income; she would consider it a sin to "invade her **principal**."

W.18 Compliment and Complement

Both words can serve as either a noun or a verb, and both form the adjective by adding the suffix *-ary*. But a *compliment* is an expression of admiration, appreciation, or respect, while a *complement* is that which must be added to make something complete or to supply its deficiencies. A ship's *complement* is the full force of men and women needed to run it.

> Djamila and Djamaal decided to run for office together, for her quickness was the perfect **complement** to his seriousness.
> The S.S. Perdita sailed without a full **complement** of trained navigators and went around Cape Horn instead of the Cape of Good Hope.
> Francoise's ability as a writer **complements** her love for literature to make her a very strong English student.
> **Compliments** on the food are always gratefully received in the kitchen.
> The **complimentary** dinner we were fed on the airline, in appreciation of valued customers, was really more of an insult.

W.19 Stationary and Stationery

Stationary is an adjective meaning *keeping in the same place; not moving*. The noun *stationery* means *letter-writing paper*, more broadly *supplies needed for writing*, or more broadly still *office supplies*.

*The ancients thought the sun turned around the earth; we say that the earth turns around the sun. In reality neither earth nor sun remains **stationary**.*

*It is a mistake to write business letters on pink **stationery** with pictures of flowers and bunnies.*

*Office Depot sells **stationery** of all kinds, but I still couldn't find the kind of paper clip I wanted.*

W.20 Affect and Effect

Both words can be used as nouns or as verbs. Let's start with the verbs. *Affect* means *have an impact on, touch, move. Effect* means *accomplish, get done.*

*There is no doubt that the depletion of the ozone layer will **affect** our climate.*

*Olive's moving performance as "Mad Margaret" **affected** the audience greatly.*

*Emma Biscious will **effect** numerous important changes, such as the creation of a presidential parking spot, during her term as Glee Club President.*

Used as a noun, *effect* means *result, outcome, something done.* In any discussion of why things happen, we analyze causes and *effects.* The noun *affect* is a term used in psychology to mean the degree or kind of emotional response a person is seen to have. Some schizophrenics, for example, are said to be "affectless," meaning that they seem to have no emotional response whatsoever.

*It's amazing how powerful an **effect** on your state of mind a few A's can have.*

*Calvin exhibits very little **affect**, but he feels things deeply all the same.*

Words to Watch Out For 17-20: Exercise

If the sentence is correct, write "C." If there is an error in word usage, correct the error.

1. A green salad compliments a tasty stir-fry of tofu, but the principle of a nutritious diet does not depend on particular foods.

2. Morton says that he has no trouble with that particular rule, since it does not affect him, but he objects on principal. _C_

3. When Mike invested his principal in the van from which he sells office supplies around the city, people joked that his business is not stationery.

4. The principal has stated his intention to effect many improvements in the quality of life at school. _C_

5. Janine gets many complements on her dead-black stationery, which effectively matches the downtown "loft-look" of her room, wardrobe, accessories, and make-up.

6. Some people think Otto never moves on account of laziness, but he claims he remains stationery on principle.

7. Paying someone random or generic compliments will not have the desired affect.

8. An essential principle of flattery is to know what the "flatteree" wishes to hear, but a complimentary skill, effective phrasing, is also key.

9. In order to effect an ethical outcome to the genetic engineering case, a group of medical schools have filed a brief with the court, even though they are not principals in the suit. _principles_

10. Olive reacts to everything with exaggerated affect, while Otto's principle response is boredom. _C_

11. Bismo has stayed stationary for so long in his studies that some people say his intellectual ship set sail without a full complement of wits. _C_

12. "I will not let this affect my mood; I will instead practice the principal of detachment," said Otto, when everyone but he received a complimentary lapel pin.

Words to Watch Out For 21-24

W.21 Effective, Efficacious, Efficient

All three of these adjectives derive from the noun *effect* (see W.20). *Effective* and *efficacious* are quite close in meaning. They both mean *capable of achieving a desired effect*. *Effective* can be used of persons or of actions, *efficacious* used only of actions.

> *Ms. Rackham is very* **effective** *at extracting confessions.*
> *Inflating grades is not really an* **effective** *way to build confidence, for students measure their achievements against those of others.*
> *A drink made from mint, egg yolks, hot water, and lots of ginger proved very* **efficacious** *in curing Khadija's cold.*

Efficient means *achieving results with the least effort or expense*. It too can be used of either persons or the means they use.

> *Head-banging is an effective way to gain attention but not a very* **efficient** *one, since it costs both effort and pain.*
> *Howie Getz-Tewitt is so* **efficient** *that he can shuffle as many papers in forty minutes as most people can in two hours.*

W.22 Eminent, Imminent, Immanent

All three are adjectives. *Eminent* means *highly placed, important, conspicuous*. *Imminent* means *about to happen*. And *immanent*, the least common of these words, means *in-dwelling, pervasive* and is most often used in discussions of the way in which spiritual or metaphysical entities inhabit the physical universe.

> *Robert Steel occupies such an* **eminent** *position in the world of letters that it is shocking to learn how much he has plagiarized from others.*
> *When the elevator cable parted with a twang on the sixty-seventh floor, we had an uncomfortable feeling that an unpleasant experience was* **imminent**.
> *Many people who visit the oracle of Apollo at Delphi get the feeling that something sacred is* **immanent** *in the very rocks and trees of the site.*

W.23 Sight, Cite, Site

Sight is a noun and a verb. The noun means *the act of seeing, the ability to see,* or *an object of seeing, something to be seen*. The last meaning is active, for instance, in "sightseeing." As a verb *sight* means *catch sight of*.

> *After John Milton had lost his* **sight**, *he dictated his poetry to his daughters.*
> *Among the* **sights** *to be seen in Marrakesh, the ones not to be missed are the Koutoubia tower and the Medersa Ben Youssef.*
> *A spouting whale was* **sighted** *on our third day out from Bar Harbor.*

Cite is a verb with a few distinct meanings. It most commonly means *refer to*, as when a writer or speaker refers to someone else's words. *Citing* differs from *quoting* in that *quoting* always brings in the exact language of the original, while *citing* more usually simply mentions or perhaps paraphrases the text where a particular passage may be found. *Cite* can also mean to mention a person either in commendation or in accusation ("citation for bravery," "traffic citation").

> *My English teacher always **cites** Oscar Wilde to back up any point at all.*
> *Florence was **cited** by the Lions' Club for her work in bringing art to Red Hook.*
> *Ollie McStake has been **cited** for various "moving violations," although his car is almost always stationary.*

Site is a noun and verb. The noun means *place, location where something will occur or had occurred.* The verb means *put in a particular location.*

> *The **site** of Chartres Cathedral was used by pagan cults for centuries before the Christians decided to build there.*
> *The new administration building has been **sited** where it should receive its share of fly balls.*

W.24 Council and Counsel

Council is a noun meaning *a group of people who make decisions or recommendations. Counsel* can be a noun, meaning either *a piece of advice* or *someone who gives legal advice,* i.e. an attorney; or it can be a verb meaning *advise.* To *keep your own counsel* is an idiom meaning *not to let others know what you are thinking.*

> *The trustees adopted the recommendations of the Administrative **Council**.*
> *When the Unabomber was tried, he did not want to retain **counsel** but insisted on conducting his own defense.*
> *Seeing that her enemies were heading for destruction, Paula Titian kept her own **counsel** and did not interfere.*
> *His parents' wise **counsels** had, he felt, kept him from gaining any success.*
> *Many adults **counsel** courses of action they themselves would never have the courage to follow.*

Words to Watch Out For 21-24: Exercise

If the sentence is correct, write "C." If there is an error in word usage, correct the error.

1. Last summer, when the reservoirs dropped to only 10% of their usual level, drought was immanent, and no efficacious remedy could be found.

2. On account of the rain delay, her efficient schedule began to unravel, and she was late not only for the moon walk but also for the suspended animation exercise.

3. The site of Woodstock '99 was once a farm; but like the place where the original Woodstock festival was held, it is now a shrine where dead rock stars are often cited.

4. The council offered counsel to the Glee Club President as she attempted to select a site for the recital of her oratorio.

5. Because of the imminent visit of the eminent visitor, the railroad station is closed to regular commuter traffic; and all citizens are being councilled to remain in their homes.

6. Two minutes before the dawn of the new millennium, the doom-predictor stood on the cite where the Second Coming was expected and said, "The end is eminent!"

7. Nobody wanted to retain Harvey Blunderman as counsel in a capital trial, for though his voice was loud, his defense was inefficient, and his client was invariably executed.

8. Georgia was cited so often for excellent essays that she became the imminent authority in her class on writing, and many came to ask her for her counsel.

9. I give all my students the same counsel: become a more efficacious reader by getting a grasp of the whole sentence before you tackle the words.

10. What makes these sentences particularly effective is the fact that each contains more than one site where a student must stop and ask if there is an error.

11. The temples at Angkor Wat are more than just a sight for tourists to snap pictures of; the spirit of a whole culture and history are imminent on this majestic site.

12. Citing rules that the High Council of Grammar Elders had never authorized, Mr. Scroomup so effectively confused his students that total grammar breakdown was eminent.

Words to Watch Out For 25-28

W.25 is another pair of sound-alikes. With W.26-8 we get into a different sort of problem, the misuse of the preposition *like*. So, like, study these carefully.

W.25 Lead and Led

The verb *lead* (opposite of *follow*) forms its past tense and past participle in *led* (unlike *read*, whose past tense and participle are also spelt *read*). The noun *lead* is the name for the famously heavy metal whose symbol in the periodic table is Pb.

> That tyrant is being tried in The Hague for war crimes because he **led** his country into disastrous wars for what he claimed were patriotic reasons.
> The cake looked good but weighed in her stomach like **lead**.

W.26 Like and As

The use of *like* in place of *as* is a very common error. *Like* is a preposition meaning *resembling, similar to*. It is used to introduce an adjective phrase that asserts a likeness between two nouns or pronouns.

> She wore a hat **like** a basket of flowers.
> There's no business **like** show business.

The phrase "like a basket of flowers" is an adjective modifying "hat." "Like show business" modifies "business." Whenever you are tempted to use *like*, try substituting *resembling* and see if your sentence still works. What about these?

> She dances **like** a bomb exploding.
> He breathes **like** a galloping horse.

Here we're in tricky territory. It might seem that the phrases really modify the verb, in which case they should be adverbial clauses of comparison: "as a galloping horse [breathes]." But in fact the phrases are best seen as predicate adjectives (even though "dances" and "breathes" don't seem like linking verbs), because they are meant to describe the subject. So when can't you use *like*?

> I wish I could speak correctly, **like** my friend does.

Like never introduces a clause; only a phrase. *As* is what we want here. *As* is a subordinating conjunction used to introduce a clause of comparison, with the meaning *in the way that*.

> I wish I could speak correctly, **as** my friend does.

W.27 Like and As if, As though

This error is even more common than *like/as*.

> Mr. Severe the overseer looked **like** he was going to whip us.

Like is a preposition, remember; it can't introduce a clause. Use *as if* (or *as though*).

*Mr. Severe the overseer looked **as if** he were going to whip us.*

Note: After *as if* and *as though* you will also find the verb form *were* where you might expect *was*, as in the last example. This usage is the contrary-to-fact subjunctive, discussed in Chapter X, Rule 80.

W.28 Like and Such as

What's wrong with this statement?

*Julie won't eat meats **like** pork, lamb, veal, and beef.*

Try plugging in "resembling" for *like* and you'll see the problem. Pork, lamb, veal, and beef are not meats *similar to* the ones Julie won't eat; they are *examples of* the kinds of meat she won't eat. *Such as* is a handy preposition for this situation.

*Julie won't eat meats **such as** pork, lamb, veal, and beef.*
*The number of explosions in action movies **such as** <u>Mission Impossible 2</u> often seems excessive.*

Words to Watch Out For 25-28: Exercise

If the sentence is correct, write "C." If there is an error in word usage, correct it.

1. Like an idiot the prizefighter lead with his chin, as if he imagined that "Iron Mike" would be too polite to swing at it.

2. As if she had really been born with a silver spoon in her mouth, Aunt Consuela, like her sister Adelaide, brushes with Gorham's polish instead of toothpaste.

3. Jennifer was going to get a tattoo, as Marge had done, but the tattooist acted like it was a crime to write "I love Mom" and asked if she wouldn't like something cooler done, such as having her lip pierced.

4. When hunger led Harry to open the heavily wrapped cheese, it was suddenly like forty athletes had taken off their shoes simultaneously.

5. "I would like to write like Jane Austen wrote," said Mrs. Woods, blushing like a bride with excitement.

6. Nothing that Ed had heard about Lydia had lead him to guess that her tastes in music and movies would be so exactly like his own.

7. Mr. Brasspartz sells "door furniture" like knobs, latches, peepholes, letter-slots, and hinges, and these items sell like hotcakes.

8. Don't give me looks like that, when I've led you through this grammar maze like you were my own child.

9. Mr. Wertheim has led me to understand that all makes of printer, like Epson, Hewlitt-Packard, Canon, and Apple, use most of the same parts.

10. Sylvie, speaking in a throaty voice like she always does when in love, said, "Jean-Pierre-Luc-Henri, lead me at once to ze rose garden."

11. I work like a dog on my essay, and then my teacher inspects it as though it were full of crawly worms.

12. The lead piping that once led water into many British towns, such as Exeter and London, made the water so toxic that Brits began to behave like they were bonkers.

Words to Watch Out For 29-31

W.29-31 explain more usage errors with connectives used to subordinate one idea to another.

W.29 Due to and Because of, Because, or On account of

Another widespread usage issue involves these connectives, which all express a cause. *Due to* is often incorrectly used to modify a verb:

> The baseball game was called off **due to** rain.

But *due* is an adjective meaning *owing*; an adjective cannot modify a verb. Let's first look at a sentence where *due to* is used correctly.

> We are expecting an abundant harvest *due to* the heavy rainfall this summer.

Due here modifies the noun *harvest*. But if you want the phrase to modify the verb, use *because of* or *on account of*.

> The game was called **because of** rain.
> The game was called **on account of** rain.

Or you might consider turning the phrase into a clause and using the subordinating conjunction *because*.

> I lost the job **because** I was timid.

This sounds more direct and forceful than "I lost the job because of my timidity."

W.30 The reason is because

This phrasing is due to the carelessness that kept the writer from noticing the redundancy: both "the reason is" and "because" express a cause. Just say, "The reason for X is Y," or "X is so because Y."

> **Wrong: The reason** Olive is broke **is because** she spends like a drunken sailor.
> **Better: The reason** Olive is broke is her spending like a drunken sailor.
> **Better yet:** Olive is broke **because** she spends like a drunken sailor.

W.31 Being that

Never use *being that* as a way to express a cause. Use *since* or *because* instead.

> **Wrong: Being that** I left my books in a bar, I couldn't do my homework.
> **Right: Since** I left my books in a coffee shop, I couldn't do my homework.

Words to Watch Out For 29-31: Exercise

If the sentence is correct, write "C." If there is an error in word usage, correct it.

1. Being that you have not shaved, I wonder if the reason is that you are trying to grow a beard.

2. Alice the parakeet is an excellent flyer; but due to molting she is temporarily grounded.

3. The picnic blanket was washed with extra softener due to Herbie's desire to be kind to the ants who would undoubtedly arrive the minute the food was unpacked.

4. Being that you discharged hundreds of gallons of pollutant into the water, you are required to effect a complete cleaning of the area.

5. The reason the exam has been moved to the gym is because students perform better when inhaling the atmosphere due to generations of sweating bodies.

6. Being that which no one could look upon without loathing, Count Dracula pulled on his Tom Cruise mask and went out into the world.

7. Due to the discovery of an Indian burial ground under Tillinghast Hall, Dr. Mullady has announced that the whole building will be moved to the infield.

8. The deficiencies in these exercises are entirely due to the authors' carelessness, being that we are only human.

9. The reason there are nine problems in this exercise instead of twelve is because there were three rules instead of four.

Words to Watch Out For 32-36

The verbs in these pairs are often confused with one another.

W.32 Lie and Lay

Lie means **be** at rest in a horizontal position, while *lay* means to **put** (something) at rest in a horizontal position. Therefore *lay* takes a direct object while *lie* never does. Can you still say, "I was *laying* on my bed when the phone rang"? No, you need to say *lying*, because it was you at horizontal rest on the bed, not some object that you were placing there. The present, past, and participial forms of *lie* are *lie, lay, lain, lying*. The forms of *lay* are *lay, laid, laid, laying*. It is confusing that *lay* is both the present form of one verb and the past form of the other, so you will need to learn to keep these forms straight.

> Isn't that Marjorie's dog **lying** on the hood of that BMW? [Not *laying*.]
> **Lay** your hat there and let your scarf **lie** next to it.
> After I had **lain** in a stupor for three hours, I picked up my homework and **laid** it gently in the fireplace.

Lain, the past participial form of *lie*, probably seems least familiar to you, but it is the correct form, so make it your own.

		Lie	Lay	
Present: lie, lies		I lie, you lie, she/he/it lies, we lie, you lie, they lie	I lay, you lay, he/she/it lays, we lay, you lay, they lay	**Present:** lay, lays
Past: lay		I lay, you lay, she/he/it lay, we lay, you lay, they lay	I laid, you laid, she/he/it laid, we laid, you laid, they laid	**Past:** laid
Participle: lain		I have lain; she has lain; they have lain	I have laid; it has been laid; he has laid; they have laid	**Participle:** laid

W.33 Rise and Raise

The situation here is just like that in *lie/lay*: one of the verbs, *rise*, does not take a direct object but merely describes an upward movement performed by the subject, while the other, *raise*, means *move (something) upward*. The forms of *rise* are *rise, rose, risen, rising*. The forms of *raise* are *raise, raised, raised, raising*.

> He watched the moon **rise**, and then he **rose** from his chair and went in.
> As she was **raising** the blinds, the guy across the airshaft **raised** his too.

W.34 Sit and Set

Similar situation again. *Sit* doesn't take a direct object but is almost always followed by a preposition (*on, at, in, beside*). *Set* usually does take a direct object and means *place (something) somewhere*. There is one interesting exception: when speaking of the sun, moon, stars, planets, or constellations, *set* is used as the opposite of *rise*: "Venus is rising," "Scorpio is setting." In this case it does not take a direct object. The forms of the two verbs are: *sit, sat, sat, sitting* and *set, set, set, setting*.

> *Maria **set** her binoculars down and went to **sit** at her desk.*
> *After Ed had **sat** a long time watching television, he decided it was too late to **set** himself to work.*

W.35 Precede and Proceed

Precede is a verb meaning *coming (or going) before someone or something*, either in the order of space or in the order of time. *Proceed* is a verb meaning simply *go forward, go to the next thing*.

> *A pronoun's antecedent usually **precedes** it in the sentence, but not always.*
> *In Jane Austen's day married women **preceded** their unmarried sisters when going in to dinner.*
> *After refilling my water bottle, I **proceeded** across the Sahara.*

W.36 Imply and Infer

To *imply* something is to state it indirectly, to suggest it, to hint at it. To *infer* something is to understand what has not been directly stated, to "read between the lines," in short to pick up on an *implication*. Hence *implying* is what the speaker does, while *inferring* is what the listener does.

> *Without putting it in so many words, Mr. Schocken **implied** that Fran's costume was a little too revealing.*
> *I **infer** from your comments that you would like me to give you less homework.*

Words to Watch Out For 32-36: Exercise

If the sentence is correct, write "C." If there is an error in word usage, correct it.

1. From the light coming through the window, Audrey inferred she had been laying on the couch for hours.

2. The mayor has just banned the use of Avitrol, a poison that gives pigeons hallucinations and then precedes to kill the poor birds while they're dreaming.

3. The border dispute between the Muslims of Kashmir and the Indian government has raised much bad feeling; and the level of tension, which had laid at a fairly low level for many years, has risen again.

4. As the moon set below the horizon, Otto too set in his chair with a beer in his hand and wondered what his wife had been implying by calling him "Blotto."

5. Do the many allusions to birds and chameleons in this book infer that Dr. La Farge and his colleagues are raising these exotics?

6. Sonya Pistoff politely implied that the quantity of grammar homework her teacher had lain on her was excessive.

7. Every afternoon, after I have laid down to rest an hour, I rise refreshed and proceed to create an appalling number of difficult grammar problems for my students. *C*

8. Setting at his computer and scrolling through decades of school history, Mr. Kenner tried to remember who had preceded Dr. Weiss as principal of the Upper School.

9. Olive set down one unlicensed firearm beside the second that already laid on her vanity table.

10. Dr. Dry sarcastically inferred that I had lain around all day, doing no homework.

11. The bucket of water raising from the stream struck an outcropping of the bank and proceeded to spill its contents over the backpack Carlos had laid on a ledge.

12. Just because I said, "You have no reading to do tonight," don't precede to infer that you won't have any grammar homework.

13. From her saying, "That's it for me. It's their turn now," I infer that Olive raised twenty-three children so that she could lay around for the rest of her life.

14. The schooner *Esmeralda*, infamous as the prison-ship where many Chilean political prisoners had lain awaiting torture, preceded out of Boston harbor under power and then set its sails.

Words to Watch Out For 37-42

We'll begin with some more troublesome verbs and then go on to some distinctions that have to be made when quantities are under discussion.

W.37 Afflict and Inflict

The verb *afflict* means *make trouble for, give pain to, punish.* Its direct object is always the person(s) receiving the trouble, pain, punishment, which are usually mentioned in a prepositional phrase beginning with *by* or *with.* The verb *inflict* means *bring (something unpleasant) down upon (someone).* Its direct object is the unpleasant thing, and the person(s) slated to receive it are usually mentioned in a prepositional phrase beginning with *on* or *upon.*

> *The faculty decided to **afflict** the sophomores with longer tests and shorter lunches.*
> *Mr. Enright likes to say that his wife "**afflicts** the comfortable and comforts the **afflicted**."*
> *E. Jess Droneson, the most boring teacher in the school, **inflicts** his lectures upon juniors every day at 10:45.*
> *We can't stand my aunt, but she **inflicts** herself upon us for a month each year.*

W.38 Emigrate and Immigrate

Emigrate means *leave your own country to go live in another,* while *immigrate* means *settle in a country not your country of origin. Emigrants* leave, *immigrants* enter a given country.

> *Hundreds of thousands of Highland Scots were forced to **emigrate** to Canada by the infamous "Highland Clearance" of the late eighteenth century.*
> *Those who have recently **immigrated** to the United States must often take work they are overqualified for.*

So much for the verbs. The usage issues to be discussed next arise from the fact that English nouns are of two sorts: the one naming countable items and the one naming things that cannot be counted. "Count-nouns" is a useful term for the first. Anything you can count is a count-noun: people, trees, french fries, movie stars, pagan deities, tests, and so on. The other sort of noun cannot be counted: money (as opposed to dollars), sleep, sand, water, air, friendship, furniture (as opposed to chairs and beds) and so on. Some "no-count-nouns" can be used as count-nouns: "My hair is falling out. I found twenty-seven hairs in my brush this morning." Here's an easy test to apply: if you can put the indefinite article *a* or *an* before the noun, then it's a count-noun.

W.39 Amount and Number

The noun *number* is used to refer to a quantity of count-nouns. The noun *amount* is used to refer to a quantity of no-count-nouns.

> *The **number** of friends Katie makes can be explained by her kindness.*
> *The **amount** of trouble Enna Doghaus gets into is really staggering.*

Trouble is a no-count-noun even though in another context you could speak of "troubles" and count them; then you would use *number:*

*"The **number** of troubles afflicting the sophomores rejoices my heart," exclaimed Monsieur Martinet.*

W.40 Few, Several, Many, Much

All of these words serve as either adjectives or pronouns. *Few, several* and *many* must modify or replace count-nouns. *Much* must modify or replace no-count-nouns.

> **Few** *of those golf clubs ever get much use.*
> **Several** *pigeons have landed on my window-ledge.*
> *Olive is not on speaking terms with* **many** *of her relatives.*
> **Much** *of Otto's training has been in elevator maintenance.*

So what about *any, most, all, none, some?* These are the "AMANS," and when an "AMANS" pronoun is the subject of a sentence and is modified by a prepositional phrase, the verb will be singular if the noun in the phrase is singular – in other words, a no-count-noun – and plural if the noun in the phrase is plural – in other words, a count-noun.

W.41 Less and Fewer

Both serve as either adjectives or pronouns. *Less* is used only with no-count-nouns and *fewer* only with count-nouns.

> *Dominic had* **less** *money than he'd thought.*
> *Damien had* **fewer** *CD's than he'd thought.*

More, you'll notice, works with either.

W.42 Between and Among

These are prepositions, and the distinction between them is one of the very few survivals in English of the dual form (as opposed to plural). Count your blessings. Use *between* when talking of two entities, *among* when referring to three or more.

> *Several events have created friction* **between** *Congress and the White House.*
> *There is no agreement* **among** *the state legislators about how to resolve the budget dispute.*

Words to Watch Out For 37-42: Exercise

If the sentence is correct, write "C." If there is an error in word usage, correct the error.

1. Monsieur Martinet has afflicted a huge number of vocabulary quizzes on his unhappy students.

2. Many of the students in that class are thinking of emigrating to Poland, since less than four are actually passing.

3. When the sophomores learned that a third year of grammar study would be inflicted upon them as juniors, a unanimous impulse to protest arose among them.

4. When Jalil's grandmother first emigrated from Pakistan, she could not believe the amount of documents she had to fill out in order to enter another country.

5. There were fewer lives lost between all the combatants in World War One than in the influenza epidemic that followed it.

6. When she put on her first sleeveless shirt of the season, Didi noticed many more moles on her arms than the amount she had counted last year.

7. "The number of inflictions that have been laid upon us," shouted the preacher, "proves that we are the children of Satan!"

8. "We must immigrate out from the Nation of Sin," he went on, "and live among the righteous and the godly."

9. Olive prefers to live in a place where there are less of the righteous and godly inflicting their views upon the rest of us, who are by far the greater number.

10. Olive and Otto have settled it among themselves that they will never be righteous or godly if they can help it and that they will make do with the fewest possible rules.

11. Lucy Nagel, who had been afflicted as a child with polio, died recently after spending the greater number of her ninety-five years in bed.

12. Few people have ever shown a greater amount of courage and good humor than Lucy, who divided her time between reading, conversation, brief outings in a special wheelchair, and remembering the vast number of people she loved.

Words to Watch Out For 43-46

The first of each pair of forms is false and not available for formal writing. Use the second.

W.43 Should (Could, Would) of and Should (Could, Would) have.

Should, could, and *would* are helping verbs and must be followed by the verb itself. This error arises from the similarity in sound between *of* and *have* as it's often pronounced: *should've*. Don't use that contraction in formal writing.

> They **should have** told us where they were going.
> I **couldn't have** made myself clearer.

W.44 Eachother and Each other

There is no such form as the single word "eachother." *Each other* is a compressed appositive phrase like *one another*.

> They told **each other** that he could not possibly quiz them again so soon.

Each other is appositive to *they*.

W.45 Thusly and Thus

Thus is already an adverb meaning *in that way, therefore*. The *-ly* adverbial ending is thus redundant.

> Othello demonstrates how he handled a Saracen when he exclaims, "I smote the villain **thus**," and stabs himself.

W.46 Different than and Different from

Than is a subordinating conjunction that introduces a clause of comparison. When *than* follows an adjective, that adjective has to be a comparative: "stronger than your big brother is." Since *different* is not a comparative, use the preposition *from* after it.

> Nastine's world-view is **different from** most people's, for she likes war.

Words to Watch Out For 43-46: Exercise

If the sentence is correct, write "C." Wherever you find an error in word usage, correct it.

1. Colin and Kathy were so shy that they wouldn't ever of gotten to know eachother if a friend had not locked them in a room together.

2. There were three shooting rampages in Atlanta in 1999; thus it would of seemed fair at the time to conclude that crimes were on the rise there.

3. Yet Atlanta is not so very different than other cities and does not have many more crimes than, say, Boston.

4. Some citizens argue that controlling the sale of automatic weapons would do nothing to prevent killing sprees, but the people who reason thusly have trouble accounting for Atlanta, Littleton, and the July 4th killings in Chicago.

5. Mrs. Reed's theory about the phrase "eachother" was different than mine: she thought it should be used only for groups of three or more, and that "one another" was the proper phrase to use for two people.

6. Grammar is not too different than skiing, in that you feel like a clumsy fool at first.

7. You and the other people tangled together in the snow keep telling each other what you should of done to avoid the collision.

8. Since chameleons don't much care for eachother's company, I have had to put my two in separate window-gardens.

9. They get along thusly by never seeing one another, and in this they are no different than many people I know.

10. I could of just put both of them in a tank and let them work it out among themselves, but chameleons can't handle that kind of stress.

11. Every morning I spray the trees with water until the leaves are dripping; the chameleons sip the drips and get their water thusly.

12. Dr. Johnson's ideas were different from those of Bishop Berkeley, who claimed the physical world to be an illusion; Johnson kicked a stone in the road and cried, "Thus I confute him!"

13. Being that a lot of grammar problems took Otto less hours than they should of, he decided that after all he was not so different than Grete the Grammar Goddess and thusly entitled to ask her for a date so they could get to know eachother..

Words to Watch Out For 47-50

The first set of forms is false and not available for formal writing. Use the second.

W.47 NOT Sort of, kind of BUT Rather (quite, somewhat)

Everyone says *sort of* or *kind of* to qualify a statement one is not entirely committed to. "He's kind of cute." In formal English substitute *rather, quite, somewhat.*

> That teacher is **rather** sadistic.
> George was **somewhat** annoyed to find his bookbag at the top of the flagpole.

W.48 NOT These sort of, These kind of BUT This sort of, This kind of, OR These sorts of, These kinds of

It's not uncommon to hear someone say, "I have trouble with these sort of math problems." But *this/these* is an adjective that must agree with the noun it modifies. In the example *these* was used because *problems* is plural, but *these* doesn't modify *problems*. Figure out if you're talking about one sort or kind, or more than one.

> I have trouble with **this sort of** math problem (or with **these** math problems).
> Gorgonzola and Stilton are very smelly; Olaf will not eat **these kinds of** cheese.

W.49 NOT Try and BUT Try to

In casual speech it's normal to say, "I'll try and have it done by tomorrow." But the speaker doesn't mean that he or she will both *try and have* as two separate actions. Use *to have* in this situation, an infinitive phrase to serve as the direct object of *try.*

> Olive did not even **try to** hear her son's excuse but reached for the whip.

W.50 NOT A lot, Alot BUT Much, Many

The one-word form *alot* simply doesn't exist. The two-word form *a lot* does exist and means *a piece of real estate, a collection of objects for auction*. It does not mean *many* and it is not an adverb meaning *much*. We often hear sentences like these:

> A lot of my friends are going to perform in the play.
> I don't know a lot about Asian history.
> She likes him a whole lot.

Get rid of *a lot*. Find a substitute.

> **Many** (or **Quite a few**, or **A number**) of my friends are going to perform ....
> I don't know **much** (or **a great deal**) about Asian history.
> She likes him **very much**.

Words to Watch Out For 47-50: Exercise

If the sentence is correct, write "C." If there is an error in word usage, correct the error.

1. Bing Jeter likes chips and fries a whole lot, but if he doesn't try and restrain that liking, he is going to end up one obese boy.

2. The good news is that once you've really learned grammar, you don't have to think about it alot anymore, and thus you save time.

3. I hear a lot of writers moaning, "Oh, if I had only learned those usage rules when I was a kid, I wouldn't have to worry about those sort of problems now."

4. I bought quite a few trees and plants for my chameleons and installed a lot of lights for them to bask under; these purchases were kind of expensive, but love demands these sorts of effort.

5. My chameleons get kind of annoyed if I spray them by accident, so I try and spray near them.

6. These kind of chameleons are found all across North Africa and even into southern Europe; they are alot different from the sorts of chameleon you find in Madagascar.

7. They are kind of fastidious in choosing the places where they poop; if all pets behaved thus, the city would be a lot cleaner than it is.

8. Ida Leiser is running to Sotheby's, because a lot of Marilyn Monroe's possessions, such as tweezers and pill bottles, is being put up for auction today, and she collects those sorts of things.

9. Olive and her friends played baseball on a lot behind the bowling alley, but first they had to clear away alot of broken glass.

10. Some people think that Otto is sort of weird on account of the sort of clothes he wears, but they should try and not make judgments based on appearances.

11. It's been overcast for ten days; my chameleons won't even try to eat in this sort of weather.

12. A lot of the grammar you're taught in English sounds kind of funny at first, but if you try and master the principles, you gain more control over your expression.

Review exercises

Here is another set of exercises, to help you cement your editing skills, build confidence, and have some more fun with English usage. The format is the one you know: sentences to edit. Any sentence will either be correct or contain an error of the type named in the heading. If the latter, correct the error.

I. Apostrophes

1. Mendacia swore she had left the overdue essay at her sister and brother's-in-law house.

2. Everyone laughed at the Vitale's for thinking that SUVs are Sealed Underwater Vehicles.

3. All those sheeps' wool is especially long and fine.

4. When that weird Mac computer of ours reads a document written in Word for PC's, it turns all the apostrophes into O's.

5. The Explorers Club has many members who do their exploring in a comfortable armchair.

6. Mr. Dimbulb listened to Maria's report but had no way of grasping those fine insights of her's.

7. Most men's stores nowadays do'nt carry celluloid collars like the ones on my grandfather's shirts.

8. You can be sure that Frieda and Horace's textbooks will be neatly arranged in those two spotless lockers of theirs.

9. Two thirds of Gladys' friends can't remember a time when she did not hold the attorney-general's position.

10. In the "Roaring 20's" many American writers decided that the U.S. was'nt where they wanted to do their roaring and went to Paris instead.

11. "That decision isn't ours; it's Mr. Speinliss'," said Mr. Woffels.

12. Everything any of you say stay's within these four walls; I won't breathe a word of it to the Netherlands' agents.

13. Professor Knox' students were trying to calculate fish's intelligence, but they're results were thrown off by the unexpected intellectual power of sardines' minds.

14. Let's just say that the last three summer's weather hasn't confirmed every scientist's suspicions about global warming.

15. Why do lawyers' firms use so many &'s in their names, instead of *ands?*

16. Henry doesn't like the new list of the apostrophe rules on the school wall; and he ran down the hall crying, "Its insulting to think that I can't remember how to use that stupid little symbol without consulting a written rule."

17. A few years ago the engineers working on Apple Computer's operating system decided that Unix's capabilities were greater than their's.

18. When Jorge heard about the new J. Lo DVD, he decided that an autographed copy would be worth at least two week's salary; not surprisingly, his wife disagreed.

19. I hate the way that celebrity signs her name; the little circles over the *j's* are just too precious.

20. Olive's and Otto's refrigerator is a war zone, with Otto's beer bottles pushing out Olive's salamis.

21. The girl's gym in that school is not only a disgrace but also a violation of the law because the boys' gym is larger and better maintained.

22. Chou's father-in-law's eldest brother's new baby is related to me, but for the life of me I cant figure out how.

23. The childrens' little feet pattered overhead all night the last time Morgan went on vacation, but the motel owner was not particularly sympathetic to her complaints.

24. On April 1st Ignatius went to a restaurant and ordered "fishes' feet," but the waiter was not able to find any and went to ask the manager for help.

25. Please do not spill any coffee on that term paper when you read it because it represents at least twenty hour's work.

II A. Subject-Verb Agreement

1. Omar told Fatima that her greatest beauty were her almond-shaped eyes.

2. The entire French Fries Appreciation Club, minus Stoatly and the Needlebaum twins, are going out to appreciate some curly yam-fries.

3. Under several layers of clamshells, arrowheads, and bits of pottery lie the intact tomb of twelve kings.

4. There was, in spite of all the confusion in the case, no real questions remaining to be answered.

5. The leader of those clowns, incompetents, and bozos have never even apologized for painting the White House orange.

6. Gloria, not the critics and professors, was the harshest judge of her own writing.

7. Ironically, the smallest members of the French Fries Appreciation Club eats the greatest number of fries.

8. How many fries do you guess is consumed in a single half-hour by the FFAC?

9. There have been a wide range of estimates made of how far all the fries eaten this year by the FFAC would reach, if placed end to end.

10. Francois Freiberg, the FFAC's president, together with several henchpersons, has put the distance at twelve hundred miles, or from here to Chicago.

11. Other members of the FFAC, the fastest-growing club in both numbers and waist-size, argue that the real distance, measured in kilometers, are more like 800.

12. There is, it is reckoned, about forty fries in the average "large fries" container.

13. Freya Friedberg, the scientifically gifted sophomore who is also the most serious fry-appreciator of all the FFAC's members, have measured thousands of fries.

14. Freya, with the assistance of her friends Frieda Frye, Fritz Fried, Fred Friedman, and Farida Frytag, have authored a study to be published in *Deep Fat*, the club's publication.

15. Her conclusions in that monumental study, which is filled with graphs and photographs, give the average length of a french fry as 7.113 centimeters.

16. There are needed only a little in the way of brains to work out the total length of a "large fries" batch at 284.52 centimeters.

17. At the outbreak of the Spanish Civil War General Franco's Army of Africa, as well as some units of native Moroccan troops, were quick to invade Spain.

18. There are a box of jelly doughnuts on the table over there next to the Singing Walnuts, who are trying to compete with the California Raisins for a job in commercials.

19. The worst aspect of daycare in that area near the California-Mexico border is poorly trained childcare workers.

20. The excitement Salvatore and Maria feel at demolition derbies are not going to be reduced by the distance they must travel to get to them.

21. Because Millicent loves macramé, a set of 4509 how-to and pattern books are our present to her as she weds Mackerel, who does not love macramé but is willing to put up with it.

22. Tammy, as well as a hundred other nuclear physicists, look to Albert Einstein for inspiration in science but fortunately not in hair-dressing.

23. The green pencil, which is one of the many writing implements resting on the shelf next to my collection of Antonio Banderas biographies, need sharpening.

24. Up on the east side of the office building, near the parked cars and the striking parking lot attendants, was Donald, along with his friends the Gorilla Brothers.

25. On the counter were a heaping plate of chocolate cookies for my twelve-year-old cousin and her incredibly annoying friends.

II B. Subject-Verb Agreement

1. Abercrombie & Fitch sell clothes with the rugged look that quite a few couch potatoes like.

2. Every book and notebook in Jelilah's locker is sticky with grape jelly.

3. Kurt's computer, his CD player, and his love-life is completely messed up.

4. Each girl and boy in the seventh grade have been commended for dressing modestly.

5. There is neither fresh bread nor tasty pastries for sale in that bakery.

6. The ranting and complaining that used to flow out of Ira's typewriter, in the old days, now goes out over AOL instead.

7. Whether Ted Thrust or Emma Parry become captain of the Fencing Team, we can expect some backstabbing during the elections.

8. For the first time in the school's history, the Head of the Upper School and the senior class dean are the same person.

9. Mr. Bill or his two favorite students are expected to introduce the motion in the Governing Council.

10. The law firm of Winthrop, Stimson were once called Winthrop, Stimson, Putnam & Roberts.

11. Does either Freya Friedberg or the other members of the French Fries Appreciation Club ever stop to think how much salt and grease is on those fries?

12. Smith, Barney have been chosen as the brokerage house to invest the assets of the FFAC.

13. Shrewd investment or a strong bull market have made millionaires of those Fries Appreciators.

14. Every officer and member of the FFAC now wear a gold lapel pin in the shape of a french-fry, and either diamonds or something that looks like them represents the salt crystals.

15. Ketchup red, mustard yellow, or Russian-dressing pink are the most popular color for lipstick now.

16. Each radio and CD player in that store have very large amplifiers, and if you buy one, I hope that you will also buy a pair of earplugs for me.

17. I have read every report from every brokerage now trading on the Internet; Kinkel & Daughters are my choice because the company makes a huge profit all the time.

18. Whether the hunters or the rhinoceros charging them are the first to lose nerve, I'm climbing that sturdy-looking tree.

19. The congressional black caucus and its leader are planning to investigate alleged violence against minorities by members of that police department.

20. Peanut butter and jelly are the theme of a restaurant that just opened downtown, but needless to say, this favorite of children everywhere is priced at a luxury level.

21. The hand-pieced quilt and embroidered comforter that my grandmother brought out of Poland is the only thing she has left from her husband's family, which perished in World War II.

22. After a long, arduous campaign for class clown, the winner and still champion are Davey Fitzpatrick, who can swallow soapsuds while blowing bubbles with his nose.

23. Since Olga has just ripped the very last tent that was waterproof, Noah is sending her to the store; fortunately, Sears are having a Memorial Day sale on all camping gear.

24. Each dancer that finished showering were personally invited to report for table-waiting duty in the cafeteria.

25. Either Spinderella or her cousins is expected to polish all those glass slippers before the palace's going-out-of-business sale.

II C. Subject-Verb Agreement

1. Absolutely no one among the members of the French Fries Appreciation Club are willing to be seen in McDonald's or Burger King any more.

2. Some of the money that the FFAC made investing in securities has been set aside for a trip to Belgium, which many believe to be the homeland of fries.

3. Three quarters of the members of the club also supports a "fries tour" of France.

4. Every single one of the eighty-nine Fries Appreciators have different ideas about which kind of french-fry is tastiest.

5. Most of the "shoestring" and "curly-fries" fans think the thick "steak-cut" fries are inedible, while a few, a less rigid bunch, eat them when there is none of the "shoestring" or "curly" sorts to be had.

6. Nobody among the "steak-cut" fanciers eat in the same place as a "shoestringer."

7. One or the other of these two parties are always making trouble in the FFAC's daily lunch meetings, and none of the "medium-size fries" people or the "eat-anything" gang have been able to restore harmony.

8. Has all of you poor sweating usage-hogs heard enough already about the French Fries Appreciation Club?

9. All of the library's collection of books with paintings of nudes have disappeared.

10. Any of the librarians is likely to be short-tempered until every one of those books has been returned.

11. Neither of the art-history teachers, Mr. Yates or Mr. Schlesinger, have been able to supply the librarians with a clue about who the thieving art lover might be.

12. All of the French Fries Appreciation Club are under suspicion, however, because a few of the books on the same shelf were spotted with grease.

13. Are there not, among all the vocal complainers in the tenth grade, someone who will protest the random and unnecessary mention of the French Fries Appreciation Club in the last problem?

14. Each of the deans have been grilling suspects for the last three days, but nothing like a confession has yet been obtained.

15. Most of the deans' time have been spent listening to carefully constructed alibis, but Dean Delanty thinks some of the witnesses are close to cracking.

16. Several of the jokes told in that assembly by the funniest girl in the senior class was condemned by her male classmates.

17. All of Uncle Demetrius's coins, as well as the carpet supposedly given to him by Ali Baba himself, is going to be in the next auction at Sotheby's.

18. All of the air in Ali Baba's caves are scented with just a hint of treasure.

19. Every one of the parakeets in Alice's how-to-fly-like-a-real-bird class are learning how to fly more efficiently, but someone has a bad habit of dropping used feathers on the floor.

20. Were neither of you worried when your chemistry experiment whistled at you?

21. Even one of the hundreds of sandwiches on those carts is enough for a complete meal because the chef stuffs in too much cheese and meat.

22. Both of the plays that Oscar wrote is good enough to receive an award, but neither is eligible for an Oscar because that award is reserved for films.

23. Anybody in the United States have the possibility and opportunity to wave the flag, so long as the flag does not enter anyone else's eye.

24. Neither of the home runs that Belter hit last night were as long as the one that Driver belted on Tuesday, but Belter's hits enabled his team to win the game.

25. Some of the cherries in the pie that was blown eight miles in the hurricane is splattered all over the sidewalk, but George Washington's tree is still standing.

II D. Subject-Verb Agreement

1. The number of orders of "large fries" eaten by one member of the FFAC in a year come to 1,092, according to Freya Friedberg.

2. The members of the club disagrees as to whether she may have underestimated.

3. The club is unanimous, however, in finding that over a thousand orders of "large fries" is an awesome quantity of fries for one person to consume.

4. You will remember that 40 individual fries makes up such an order and that there are 89 members in the club.

5. Taken as a whole, therefore, the membership of the club consumes just under four million fries per annum.

6. Many in the club think that the total number of fries consumed are well over four million.

7. The majority of those fry-hogs doesn't care.

8. The Fry Distance Measurement Committee, chaired by Freya and staffed by students with rulers, have determined that the fries eaten in one year, if placed end to end, will extend 276.52 kilometers

9. Because 276.52 kilometers is far less than had been claimed, the club is still debating the validity of the Measurement Committee's methods.

10. While this debate rages a number of members, as many as a half, is still dipping their favorite kinds of french fry into the special house ketchup.

11. Don't you think that six hundred and sixty-six high-school students are a rather ominous number?

12. The number of football injuries has remained steady for the last four years, but the soccer team have been plagued with accidents.

13. A number of American voters is growing impatient with the choice of candidates they are offered.

14. Why does the majority of these grammar problems discuss a completely fictitious club of idiots obsessed with french fries?

15. My family, the Pierces, disagrees with me about my getting a silver stud put in my tongue.

16. Frasier's family has decided to let Niles enter the Kentucky Derby as long as he agrees to ride a horse.

17. A number of network executives is in favor of renewing that nature show for another year, despite the declining ratings, because *Frogs* has such a loyal audience.

18. Despite arguing non-stop for over an hour, the committee has not been able to agree about whether or not to admit you to driving school.

19. Although Egbert really likes blowing bubbles, he thinks that twenty dollars is too much to pay for a simple stick of bubble gum.

20. The jury have finally agreed that, in light of all the evidence, the only possible lunch order is vegetarian lasagna.

21. "Five hours of writing are all I have to do tonight," said Poppy with a rueful grin.

22. The faculty Commission on the Status of Chewing Gum has decided that nothing it can do is likely to solve the problem of gummy wads stuck to the bottom of chairs.

23. According to the United States census statistics, the number of Americans who own more than one computer are growing every year.

24. In honor of his grandson's fifth birthday, Dr. Legovitch bought five gold coins, and the five coins now rests on little Leggy's dresser.

25. After a tough workout on the field, the baseball team is simultaneously hitting, pitching, and fielding in order to be in tiptop shape for the big game.

III. Pronoun-Antecedent Agreement

1. It's not everyone who knows what style of glasses truly suits them.

2. In 1984 the Reptile League was formed in Turtle Bay to pursue their mission of promoting the happiness of all reptiles.

3. If any reptile owner is found mistreating their pet, they are looking at three months in jail.

4. Each of the delinquent reptile owners is given one of those lectures that makes you feel like one of the insects that are fed to reptiles.

5. The Reptile League keep their binoculars trained on every known reptile owner so that each turtle, lizard, and snake can lead their lives in a suitable environment.

6. Neither the ground-dwelling chameleon nor the arboreal variety can stand much variation in the temperature of their habitat.

7. Chameleons in the species called "the panther chameleon" is especially prized for the vivid colors it can turn.

8. A chameleon can be in the same room as a person and remain entirely invisible to them.

9. The idea that chameleons change color to blend with a plaid background is one of those myths that are very hard to kill.

10. The male "Jackson's Chameleon" is not the only chameleon that grow horns on their heads.

11. Every snake and lizard in both hemispheres shed their skins regularly.

12. I, who am daily learning more about chameleons, can inform you that a chameleon, like an adolescent, is very susceptible to stress and can be fierce in defending their territory from others of their kind that are seeking to invade.

13. Every one of the students in this room will finish this exercise knowing more about reptiles, and particularly chameleons, than they did when they began it.

14. Neither the catcher nor the umpire were expecting the pitcher to throw an iguana at them.

15. This is the only one of the exercises so far that hasn't mentioned the French Fries Appreciation Club.

16. "Now that we know about the tornado, I advise everyone to hold onto their hats and immediately descend the steps to the root cellar," said Auntie Em.

17. Ms. Tuber, our esteemed music teacher, could not believe that anyone had left their tuba – her favorite instrument – at home on the day before the big concert.

18. "Have neither of the girls any sense of commitment to their orchestra, any sense of responsibility for the tuba?" Ms. Tuber asked more in sorrow than in anger.

19. Either Dmitri or his fellow tuba player Igor had brought their music, but Ms. Tuber was not consoled.

20. None of the violinists asked themselves whether or not the tubas were worthy of being in the same orchestra, but all of the oboists were adamantly opposed to brass instruments anyway and seized the opportunity to call for expulsion.

21. "Is it you who claims that we should play only with the jazz ensemble?" inquired Igor pugnaciously, hands on hips and lower lip sticking out a mile.

22. Some sections of the orchestra were growing impatient, but neither Igor nor the chief oboist was willing to change their position.

23. "Each of the orchestra members has been forgiven their mistakes in the past," said Ms. Tuber, who was unwilling to lose her favorite band members permanently, however angry she might be at the moment.

24. The principal saved the day by saying that if anyone who had forgotten an instrument wanted to practice, she would work with them after school.

25. Did the band begin their concert with confidence?

IV. Punctuation with Quotations

1. In Britain quotation marks are called, "Inverted commas," and you can see why.

2. When the fox saw the crow, the fox wondered, "Where did he get that cheese"?

3. "Your feathers are beautifully lustrous," said the fox to the crow, "your song must be equally lovely."

4. Did the crow ever think, "He's just flattering me to make me drop this cheese"? *C*

5. "Sing for me, I beg you!," the fox implored the crow.

6. The crow said to himself, "This fox really needs to get a life;" still, he opened his beak and sang.

7. The fox would have shouted, "Thanks for the cheese!," had his mouth not been full.

8. The crow told his wife, "I finally got rid of that damn cheese". *C*

9. She was pleased, since the cheese was well past its "sell-by date."

10. She commented that, "It was starting to smell like a gas leak."

11. "That is the worst smelling fox I've ever met!" The creatures in the forest exclaimed as the fox ran past.

12. The fox was wondering if, as the poet put it, "someone had blundered;" the thing in his mouth was choking him with its noxious fumes.

13. "I've never in my life," he told himself, "eaten cheese. I'm a carnivore, not a cheesivore"!

14. Soon the environmental police's squad cars' sirens were wailing, and loudspeakers were bellowing, "pull over, Buddy!"

15. All the forest creatures called the environmental cops "pigs", because they really were pigs.

16. After completing this exercise, one girl turned to another and commented, "How cheesy was that fox and crow story, Marissa"?

17. Why, when the Adamsons have a perfectly good garage, do they insist on saying, "We need a carport?"

18. Cinderella asked the prince "Why do you think that one little glass slipper is enough basis to propose marriage?"

19. "You grabbed my finger when you were only an hour old", Mr. Glass told his daughter, who was not at all interested.

20. The muggers' statement that it was, "nothing personal" did not make Andrew feel better about losing a wallet filled with antique baseball cards.

21. The citizen who captured the mugger added, "just because you want something, there is no reason to believe that you will get it."

22. "The baby's maternal grandparents bought her a Knicks pennant," said Mimi, "the paternal grandparents bought her a Lakers sweatshirt."

23. Jerzy said, Poland is my home, but Lech was not impressed.

24. "Aren't you tired of all these ridiculous grammar sentences"? asked the teacher who was responsible for writing them.

25. "The next trip to the shopping mall will be my last," promised Elvis, "I know that my appearances cause too much of a ruckus."

V A. Pronoun Case

1. Fritz Fried claims that nobody but Frieda Frye and him is able to put an entire order of "large fries" in his or her mouth all at once.

2. "Ms. Nemo, the student body class as a whole is complaining about us putting in these sentences about french-fries," said Dr. La Farge.

3. As the principal drew out his nickel-plated .44, Dr. La Farge was forced to confess: "The author of the french-fry sentences was I and none other."

4. But when the punishments were being decided, La Farge declared that both authors, Ms. Nemo and himself, should be given the same number of lashes.

5. Opeoluwa protested, "These references to french fries mean nothing whatsoever to Dmitry and I, since we are not French."

6. Shana said, "Us non-potatotarians are offended by constant references to potatoes fried in hot fat and heavily salted for consumption by you and me."

7. Lauren said that all the couch potatoes in the tenth grade – Sulin, Tomas, and she – agreed that no one could be more outraged than they at this abusive behavior.

8. The Chinese were not the least bit happy with us bombing their embassy in Belgrade during the Kosovo war.

9. E. Drather Steele claimed that aliens with claws had commanded three students – Chitra Kopyitova, Speedy Z. Rocks, and he – to produce the same exact essay.

10. "They don't give us underclasspersons a moment's peace," complained Becca; "in fact, there are some of us, like Clarisse and I, who get asked to do everything."

11. Angelica is upset because her boss trusts the computer more than her, and Angelica is angling for a promotion and a serious raise.

12. Trotsky felt confident that large-minded men such as Stalin and himself could work out their differences.

13. Molly had mixed feelings about him singing "You Say It's Your Birthday" on her special day.

14. "Machine Gun" Kelly denied that it had been him who had sprayed bullets through the window of the barber shop and added that the police surely had better things to do than to persecute "us weapons specialists."

15. "You may not remember him being in class, but at least two witnesses, Leah Deliah and I myself, will swear that the guy in the back row was he," said Perja Rhee.

16. Those thugs - Otto and him – are responsible for fifteen burglaries.

17. He is a better actor than Gregory Peck, but Gregory Peck is more handsome than him.

18. Neither Dawson nor I have much acting experience, but it is not fair to say that he is better than me in that commercial.

19. The students in the play – Gigi, Jean, and him – are to be excused from all classes for the last two days before the show.

20. When Howie Yadoon picked up the phone and asked who was calling, a stranger's voice replied in a thick Transylvanian accent, "Vhat do you think? It is me."

21. If you need a tour of the Brooklyn Navy Yard, give Otto or myself a call; and we will explain every single aspect of the yard's history to you in excruciating detail.

22. The dance teacher gave tickets to we boys so that we could attend the ballet with our friends.

23. Between you and I, I don't think that the American public is educated enough to use pronouns correctly.

24. I admire the Romans, but I resent them inventing pronoun case.

25. April thought that she had seen Godzilla in the parking lot, but because The Monster Channel had reported he was in Tokyo, April decided that it could not have been him.

V B. Pronoun Case: Who/whom

1. Anjali can never remember who she's lent her calculator, but she wishes whoever it is would return it.

2. Mr. Dimbulb is a thinker whom many consider to be "not the sharpest quill on the porcupine."

3. You never can tell whom it will be who will rescue you in the moment of crisis.

4. "Machine Gun" Kelly knows who he can trust and who he has to shoot.

5. Leah Deliah is one of those people who tell several different stories and whom therefore no one believes can be trusted.

6. "Whomever you wish to invite will be welcome," said Scrooge, who people had always believed miserly and mean.

7. There is no one to whom teachers listen with more delight than a student who knows what he or she is talking about.

8. It sometimes seems as if gun salesmen will sell even automatic weapons to whomever can pay for them.

9. To be popular means to be one of those figures whom most people think most other people admire.

10. The issue of who should run the French Fries Appreciation Club is becoming acute, now that Francois Freiberg, whom we think first founded the club, is getting ready to graduate.

11. Friedrich deVries thinks it's he who the club should elect, since it's he who introduced them to fried sweet potatoes.

12. Nobody whom Emma ("Em") Bezzle, the club's treasurer, has shown the accounts can make head or tail of them.

13. Emma, who no one suspects of stealing, has worse handwriting than anyone whom we can remember occupying that office.

14. One must not blame Emma, who, it must be kept in mind, the club's by-laws require to record all income and expenditure with a french fry dipped in ketchup.

15. Not everyone in the club is aware of whom it is that, late at night, keeps track of the club's extensive portfolio of investments, especially the shares in Spuds, Inc.

16. I know you think that you know whom I like, but whom you think I like doesn't matter to me.

17. "Whom shall I say is calling?" said the secretary politely as she filed her nails and checked her stock options.

18. Supergirl, whom everyone in Metropolis is sure flies more quickly than Superman, plans to enter the Superhero 500 next Memorial Day weekend.

19. The English assignment was to write a novel about whoever the student believes is the most important person in history.

20. Naturally, the English teacher, whom everyone realizes is pro-environment, wants the students to write about Rachel Carson or whoever else made a difference in the way we think about ecology.

21. Helga is a skilled debater whom everyone thinks is going to be a member of the supreme court one day.

22. Virginia Woolf is one writer who everyone thinks is an amazing stylist and a creative artist.

23. "Do you have any zucchini in that basket?" asked the chef who was planning to create a casserole.

24. Who do you think will be the best tennis player in the tournament?

25. Noah wants to take whoever really wants to travel on the ark, but Mrs. Noah says that he should take whoever has a ticket.

VI. Punctuation with Independent Clauses

1. Ernie has one of those transparent faces, he can never get away with a lie.

2. Straw shoes may not be practical for long walking, however, they certainly do look sharp on the feet.

3. Please call and leave her a message for Frederika Frizell has gone to the soup kitchen to distribute fries.

4. Frederika eats nearly half of the fries herself, nevertheless, the homeless men and women still get plenty.

5. She hasn't come home yet she was due back an hour ago.

6. David thought that the drivers of the luxury cars passing him were pretentious, and resolved never to own a Lexus or BMW.

7. The building across the street has a domed turret, it's one of the oldest houses on the Upper West Side.

8. The painters smoothed out the plaster with broad plaster knives, and then sanded it down with a belt sander.

9. Laura stood cursing in eight inches of snow, no one had phoned her to tell her school had been cancelled.

10. Robbie never manages to pass his road test, however much he practices parallel parking.

11. He's not sure how to put the car in reverse, he can't remember which way to turn the wheel either.

12. Remember to put on your seat belt, you might take a trip through the windshield otherwise.

13. No one in the French Fries Appreciation Club is cold-hearted but Frederika Frizell is an especially caring young woman.

14. Chameleons are slow to get there, but brilliant in choosing the best route.

15. Though Frederika had, in fact, packed her walkman, her homework, her bottle of water, and a full range of hair tools, she then, in a moment of distraction, forgot the bag in which she'd packed them, and left home with only thirty pounds of fries.

16. Apologizing profusely, Marc Antony presented his favorite pet to Cleopatra, and then explained the care and feeding of poisonous reptiles to the fascinated queen.

17. The slippery slipper slid on the banana peel, the boots booted a mango before landing in hot water.

18. Four long, treacherous rounds lay ahead, but Rocky was not afraid of the future.

19. He found a new pair of shoes in the closet but he did not know when or where they had been bought.

20. Josh shook the soda for at least ten minutes, consequently we were all wearing soda for the remainder of the afternoon.

21. Buffy is facing too many vampires she can't keep up with the flow of those pesky bloodsuckers.

22. Since we had already invested in that stock, we followed its progress closely, but no one could have predicted that downturn.

23. After lighting the birthday candles on her grandmother's cake, Angie sang "Happy Birthday," and ate three large pieces.

24. The famous actor-turned-politician spoke for an hour or so to the political fundraisers, and urged them to "get out the vote" and "bring home the bacon" for the party.

25. Harriet thinks her pet horse is the best-trained animal in the world, indeed she thinks he is the best trained animal in the entire universe.

VII. Pronoun Reference

1. In these grammar exercises it seems as if they throw in sentences about fries whenever inspiration fails.

2. Frederika Frizell told Frances Frytag that she was a sure bet to win the fry-eating contest.

3. Laura can walk on her hands and whistle "I Did It My Way," which astounds everyone but her intimate friends.

4. To be certain that her students don't see her tests in advance, Ms. Fierfel locks them in her filing cabinet.

5. Titus Wadsworth is a mighty rich man, but he never gives any of it away.

6. In Ana's match with Chitra, she won every set 6-0.

7. Amin always edits the grammatical errors and spelling errors out of his essays before recopying them.

8. In one street in Marrakesh they sell buckets made from old tires.

9. Bert ordered his brother Brett to stop wearing his shorts.

10. J.B. has a habit of screaming, "SCORE!" when he gets a problem right, and this gets on everybody's nerves.

11. Because her mother had such a brilliant career as a harpist, Carol never learned to play one but took up the tuba instead.

12. Mending socks is a laborious chore, which Victor avoids as much as he can, although they all have holes in them.

13. A chameleon was watching a cricket when it shot out its tongue and ate it.

14. On Old Macdonald's farm the pigs have started to say, "Moo, moo," just to annoy him.

15. Farida knows fries will make her gain weight, but it doesn't keep her from eating all she can of them.

16. The policeman arrested a suspect for the murder, but he did not take the matter seriously enough.

17. In Charlotte Brontë's novel it says that Jane Eyre is an orphan.

18. In *The New York Times* article by Otto and Olive, they report that pronouns have truly gone out of style.

19. He walked nonchalantly out of the police station, which insulted the various felons who were waiting to be locked up.

20. When she walked into her surprise party, Connie screamed with joy, which made all the work and preparation worthwhile.

21. In William Shakespeare's plays he shows the true nature of humanity.

22. In Otto's favorite pawnshop they don't accept guitars without strings.

23. Lizzie slugged Anthea because she was acting strangely.

24. Otto tried to eliminate all pronouns from his writing, which was a fruitless pursuit.

25. The seven-foot basketball player was guarded by the seven-foot-six-inch guard, and he was quite successful.

VIII. Modifying Errors

1. To be sure a modifier is not "dangling," it must be given one other clearly identifiable word to modify.

2. The man hiccuping uncontrollably searched the room for something to give him a shock.

3. He only found a very ugly lamp, which did not even slow the hiccups down.

4. All special-effects engineers are not careful to get the right lighting on their models.

5. When creating a computer animation of a human being, it is essential to make it move as humans really do.

6. My uncle often answers the doorbell that chimes in his underwear.

7. Malika has nearly crocheted half the bedcover she plans to sell.

8. Caught in a gust of wind, Elvin's hat just blew away.

9. My mother dressed the wounds where I had scraped myself with different sizes of Band-Aid.

10. To be sure of getting into that movie, call ahead and reserve your ticket.

11. The caves near Taza in Morocco are dangerous enough even to daunt the most experienced explorer, let alone a beginner.

12. The convicted jaywalker was sent to the maximum-security prison where he would spend the next fourteen years in a van with bars on the windows.

13. While staying with her uncle, Gina learned that he knew whole operas by heart but didn't even know the most famous ballets.

14. Eating quickly produces gas.

15. Michael only eats meat when he's having dinner at a friend's house.

16. Squinting into the sunlight reflecting off the pristine, white sand, the sunglasses did not really protect Agatha's eyes.

17. Olive dropped some coins in the street fiddler's violin case that she had just taken out of the bank.

18. To write a complete list of everything a college-bound senior has to do each night, an extra-large bottle of ink is helpful.

19. My Aunt Beatrice went to Reno, Nevada, but she only had one hour to gamble.

20. Playing the viola in the nursing home, the shouts of the residents drove the little girl to abandon her instrument.

21. The shoe that Esmeralda bought last week needed to be repaired.

22. When buying boots for the Alaskan winter, it is especially important to have both a right and a left boot.

23. Sally had nearly finished her term paper; but then the phone rang, and she stopped typing.

24. To dance the tango correctly, a long-stemmed rose should be clenched between the teeth.

25. Rita found the husband in the desert she had been looking for.

IX. Punctuation with Essential and Nonessential Elements

1. The French Fries Appreciation Club or FFAC has some members who are seriously overweight.

2. The FFAC's new president Lettice Knotby-Luzas has suggested that all club members exercise.

3. The physical activity, that most FFAC members choose, is yoga.

4. Coach Mike, the genial and popular yoga instructor, urges beginning yogis not to try the advanced poses, where you wrap your leg behind your neck.

5. Beginners to avoid injury should take frequent breaks and study their classmates who have mastered the form.

6. Everyone, taking Coach Mike's Yoga Foundations course, starts by learning "Mountain Pose."

7. Mountain Pose, called tadasana in Sanskrit, is a standing pose, that requires more concentration than you might expect.

8. You may think that all you have to do is stand, keeping your feet together.

9. Sounds easy, but the large guy, standing in the back row, regularly tips over.

10. He's falling because the work to be done in this pose which he's not doing involves rooting down through your feet, rolling back your thighs, tucking your tailbone under, and shifting your shoulders onto the back body.

11. Coach Mike's favorite student Wendy enjoys the pose known as "Baby Dancer."

12. In "Baby Dancer," a balancing pose, you start in Mountain Pose and then raise one arm and bend your knee, the one on the other side.

13. Then you strengthen the standing leg working to create a band of muscle above the kneecap until you have reached the point where you feel stable.

14. Next, you catch the instep of your raised foot with your hand, the one on that side not the lifted one.

15. Finally you push back the foot, that you're holding, and fold forward from the waist to create a backbend.

16. It is important to keep your hips squared during this pose which is relatively advanced.

17. The big guy who stays in the back row where he won't be so visible regularly falls over during this pose also.

18. He's heavyset, but Frank Frye who is the FFAC's Secretary of Health is even heavier.

19. Of course Frank has an advantage in his feet, which are immense, and in the training that he received in ballet.

20. "Work at a level, where you feel challenged but not overwhelmed," cautions Coach Mike, picking up the back-row guy for the eighth time.

21. Mike's wife Robin, who is also a yoga instructor, is an expert on aromatherapy, a practice that uses essential oils to promote energy and harmony.

22. The oil called bergamot used to flavor Earl Grey tea is a favorite of Robin's and one that she often uses in the mixtures that she creates.

23. When Robin teaches a yoga class that contains more than four FFAC members, or "Friars," she has them apply a fragrance that masks the smell of cooking oil which she calls "definitely nonessential."

24. You knew that an exercise that mentions essential oils in a lesson, where essential and nonessential elements are the topic, would have to have at least one joke about nonessential oils.

25. An exercise where the yoga instructions are based on the experience of this author, who is an English teacher, not a qualified yogi, should be used to improve the usage skills that will make you a better writer, not as a guide to the ancient practice yoga.

X. Verbs

[Note: All three lessons of Chapter X are covered in this exercise.]

1. Olive informed Otto that the techno music he was playing is not her favorite.

2. She insisted that he should turn it off.

3. Otto refused, saying that he was listening before she came in.

4. "If I was eager to listen to repetitive machine noise," Olive retorted, "I would listen to my dishwasher."

5. Otto and Olive argued about music for an hour; at last he tells her there's no disputing about tastes.

6. Agreeing at last to disagree, they went on to discuss why people find other people's music so hard to listen to.

7. Olive suggested that everyone thought music was a good thing, so why not enjoy it all?

8. "I wish I were able to hear a piece of music the first time I listen to it," said Olive.

9. "Right," agreed Otto. "I ask myself how many songs I might have really liked if I would have given them a chance."

10. Otto asked Olive what she thinks makes a piece of music good or bad.

11. "I never know," she answered, "until I listened to it several times."

12. "A song that strikes me as stupid now will become a favorite by the time I will have listened to it repeatedly."

13. Having said that, she went on to qualify the observation she just made.

14. "Maybe the song just gets stuck in my head after I listened to it twenty times."

15. "Then I find myself wishing I had better sense than to put that tune on my MP3."

16. Otto thought that now it is his turn to quote Shakespeare's *Antony and Cleopatra*.

17. "Right after Cleopatra asked for music in Act 2, scene 5," he said, " she called it 'moody food for us that trade in love.'"

18. "But as soon as a musician has started to play, she commands that he 'leave it alone' and adds, 'Let's to billiards.'"

19. "So here's my question: has the music changed her mood from a need for love to a need for billiards, or does her change of mood make Cleo wish that her musician stop?"

20. Olive suggested: "If he was playing techno, I can see where Cleo might prefer to shoot some pool."

21. By the time Otto figured out a snappy reply, Olive went on to say, "But I think it matters where you are when you hear a piece of music."

22. "Browsing in a bookstore," she went on, "I've heard a tune I liked that I would have turned off if I would have heard it on the radio."

23. "Sometimes you're freed to hear music by the fact that a stranger has chosen it," agreed Otto, "and sometimes it bothers you so much you politely request that the perpetrator should die."

24. "If someone was deliberately trying to color my mood with music," mused Olive, "I would not enjoy that tune."

25. Otto declared that there were always plenty of people who tried to control a space by filling it with their music.

XI. Parallelism and Comparisons

[Note: Both lessons of Chapter XI are covered in this exercise.]

1. Toned up by yoga and because it also brought them into balance, the "Friars" held a dating-behavior seminar.

2. Once the fries had been a more absorbing interest to them than any matter they could imagine.

3. A few holdouts wanted to stay focused on fries; something new was what was now wanted by most others.

4. The Friars came up with several proposals: windsurfing, ice-climbing, and to teach themselves italic calligraphy.

5. But Lettice Knotby-Luzas, as always forceful and she has an imagination too, said, "No. We must master the protocols of dating."

6. "Relationships," she added, " are just as important as, if not more important than, anything we could be doing."

7. "We may either choose to snack on fries or on celery, but we all need love."

8. "Love, though not problem-free, gives us more pleasure than problems," she declared.

9. So the Friars hired Layla the Love Guru to instruct them in some dating do's and also in what you ought not to do when dating.

10. "First, remember that your date has just as many fears, interests, ideas, tastes, and personal history as you," Layla began.

11. "He or she will be going into the date just as nervously if not more so than you are."

12. "All of us start off scared that our dates not only will try to take control of the situation but to impose their needs on us."

13. "To have judgement passed on us, to be treated coldly and insultingly, and knowing that malicious gossip will circulate about us as soon as the date is over: these are outcomes that everyone dreads."

14. "Because we neither want to feel rejected nor used, some of us will be tempted to project our own power, wearing a mask of supercool indifference or confidence."

15. "Others will reveal all their weaknesses at once, hoping either to gain sympathy or, failing that, they'll at least control the moment of their exposure."

16. "The defenses your date will put up are at least as formidable if not more so than the Great Wall of China, so what do you do?" asked Layla the Love Guru.

17. Fritz Frost raised his hand and said, "You'd both have to make her defensiveness seem unnecessary and unattractive."

18. "With that approach," remarked Fedora Frankly, "you will be sure to get fewer dates than any boy in this room."

19. "I think you must first address the person behind the mask," said Fred Forthwright, "and then your own mask must be dropped."

20. "Fred's approach will work much better than Fritz," approved Layla the Love Guru.

21. "But what do I talk about to this unseen 'person'?" asked Fritz, who as usual was stubborn, combative, and wanted to be endlessly talking.

22. "There are three rules to follow," Layla instructed them," on any date: first, don't talk about yourself the whole time; second, don't talk about yourself the whole time; and third, the whole damn evening should not be spent in talking about yourself."

23. The other Friars understood Layla much better than Fritz.

24. "Picking your nose, belching, and cracking endless 'dumb-blonde' jokes are not only contraindicated as tasteless and offensive but because they get you dumped on the spot."

25. "Of all the love rules I have ever been given," said Fairley Fonda admiringly, "yours are far better, Layla the Love Guru!"

XII. Double Negatives

1. I can't hardly believe there's anyone who still doesn't know not to put two negatives in one sentence," complained Mr. Stickler one day in the Faculty Lounge.

2. "Well, some morons deny that studying grammar has no value and would do away with it completely," said Dr. De Kreppit, raising his nose from his dictionary.

3. "I can't help but imagine that they are very ill-bred people," said Harry Stowcratt.

4. Meanwhile, outside the lounge, Eve Strappa was asking, "Can you help wondering what our teachers talk about when they're alone?"

5. "I can't understand what they say barely at all, even when they're with us," said Ivan O'Clew.

6. "Don't English teachers never talk about nothing but sex, as if poetry were all pornographic?" protested May Denly-Blucher.

7. "I don't think they can't help it the least little bit," answered Trudi Traumdeutung, "for they don't have any internal censoring mechanism at all."

8. "I cannot but suppose that the teachers think the names they invent for us are humorous," sniffed Knowles Outerjoint, who is easily miffed.

9. "Yeah, and we're forbidden to make not even a single joke about ridiculous names such as De Kreppit and Fierfel!" agreed Max Kostik.

10. As I sat writing in the lounge, I was so shaken by what I couldn't help overhearing that I could do nothing but end this exercise early.

SAT-style exercises

Since March 2005, the SAT I (also called the SAT Reasoning Test) has included a section on writing. Test-takers will write an essay and answer grammar questions. Those who have mastered the material in this book are well equipped to handle the SAT grammar sections, which contain three types of questions:

Paragraph revision (see exercise A below). The SAT presents you with an essay that resembles the first draft of a student's work. The essay is followed by questions about specific sentences or about the order and structure of the paragraphs.

Error identification (see exercise B below). In this type of question you must identify, but not correct, a mistake in grammar or determine that the sentence is error-free.

Sentence revision (see exercise C below). In sentence revision questions a portion of a sentence, or in some cases an entire sentence, is underlined. Four revisions follow. You may choose to change nothing, in which case A is the answer, or you may choose another version from choices B – E.

Here are some exercises to help you review the usage principles you've learned in formats like those used on the SAT.

Exercise A, Paragraph Revision.

Directions: Read this essay, which resembles the first draft of a student's assignment. Then answer questions 1 – 8 below.

(1) These days the airways and other media are filled with charges of unfairness. (2) People from both sides of the political debate claim that their view, not the ideas of the other side, are unfairly kept out of the public's knowledge. (3) The opposite attitude gets more time than them. (4) In a democracy it is important for citizens to know if this is going on (5) Only informed citizens can make the right choices on election day.

(6) How can the media be judged? (7) One way is to measure how much air time or how many articles are given to each side of a argument. (8) If people who favor a new power plant speak for three minutes, then people who are against it should have three minutes too. (9) But even this method isn't good enough all the time. (10) Maybe a whole town almost supports the plant and only ten people don't. (11) Then they shouldn't get as many minutes because they are not equal in size.

(12) The ideas of ten people can make a real difference. (13) If a local television station broadcasts the objections to the power plant, the rest of the inhabitants of the town may change their mind. (14) Some of the greatest changes in history have stemmed from the pressure of minorities for righteous causes. (15) The ideas from some protest groups may simply be right.

(16) In my opinion, I believe that most news sources try to be fair. (17) A station manager or an edi-

tor must consider the facts, whether they are true or just trumped up charges. (18) The news report must say whose opinion is being reported and also include information about the background of the person making the statement, the audience can then decide what to think. (19) In a democracy, people should hear more opinions, not less, even at the risk of giving attention to ideas that aren't well thought out.

1. The best revision of sentence 2 is

   (A) A few people from both sides of the political debate claim that their view, not the ideas of the other side, are unfairly kept out of the public's knowledge.
   (B) People often claim that their views, not the ideas of the other side, are unfairly kept out of the public's knowledge.
   (C) People often claim that their views, not the ideas of the other side, is unfairly kept out of the public's knowledge.
   (D) Their views, not the ideas of the other side, is unfairly kept from the public, according to claims.
   (E) Politicians from both sides claim that their view, not the ideas of the other side, are unfairly represented.

2. What is the best way to combine sentences 4 and 5?

   (A) In a democracy it is important for citizens to know if this is going on and only informed citizens can make the right choices on Election Day.
   (B) In a democracy it is important for citizens to know if this is going on because only informed citizens can make the right choices on Election Day.
   (C) In a democracy it is important for citizens to know what is going on because only informed citizens can make the right choices on Election Day.
   (D) In a democracy it is important for citizens to know what's what, therefore they can make informed choices on Election Day.
   (E) Democratic citizens can make informed choices on Election Day.

3. In paragraph 2, the power plant example

   (A) should include the name of the plant, the type of energy, and other details
   (B) explains the issues of fairness in media time allotment
   (C) is too general
   (D) illustrates the author's ideas about the right amount of time that the media should give to energy issues
   (E) should be eliminated and a more general explanation substituted

4. How should sentence 10 be changed?

   (A) A whole town supports the plant and only ten people don't.
   (B) Maybe almost everyone in the town supports the plant, excepting ten people don't.
   (C) Maybe almost everyone in the town, excepting ten people who don't, support the plant.
   (D) Perhaps everyone in the town, with the exception of ten people, support the plant.
   (E) Perhaps everyone in the town, with the exception of ten people, supports the plant.

5. The best revision of sentence 12 is

   (A) Although the ideas of ten people can make a real difference.
   (B) On the other hand, the ideas of ten people can make a real difference.
   (C) It is crucial that you keep in mind that the ideas of ten people can make a real difference.
   (D) You should keep in mind that ten people with ideas can make a real difference.
   (E) Ten people can make a real difference, however, with their ideas.

6. Which sentence, if any, should be omitted from paragraph four?

   (A) 16
   (B) 17
   (C) 18
   (D) 19
   (E) no change

7. What changes, if any, should be made to sentence 17?

   (A) A station manager or an editor must consider the facts, whether they are true or just trumped up charges. (No change)
   (B) A station manager or an editor must consider the truthfulness of a group's charges.
   (C) A station manager or an editor must consider the facts, if they are true.
   (D) A station manager or an editor must consider if the facts are true or not.
   (E) Deciding whether charges are true should be done by the station manager or editor.

8. How should sentence 18 be edited?

   (A) The news report must say whose opinion is being reported and also include information about the background of the person making the statement, the audience can then decide what to think. (no change)
   (B) The news report must say whose opinion is being reported and also include information about the background of the person making the statement, then the audience can then decide what to think.
   (C) To help the audience decide what to think about an issue, the news report must say whose opinion and what the background of the person is.
   (D) The news report must identify the source of each statement, including the background of the source, so that the audience may evaluate it.
   (E) The news report must identify the source of each statement, including the background of the source, so that the audience may evaluate the information.

Exercise B.

Directions: Choose the letter that corresponds to the section of the sentence containing an error. If the sentence is correct, choose E.

9. My best friend <u>went to Kenya</u> for <u>vacation, but</u> she <u>only brought me one</u> elephant
   A   B   C

   <u>as</u> a souvenir. <u>No error</u>.
   D   E

10. The team <u>members decided</u> to elect Derek, <u>who everyone</u> respects, as captain
    A   B

    <u>because they are</u> sure he will lead <u>wisely</u>. <u>No error</u>.
    C   D   E

11. <u>Both Daddy and</u> his brother like *Dada* <u>art, but</u> Dad <u>thinks</u> <u>he</u> should invest
    A   B   C   D

    in surrealist works. <u>No error</u>.
                          E

12. <u>Alex, not the other</u> contestants on *Jeopardy,* <u>know</u> all the <u>answers but</u>
    A   B   C

    <u>none of the questions</u>. <u>No error</u>.
    D   E

13. In Jonathan <u>Swift's</u> famous satirical novel, <u>*Gulliver's Travels,*</u> <u>he</u> tells the
                 A   B   C

    story of <u>Gulliver, who</u> was marooned on a desert island. <u>No error</u>.
             D   E

14. When Goya <u>had finished</u> his painting, <u>he gave it</u> to the <u>king, and</u> the king
                A   B   C

    <u>hanged it</u> on the wall of the castle. <u>No error</u>.
    D   E

15. Until recently <u>most American women</u> took <u>their husbands' names</u> when they
                     A   B

    married, <u>which</u> often <u>caused women to lose track</u> of their old friends. <u>No error.</u>
             C   D   E

16. When <u>he was preparing</u> for a trip to Antarctica, <u>Ferdy went</u> to Abercrombie and
           A   B

    Fitch<u>, the wilderness store,</u> where he found <u>its</u> tropical gear on sale. <u>No error</u>.
         C   D   E

17. <u>Before he</u> corrected <u>himself, the</u> winner of the Nobel Prize for
    A   B

    Mathematics <u>explained that</u> three plus four <u>equaled</u> ten. <u>No error</u>.
                 C   D   E

224 — SAT Style Exercises

18. <u>This year</u> the number of date <u>palm trees that</u> Ty <u>drew on his</u> notes <u>are</u>
        A   B   C   D

     greater than you'd think. <u>No error</u>.
                               E

19. The <u>boy's loud voices</u> could be heard throughout the <u>hallway; therefore,</u>
            A   B

     the teacher <u>shouted, "Quiet down, fellows!"</u> <u>No error</u>.
                    C   D   E

20. Neither of the <u>lawyers spoke</u> about <u>the effect</u> of <u>their own actions</u> in that
                   A   B   C

     <u>energy deal</u>. <u>No error</u>.
          D   E

21. The ship <u>sailed slowly</u> into the sunset, <u>irregardless</u> of the <u>danger of</u> the
               A   B   C

     <u>fog's</u> impairing visibility. <u>No error</u>.
       D   E

22. Every teenager and senior citizen in that <u>program, from both</u> the suburbs
                                             A

     <u>and the city,</u> <u>are planning</u> to write a book <u>entitled</u> *How to Talk to the Other*
        B   C   D

     Generation. <u>No error</u>.
                E

23. <u>The animals in George Orwell's *Animal Farm*</u> object to <u>Napoleon's</u> taking
                A   B   C

     more power <u>than</u> he should. <u>No error</u>.
                  D   E

24. She made <u>an illusion</u> to the fact <u>that she</u> was <u>"upset and tired"</u> after
              A   B   C

     <u>losing</u> the hundred-mile marathon. <u>No error</u>.
       D   E

25. <u>When Khalid married, he</u> told his <u>wife, "What's</u> mine is <u>yours'."</u> <u>No error</u>.
        A   B   C   D   E

26. <u>My favorite</u> <u>dog tired from his walk and completely famished</u> tried to jump
       A   B

     <u>on my lap</u> when <u>I was eating</u>. <u>No error</u>.
        C   D   E

27. Super-premium ice cream <u>has</u> a huge number of <u>calories, nevertheless I</u>
                         A   B

     love to eat <u>it</u> after dinner <u>while watching</u> television. <u>No error</u>.
            C   D   E

28. <u>When only eight years old</u>, her grandfather <u>told</u> Martina that <u>her tennis</u>
         A   B   C

    racket <u>would be</u> the road to success. <u>No error</u>.
           D   E

Exercise C.

Directions: Choose the best revision of the underlined portion of each sentence. If the sentence is best left unchanged, choose letter A.

29. Godzilla told T. Rex <u>that he has bigger feet</u>.

   (A) that he has bigger feet
   (B) that his feet are bigger
   (C) that Godzilla has biggest feet
   (D) about his big feet
   (E) that T. Rex has bigger feet

30. Everyone on the New York Liberty women's basketball team signed <u>autographs for hours,</u>
    <u>which their fans wanted</u>.

   (A) autographs for hours, which their fans wanted.
   (B) autographs for hours, which delighted the fans.
   (C) autographs for hours, and the fans were delighted.
   (D) autographs for hours, which were delightful.
   (E) for their fans a large number of autographs.

31. That song is so easy that <u>Alexei, who is musically illiterate, even knows it</u>.

   (A) Alexei, who is musically illiterate, even knows it
   (B) musically illiterate Alexei even knows it
   (C) even Alexei, who is musically illiterate, knows it
   (D) Alexei who is musically illiterate even knows it
   (E) Alexei, who is musically illiterate, even knows the song

32. The thermos full of coffee <u>broke, the coffee that I would like is</u> spilled.

   (A) broke, the coffee that I would like is
   (B) broke, my favorite coffee
   (C) broke, the coffee that I like
   (D) broke, and the coffee that I would like
   (E) broke; the coffee that I like

33. I always tell everyone right away <u>that they should answer</u> the phone cheerfully.

   (A) that they should answer
   (B) that they need to answer

(C) that they should be answering
(D) that he or she should answer
(E) to answer

34. The crocodile walked on the dry river bed, opened his giant mouth, and <u>then he bites</u> the nearest ankle!

    (A) then he bites
    (B) then bit
    (C) then he bit
    (D) then he will bite
    (E) then bites

35. The politician <u>whom we believe made</u> the greatest contribution to world peace is Mahatma Gandhi.

    (A) whom we believe made
    (B) who we believe made
    (C) whom we believed made
    (D) whom we believe had made
    (E) whom we believe has made

36. Where Britain once ruled over one country, <u>two nations – Pakistan and India – were created.</u>

    (A) two nations – Pakistan and India – were created.
    (B) two nations – those nations being Pakistan and India – were created.
    (C) two nations – Pakistan and India – had been created.
    (D) two nations – Pakistan and India – having been created.
    (E) two nations were created, those being Pakistan and India.

37. To test Pinocchio's honesty, <u>a ruler should be used</u> on his nose after each question.

    (A) a ruler should be used
    (B) a ruler is what you should use
    (C) use a ruler
    (D) you need a ruler, which should be used
    (E) a ruler that should be used

38. The <u>problem with your homework assignments are</u> the many errors in grammar.

    (A) problem with your homework assignments are
    (B) problem, with your homework assignments, are
    (C) problem being with your homework assignments are
    (D) problem with your homework assignments is
    (E) problem resulting from your homework assignments are

39. Some of the <u>computers that Harry fixed are</u> no longer in service because they have been replaced by newer models.

   (A) computers that Harry fixed are
   (B) computers that Harry fixed is
   (C) computers, that Harry fixed, are
   (D) computers which Harry had fixed are
   (E) computers fixed by Harry are

40. The book with the orange cover is the only one of the many on that shelf <u>that has an eye-catching cover</u>.

   (A) that has an eye-catching cover
   (B) that have eye-catching covers
   (C) that an eye-catching cover is on
   (D) that have been given an eye-catching cover
   (E) which is fortunate to have a cover that catches the eye

41. The king of that castle likes <u>hamburgers, consequently, hotdogs are banned.</u>

   (A) hamburgers, consequently, hotdogs are banned.
   (B) hamburgers, consequently hotdogs are banned.
   (C) hamburgers, consequently the king bans hotdogs.
   (D) hamburgers, consequently, the king bans.
   (E) hamburgers; consequently, hotdogs are banned.

42. Thinking of Prince Charming and that special night with great affection, <u>Cinderella wrapped the glass slipper she had worn in green velvet.</u>

   (A) Cinderella wrapped the glass slipper she had worn in green velvet
   (B) Cinderella wrapped the glass slipper that she had worn in green velvet
   (C) Cinderella wrapped in green velvet the glass slipper she had worn
   (D) Cinderella wrapped the glass slipper, she had worn, in green velvet
   (E) Cinderella wrapped the glass slipper she had worn, in green velvet

43. <u>The principle and I, who work tirelessly</u> to lessen your homework burden, will assign only those grammar sentences that can be corrected on the way to school.

   (A) principle and I, who work tirelessly
   (B) principal and I, who work tirelessly
   (C) principle and I who work tirelessly
   (D) principal and I, who works tirelessly
   (E) principle and I, working tirelessly

Answer Key to Guided Exercises

These are answers for the guided exercises in each lesson. Where you find errors in your work, consult the relevant rule, referred to by number after the problem. If you still don't understand why you got that problem wrong, make a note to ask your teacher.

I. Apostrophes (p. 3)

1. there ⇒ they're
2. its ⇒ it's
3. their' ⇒ their
4. C
5. C (or abbess's)
6. Womens' ⇒ Women's
7. their's ⇒ theirs
8. C
9. Its ⇒ it's (1st)
10. C
11. let's ⇒ lets
12. C
13. C
14. laws' ⇒ law's
15. C
16. there ⇒ they're
17. sheeps' ⇒ sheep's (sheep is plural)
18. hers' ⇒ hers
19. George's ⇒ George (joint property)
20. C
21. C
22. girl's ⇒ girls'
23. C
24. They're ⇒ their
25. senators' ⇒ senator's (only one name, so only one senator)

II.A. Subject-Verb Agreement (p. 10)

1. are ⇒ is
2. C
3. are ⇒ is
4. is ⇒ are
5. C
6. C
7. are ⇒ is
8. are ⇒ is
9. s ⇒ are
10. were ⇒ was
11. have ⇒ has
12. sit ⇒ sits
13. C
14. lasts ⇒ last
15. C
16. have ⇒ has
17. was ⇒ were
18. needs ⇒ need
19. Here's ⇒ Here are
20. are ⇒ is
21. C
22. C
23. C
24. are ⇒ is
25. is ⇒ are

II.B Subject-Verb Agreement (p. 17)

1. wish ⇒ wishes
2. want ⇒ wants
3. plan ⇒ plans
4. C
5. are ⇒ is
6. C
7. C
8. are ⇒ is
9. are ⇒ is
10. were ⇒ was
11. are ⇒ is
12. are ⇒ is
13. are ⇒ is
14. C
15. is ⇒ are
16. are ⇒ is
17. are ⇒ is
18. was ⇒ were
19. C
20. were ⇒ was
21. likes ⇒ like
22. C
23. Do ⇒ Does
24. C
25. C

II.C Subject-Verb Agreement (p. 26)

1. are ⇒ is
2. C
3. has ⇒ have
4. are ⇒ is
5. C
6. lead ⇒ leads
7. know ⇒ knows
8. want ⇒ wants
9. C (you eat cookies, not the box!)
10. are ⇒ is
11. despises ⇒ despise
12. wish ⇒ wishes
13. deals ⇒ deal
14. C
15. C
16. has ⇒ have
17. understands ⇒ understand
18. were ⇒ was
19. know ⇒ knows
20. Are ⇒ Is
21. were ⇒ was
22. C
23. C
24. C
25. C

II.D Subject-Verb Agreement (p. 33)

1. have ⇒ has
2. are ⇒ is
3. have ⇒ has
4. is ⇒ are
5. C
6. C
7. are ⇒ is
8. fights ⇒ fight
9. are ⇒ is
10. C
11. has ⇒ have
12. C
13. are ⇒ is
14. are ⇒ is
15. have ⇒ has
16. agree ⇒ agrees
17. C
18. are ⇒ is
19. are ⇒ is
20. were ⇒ was
21. C
22. have ⇒ has
23. is ⇒ are
24. has ⇒ have
25. are ⇒ is

III. Pronoun-Antecedent Agreement (p. 44)

1. their ⇒ his/her
2. C
3. starts ⇒ start
4. C
5. C
6. C
7. their ⇒ her
8. needs ⇒ need
9. their rifles ⇒ his/her rifle
10. has ⇒ have (teachers go crazy individually!)
11. she
12. are ⇒ is; their (2nd) ⇒ her
13. have ⇒ has, their ⇒ his/her
14. their ⇒ her
15. C
16. C
17. C
18. them ⇒ him/her
19. their ⇒ his/her
20. C
21. C
22. its ⇒ their
23. their ⇒ his/her
24. their ⇒ his/her
25. their ⇒ its

IV. Punctuation With Quotations (p. 56)

1. ⇒ says, "You have a head like a sieve."
2. "you ⇒ "You
3. on". ⇒ on."
4. tape", ⇒ tape,"
5. C
6. star?" ⇒ star"?
7. twinkle"? ⇒ twinkle?"
8. C
9. property". ⇒ property."
10. did." ⇒ did,"
11. it?", ⇒ it?"
12. "Are" ⇒ "are"
13. representative, "deregulation ⇒ representative. "Deregulation
14. C
15. boy". ⇒ boy."
16. longer"? ⇒ longer?"
17. Surprise?" ⇒ "Surprise"?
18. villain, "Foiled ⇒ villain. "Foiled
19. C
20. Elvis, "I ⇒ Elvis. "I
21. awesome". ⇒ awesome."
22. yet"? ⇒ yet?"
23. mother, "you ⇒ mother. "You
24. C
25. sentence"! ⇒ sentence!"

V.A Pronoun Case (p. 66)

1. I ⇒ me.
2. her ⇒ she
3. us ⇒ we
4. C
5. C
6. myself ⇒ me
7. him ⇒ he
8. him ⇒ his
9. her ⇒ she
10. I ⇒ me
11. him and me ⇒ he and I
12. me ⇒ my
13. C
14. I ⇒ me
15. us ⇒ our
16. C
17. C
18. C
19. myself ⇒ I
20. him ⇒ he
21. myself ⇒ me
22. me ⇒ I
23. C
24. we ⇒ us
25. us ⇒ our

V.B Pronoun Case (p. 69)

1. C
2. Whom ⇒ Who
3. who ⇒ whom
4. who ⇒ whom
5. C
6. C
7. whomever ⇒ whoever
8. who ⇒ whom
9. C
10. who ⇒ whom
11. C
12. C
13. whom ⇒ who
14. whomever ⇒ whoever
15. C
16. C
17. C
18. whom ⇒ who
19. C
20. whom ⇒ who
21. who ⇒ whom
22. C
23. C
24. C
25. who ⇒ whom

VI. Punctuation With Independent Clauses (p. 80)

Note: Of the several ways of curing comma-splice errors suggested on page 83, only one or two have been given here. Making two sentences of the clauses is acceptable, though not very graceful. Subordinating the less important clause to the main clause is a better cure. In cases of doubt, consult your teacher.

1. , however, ⇒ ; however,
2. party, but ⇒ party but
3. clothes, and ⇒ clothes and
4. player, furthermore ⇒ player; furthermore,
5. breath, unfortunately ⇒ breath; unfortunately
6. man, however ⇒ man; however,
7. field, and ⇒ field and
8. valuable it ⇒ valuable, for it or valuable; it
9. everything for ⇒ everything, for
10 C
11. C
12. refrigerator but ⇒ refrigerator, but
13. spectators, and ⇒ spectators and
14. car yet ⇒ car, yet
15. success, no ⇒ success, for no or success; no
16 Nelson but ⇒ Nelson, but
17. C
18. homework, now ⇒ homework, for now or homework; now
19. game, he ⇒ game; he or game, for he
20. uncle, and ⇒ uncle and
21. C
22. sister, according ⇒ sister; according or sister, for according
23. powder, and ⇒ powder and
24. him, I ⇒ him: I or him, but I
25. test, moreover ⇒ test; moreover

VII. Pronoun Reference (p. 90)

Note: There is normally more than one good way to edit these sentences. We have given a suggestion, drawing from several good options, but you may be able to think of other ways to get rid of the reference error. In cases of doubt, ask your teacher.

1. ⇒ Otto's plagiarizing his English papers is a shameful action.
2. ⇒ Olive nails her poems to the door to be sure that her children read them.
3. ⇒ In her diary Olive tells ....
4. ⇒ Otto told Billy, "Stop tying knots in your [or my] hair."
5. ⇒ When a policewoman was lecturing her, Olive grew angry and bit her.
6. ⇒ Otto's habit of screaming "Down with the government" annoys everyone.
7. ⇒ Before Olive eats fish, she always cleans the guts out of them.
8. ⇒ People are not supposed to tell lies, but Otto tells several a day.
9. ⇒ That Olive ... Nastine shows her fondness for that name.
10. ⇒ Nonsmokers are not tolerated in Otto's regular bar.
11. ⇒ Olive's genuine love for Otto doesn't stop her from ....
12. ⇒ Otto was seriously injured in a fistfight with ....
13. ⇒ Otto is dedicated to bowling, but Olive ....
14. ⇒ ... but Olive refused to become one.
15. ⇒ Otto's dog began to howl while Otto was walking him.
16. ⇒ The people at the police station have many stories ....
17. ⇒ It makes Olive furious when Otto tells lies about her.
18. ⇒ As the judge came into court, she was smiling, Olive noticed.
19. ⇒ A fight started when Otto wanted his room cleaned up and told his brother to do it.
20. ⇒ In *Macbeth* we learn that Macbeth hears a voice ....
21. ⇒ It infuriates Olive that her mother always calls her "Olivia."
22. ⇒ Tenant activists were arrested after releasing rats in City Hall.
23. ⇒ Olive puts nine olives in her martini because she loves them.
24. ⇒ Compared to Ms. Citrus, Margot knows far more about grammar.
25. ⇒ Do the directions say that you are allowed to rewrite the sentence?

VIII. Modifying Errors (p. 100)

Note: Here again there may be more than one good cure.

1. only knows ⇒ knows only
2. ⇒ Under the bed Otto found ....
3. ⇒ If you want to make friends ... OR: To make friends with Olive, you need ....
4. even to interest advanced ⇒ to interest even advanced
5. ⇒ who yesterday arrested Olive OR: was ordered yesterday to release her.
6. just interested in one ⇒ interested in just one
7. nearly wrote ⇒ wrote nearly
8. apartment, it ⇒ apartment, you will find it
9. ⇒ While he was singing ....
10. Olive dropped the hat in the sewer ⇒ Olive dropped in the sewer the hat
11. ⇒ In Bismo's car Otto drove to the bar ....
12. All people cannot easily ⇒ Not all people can easily
13. ⇒ In the street Olive found ....
14. While standing ⇒ While he was standing
15. even curses ⇒ curses even
16. some studying ⇒ you'll find some studying
17. ⇒ If people read quickly, they forget ....
18. nearly knows ⇒ knows nearly
19. ⇒ Otto corrected in several places the letter ....
20. When completely loaded ⇒ When the bus was completely loaded, the driver ....

21. ⇒ While Otto was sliding down a cliff-face, his suspenders ....
22. Olive slipped the bottle in her purse ⇒ In her purse Olive slipped the bottle
23. When exposed ⇒ When one is exposed
24. ⇒ The teacher that Tommy frequently angered made ... OR: ... that Tommy

angered made the boy's life miserable with some frequency.

25. Providing ⇒ If you provide OR: envelope, the letter to the publisher will look ⇒ envelope will make the letter to the publisher look

IX. Punctuation with Essential/Nonessential Elements (p. 112)

1. C
2. no commas around "that" clause
3. no commas around clause
4. C
5. C (true of all musicals)
6. commas around "televised by CNN"
7. no commas around "Archie"
8. commas around phrase "his high school"
9. C
10. no commas around title
11. no commas around "named" phrase
12. no commas around "Salem"
13. commas around "who" clause
14. commas around "that" clause
15. commas around appositive "a guinea pig ..."
16. C
17. commas around "to make" phrase
18. no commas around "who" clause
19. C (he considered those experiences funny)
20. no commas before "that" clause
21. no commas around "Sir Richard Burton"
22. no commas before "who" clause
23. C
24. commas before "which" clause
25. no commas before "purchased" phrase.

X.A. Verb Tense (p. 123)

1. seemed, decided ⇒ seems, decides
2. told ⇒ had told
3. turns, tells ⇒ turned, told
4. didn't ⇒ don't
5. C
6. is ⇒ was
7. C (first verb tells a literary event, second a historical one)
8. were ⇒ are
9. is living ⇒ has been living *or* has lived
10. finishes ⇒ has finished
11. fed ⇒ had fed
12. finished ⇒ had finished
13. will ⇒ would
14. insulted ⇒ had insulted
15. sterilized ⇒ had sterilized
16. landed ⇒ has landed
17. operated ⇒ had operated
18. were ⇒ had been (twice)
19. did ⇒ does
20. will complete ⇒ will have completed; begin ⇒ will begin
21. will blow ⇒ will have blown
22. C
23. thought, understood ⇒ thinks, understands
24. will finish ⇒ will have finished
25. danced ⇒ had danced

X.B. Subjunctive Mood (p. 127)

1. was ⇒ were
2. C
3. should be careful ⇒ be careful
4. was ⇒ were
5. C
6. hold ⇒ would hold
7. would be ⇒ were
8. would have told ⇒ had told
9. was ⇒ were
10. was ⇒ were
11. C
12. should be allowed ⇒ be allowed
13. pays, settles ⇒ pay, settle
14. would not have told ⇒ had not told
15. will be ⇒ were

X.C. Tense of participles (p. 130)

1. Sharpening ⇒ Having sharpened
2. Brushing, examining ⇒ having brushed ... and examined
3. C
4. Confessing ⇒ Having confessed
5. Sitting ⇒ Having sat

Optional sentences on passive voice (p. 130)

1. Beavers gnawed logs to make dams and stop the stream; *or,* Beavers stopped the stream with dams made of gnawed logs.
2. C (no need to identify who the builder is).
3. C (no way to identify the thief).
4. When the bees have built the ..., they bring in nectar and pollen to make into honey.
5. The editors are expressing ... on account of the number of good poems younger students have been submitting ....

XI.A. Parallelism (p. 139). Note: some other corrections are possible.

1. to clean ⇒ cleaning
2. behave impatiently ⇒ impatient
3. with contrition ⇒ contritely
4. ... about the Pentagon's five sides and miles of corridors.
5. Joshua is not only ⇒ Not only is Joshua; *or,* Joshua not only serves as ... but also plans to ....
6. to go on a fifty-mile hike ⇒ hiking fifty miles
7. because they can earn ..., go on ..., and help ....
8. nor did the lions sleep ⇒ nor the lions slept
9. ... because she had not only won ... but also been chosen ....
10. Archie threw the ball and broke the window.
11. ... for mumbling, not standing up straight, looking ..., and speaking ....
12. ... keeping ..., studying ..., and being ....
13. Either John ⇒ John either
14. but she also ate ⇒ but also ate
15. to eat ⇒ eat
16. Jamie was tall, rich, smart, and vain.
17. nor do they apologize ⇒ nor apologizes
18. Both the errors in logic and the several careless mistakes that Yuka made doomed ....
19. to go fishing ⇒ fishing
20. Either Amy or Jennifer must finish ⇒ Amy or Jennifer must either finish
21. not only famous ⇒ famous not only
22. C
23. will both be sold ⇒ will be sold both
24. but they land ⇒ but land
25. but Boris into archaeology ⇒ Boris into archaeology

XI.B. Comparisons (p. 143)

1. than any *other* baseball player
2. faster ⇒ fastest
3. as sharp as a samurai sword, if not sharper, *or:* as sharp *as,* if not ...
4. Jane Austen's *novels* are better
5. than any *other* bird in the flock
6. C
7. of hiphop *lyrics* that is ...
8. ... is more effective *than his basketball strategy, or: than Bobby Fisher's chess moves*
9. ... than my lawyer *saves me*
10. the most ⇒ more
11. C
12. ... than any *other* ex-president
13. best ⇒ better
14. ... as efficient *as,* if not more efficient than, ...
15. most ⇒ more
16. ... than *the poetry of* Countee Cullen
17. ... as many prizes *as,* if not more prizes than, ...
18. ... than the *other* gods of ...

19. ... not more intelligent *than Odysseus* (or some other wise hero)
20. hardest ⇒ harder
21. ... lost more games *than the Yankees*
22. C

23. ... tastier *than the large orange berries*
24. ... as critical of the City University *as*, if not more critical than ...
25. ... than any *other* actress of her generation

XII. Double Negatives (p. 153)

1. C
2. couldn't ⇒ could
3. help but wear ⇒ help wearing
4. cannot ⇒ can
5. nothing ⇒ anything
6. help but place ⇒ help placing

7. wouldn't ⇒ would
8. couldn't ⇒ could
9. could not but think ⇒ could not help thinking
10. doesn't know hardly any ⇒ knows hardly any

(Redundancy)

1. ... Julie had laid more tiles on the floor than ...
2. Herman, the little orange cat, wears a flea collar.
3. The police officer is now walking ...
4. ... after hours of running around town.
5. ... raise buckets of pitch up to the roof ⇒ raise buckets of pitch to the roof.
6. ... the marchers take a "dance break."
7. ... on the diplomas.
8. In the city most people have few or no lawn-mowing chores because they live in apartments
9. Way out in the country, especially ...
10. Arranged in a circle, ...
11. The school now has two new buildings.

12. ... for an exit from ...
13. The barber had become a millionaire since short hair has become trendy.
14. My four-year-old sister, exhausted, ...
15. The ocean helped the leaky boat to float.
16. ... began as a co-ed school.
17. ... weary after winning ...
18. ... to become a veterinarian.
19. ... take the subway.
20. I think Shakespeare ...
21. Hip hop is the anthem of teenagers today, just as rock and roll was of teenagers yesterday.
22. The rugs on the living room floor felt soft to Walker's tired feet.
23. There are currently ...

(SAT Style Exercises) (p. 221)

1. B	10. B	19. A	28. A	37. C
2. C	11. D	20. C	29. E	38. D
3. B	12. B	21. B	30. C	39. A
4. E	13. C	22. C	31. C	40. A
5. B	14. D	23. E	32. E	41. E
6. A	15. C	24. A	33. E	42. C
7. B	16. E	25. D	34. B	43. B
8. E	17. D	26. B	35. B	
9. C	18. D	27. B	36. A	

Glossary of grammatical terms used in this book

Because grammar is part of our glorious classical heritage, I have had to use many Latin-derived terms in explaining the principles of usage. To help you maximize your understanding of those principles, here is a glossary of common terms in alphabetical order. Not included are some (essential/nonessential, subjunctive) defined in the text.

Action verb	A word that names an action: *see, munch, rejoice, work, sleep, desire*
Adjective	A word that describes a person, place, or thing, answering these questions: what kind, how many, which one: *grey goose, four brothers, that city*.
Adjective clause	A group of words that contains a subject and a verb and acts as an adjective: a teacher *who gives tons of homework*. Usually introduced by a relative pronoun. [In some the pronoun is understood: I think *[that]* he's nuts.]
Adverb	A word that describes a verb, an adjective, or another adverb, answering the questions how, when, where, why, to what extent: *poorly* prepared, arrived *late*, *very* messy, stood *there*, *amazingly* skillfully
Adverb clause	A group of words that contains a subject and a verb and acts as an adverb: They were sweating *because they danced under hot lights*. Introduced by a subordinating conjunction.
Antecedent	The noun or pronoun to which a pronoun refers: As the *glacier* melted, its runoff lowered the temperature of the lake.
Appositive	A noun placed near another noun to help define or describe it: Emma, the *captain*, has announced ...
Appositive phrase	An appositive and the words that modify it: Emma, *the popular captain*, or Emma, *the captain of the Fencing Squad*
Case	With personal pronouns and *who*, case shows whether a personal pronoun or the relative pronoun is being used as a subject (*we*), an object (*whom*), or a possessive (*her*).
Clause	A group of words containing a subject and a verb (thus distinct from a phrase); may be independent or dependent (subordinate)
Collective noun	A noun that's singular in form but plural in meaning: family, collection, class
Compound subject	A subject that consists of two or more nouns or pronoun joined by *and, nor, or*: Ben and Jerry, They and their mother, She or I, Neither Ed nor you
Conjunction	A word whose function is to connect words, phrases, clauses: *but, if, when*
Coordinating conjunction	A conjunction that joins words, phrases, and independent clauses: *and, but, or, nor, for, yet, so*
Direct object	The noun or pronoun that receives the action named in the (action) verb: I shot *the sheriff*, That song bothers *me*.
Expletive construction	A sentence structure beginning with *There, Here, It* in which <u>the subject</u> is placed after the verb: *There is <u>a flaw</u> in your reasoning, Here is <u>the answer</u>, It bothers him <u>that his friend smokes</u>*.
Fragment	A group of words punctuated as a sentence that does not make a full sentence: She would not eat meat. Or fish, for that matter.

Gender	The singular feminine, masculine and neuter personal pronouns are gender-specific: *she, him, its*
Gerund	A noun derived from a verb by adding the –*ing* ending: I love *swimming*.
Gerund phrase	A phrase built around a gerund: *Eating too quickly* was his worst habit. *Patient digging* uncovered the treasure. (Note that gerunds can be described either by adjectives or by adverbs.)
Helping verb	Also called auxiliary verbs, helping verbs combine with participles or infinitives to create specific verb forms: The end *is* coming, The recital *has* begun, I *should* go.
Indefinite pronoun	A pronoun that refers nonspecifically to some, any, or all of a group of persons or things: *somebody, anything, everyone*
Independent clause	A clause that can stand alone as a complete sentence: Olive ate my bagel, but *I forgive her*.
Indirect object	The noun or pronoun receiving the action of the verb indirectly. Answers the questions "To whom?" or "To what?" naming the entity to whom/which the action named in the verb (usually a synonym of *give, say, tell, show*) is performed: Our classmates give *us* looks when we talk in Latin. (*Looks* is the direct object.)
Infinitive	The form of a verb that starts with to: *to speak, to care*. Acts as a noun (*To sing* is his delight), an adverb (*To succeed*, you have to study), and an adjective (She is an athlete *to watch*).
Infinitive phrase	A phrase consisting of an infinitive and its modifiers (adverbs) and/or direct object: *To win the debate conclusively*, they marshaled their facts.
Linking verb	A verb that names an identity between its subject and its complement: That boy *is* not scared. Forms of "be" are the best-known linking verbs, but other verbs such as "seem" and "become" can work this way too: She *became* a senator.
Modifier	Adjectives and adverbs and the phrases and clauses that work as these parts of speech are called *modifiers*. The word *modify* simply indicates the relation of an adjective to its noun, of an adverb to its verb. A modifier describes or limits. My older brother reads constantly: *older* modifies *brother*, *constantly* modifies *reads*.
Noun	A word that names a person, place, or thing: *coach, Turkey, corkscrew*. Nouns are used in a sentence as subjects, objects (direct, indirect, prepositional), predicate nominatives, and appositives.
Noun clause	A group of words that contains a subject and a verb and that acts as a noun. Commonly introduced by *who/whom/whose, that, if, whether, when, where, how, why*: *Whose woods these are* I think I know. I don't know *if I agree*.
Number	Nouns and pronouns have number: singular and plural: one *egg*, two *eggs*.
Object of preposition	The noun or pronoun following a preposition is its object: Otto is in *the dumpster* again. Among *ourselves* we can speak freely.
Object case	Used with some pronouns and *who* to show that the pronoun is being used as an object (direct, indirect, prepositional): *him, her, them, us, whom*
Participle	An adjective derived from a verb; used in conjunction with helping verbs to form some verb tenses. Present participle forms with –*ing*: the *flying* fish. Past participle forms with –*ed* in many verbs, in other verbs with other endings: the *frightened* child, the *fallen* boulder, the *swept* floor.
Participial phrase	A phrase consisting of a participle and its modifiers and/or direct objects, used as an adjec-

tive. That boy *noisily eating his spaghetti* is my ex-boyfriend.

Personal pronoun	A word used in place of a person's or object's name: *I, you, he, she, it, we, they.* Personal pronouns change form according to number, gender, or case.
Phrase	A group of words without a subject and a verb (thus distinct from a clause).
Predicate nominative	A type of subject complement. A noun or pronoun that follows a linking verb such as *be* and renames the subject: My uncle is a great *cook.* (*Cook* and *uncle* name the same person.)
Preposition	A function word (sometimes a short phrase) such as *in, under, among, alongside, after, except for, during, beyond.* Invariably followed by a noun or pronoun, called the object of the preposition.
Prepositional phrase	A phrase consisting of a preposition and its object and that object's modifiers. Such a phrase acts as an adjective or adverb, often to locate a person, thing, or action in space or time: *Below the thatched roof, During that jazz recital.*
Pronoun	A word that replaces a noun, its antecedent, and refers to it: I like curly fries; please give me some of *those.*
Relative pronoun	The pronoun used to introduce an adjective clause: *who/whom/whose, which, that*: Olive is a mother *who* seems unable to tell her children apart.
Subject	The noun or pronoun that performs the action described by the verb: The *van* carried all eleven of Olive's daughters.
Subject case	Used with personal pronouns and *who* to show that the pronoun is being used as a subject or a predicate nominative (subject complement): We are the losers in that deal, It is *she who* arranged that song.
Subordinate clause	A clause that cannot stand alone as a sentence; functions as an adjective, adverb, or noun.
Subordinating conjunction	A conjunction used to introduce an adverb clause: *although* you think I'm a lunatic, *when* he had spread the peanut butter, *if* you forget your keys,
Verb	A word that names the action performed in a sentence or that asserts an identity between two entities, a state of being. Every sentence and clause must have one.
Verbal	A word derived from a verb but that functions as another part of speech. Participles, infinitives, and gerunds are all verbals.